Analytic Philosophy of Religion: its History since 1955

Steven M. Duncan

Humanities-Ebooks

Humanities-Ebooks.co.uk publishes high quality academic and educational Ebooks in English, History, Philosophy and related areas.

It has a rapidly expanding list of searchable titles ranging from scholarly texts to student introductions, some of which contain colour illustrations and internal and external hyperlinks not reproducible in printed form.

For the current list please visit

http://www.humanities-ebooks.co.uk

Analytic Philosophy of Religion:
its History since 1955

Steven M. Duncan

𝓗𝓔𝓑 ☼ Humanities-Ebooks, LLP

Publication

© Steven Duncan, 2007, 2008

The Author has asserted his right to be identified as the author of this Work in accordance with the Copyright, Designs and Patents Act 1988.

Published by *Humanities-Ebooks LLP*
Tirril Hall, Tirril, Penrith CA10 2JE

First, electronic edition, 2007

Paperback, 2008, now from Lulu.com

ISBN 978-1-84760-082-0 Paperback
ISBN 978-1-84760-043-1 Ebook

Contents

About the Author	7
Preface	8
Introduction	10
What is the Philosophy of Religion?	11
Faith and Reason	14
Deductivism and Inductivism: Two Approaches to the Philosophy of Religion	21
Chapter One: Theism and Atheism	24
The Elements of Theism	25
Atheism	35
Chapter Two: Neo-Thomism and the Rise of Analysis	42
Neo-Thomism: Basic Elements	43
Reginald Garrigou–Lagrange and the Five Ways	46
The Beginnings of Analytic Philosophy	48
Stages in the Development of Analytic Philosophy	52
Analysis and Neo-Thomism: Early Encounters	57
Chapter Three: The Problem of Religious Language	65
The Thomistic Theory of Analogical Predication	65
Talk of God in the Analytic Tradition	74
The "Theology and Falsification" Debate	75
Non-cognitivist Approaches to Religious Language	84
The "Parity Argument": An Epistemological Counterattack	92
Chapter Four: The Argument from Evil and the Origin of Inductivism	98
Mackie's Argument	99
Pike and Plantinga: Refuting the Deductive Argument from Evil	104
John Hick's Irenaean Theodicy	107
The Atheistic Response to Pike and the Transition to Inductivism	111
Chapter Five: The Inductivist Paradigm	115
Basil Mitchell: The Justification of Religious Belief	115
Swinburne's Inductivist Theism: the General Strategy	119
Swinburne's Positive Argument for Theism	125

Swinburne on Evil and the Hiddenness of God	132
Swinburne on Religious Experience and Miracles	137
J. L. Mackie's Critique of Swinburne	140
Inference to the Best Explanation and the Future of Inductivism	142

Chapter Six: The Ontological Argument Redivivus ... 146
   The Classical Ontological Argument(s) ... 147
   Hartshorne, Findlay and Malcolm: The Modal Ontological Argument ... 150
   Possible Worlds ... 153
   Plantinga's Ontological Argument ... 156

Chapter Seven: The Cosmological Argument *Redivivus* ... 159
   The Leibniz/Clarke Argument ... 159
   The New Physico–Theology I: The "Big Bang" Cosmological Argument ... 162
   The *Kalam* Cosmological Argument ... 166

Chapter Eight: The Teleological Argument *Redivivus* ... 170
   F. R. Tennant's Teleological Argument ... 172
   The New Physico–Theology II: The "Fine Tuning" Argument ... 178
   The Future of the Teleological Argument ... 181

Chapter Nine: Post-Deductivism and the Rise of Christian Philosophy ... 183
   Protestant Philosophy before Analysis ... 184
   Plantinga's "Christian Philosophy" ... 189
   Foundationalism and the Ethics of Belief ... 190
   Plantinga's "Reformed Epistemology" ... 195

Chapter Ten: Philosophy of Religion Today ... 201
   Contemporary Theistic Philosophy ... 201
   Contemporary Atheistic Philosophy ... 203
   Toward a Friendlier Atheism 207

Bibliography ... 209

About the Author

Steven M. Duncan (1954–) earned his Ph.D. at the University of Washington in 1987 and has taught at various colleges and universities for the last thirty years. He is currently on the adjunct philosophy staff at Bellevue College. His other publications include *A Primer of Modern Virtue Ethics* (UPA, 1995), *Contemporary Philosophy of Religion* in the Humanities Insights series (2007), and *The Proof of the External World* (Wipf and Stock, 2008).

Preface

I well remember that when I was an undergraduate in the early 1970's, the intellectual culture in philosophy departments in the United States was one in which atheism was taken to be established beyond any reasonable doubt and incumbent on anyone who wanted to be regarded as even minimally rational. If that consensus had continued to the present time, a book such as this one would have had no more than academic interest. As it is, however, it tells the dramatic story of the revival of theism in the philosophy of religion, one that brought theism from the brink of intellectual annihilation to something approaching intellectual respectability in the space of a single generation. At the same time, if this were generally known and acknowledged among philosophers, this book would again be of only academic interest. However, I have found that many – perhaps even most – philosophers have not kept up with the dramatic changes in the field in the last thirty years and believe that the intellectual situation remains unchanged from what it was then. For these philosophers I hope this book will serve both as an introduction to the philosophy of religion as it is today and a challenge to the received opinion.

There is much more to the story than I have been able to summarize here. In particular, the contribution of philosophers to the discussion of the divine attributes[1], the problem of divine foreknowledge[2] and Christian apologetics[3], though interesting and substantial, have been left aside in what follows. Instead, I have chosen to concentrate on the two most hotly debated issues in the philosophy of religion in the last fifty years – the existence of God and the problem of evil – and to chart the course of the dialectic between these two discussions that has, I claim, completely transformed the field in the space of three decades.

I wish to thank Dr. Richard Gravil and Dr. Mark Addis for choosing to include this project as one of the first titles published by Humanities-Ebooks. Although new and as yet little tried, there can be no doubt that electronic publishing will make publicly

---
1   For a summary of current work on this topic, see Hoffmann and Rosenkrantz (2002).
2   For a good overview of current discussion of this problem, see Zagzebski (1996).
3   For an introduction to current issues in this area, see Hebblethwaite (2005).

available important contributions to scholarship that, given the expense of traditional methods of publishing, might never have seen the light of day. The present author hopes that something like this might be the case with regard to the modest volume currently before the reader, which is dedicated to the memory of his father, Merle A. Duncan, who died in October of 2005.

Introduction

For anyone with even a slight acquaintance with the field, there can be no doubt that the philosophy of religion has been one of the most active and volatile branches of the discipline of philosophy in the latter half of the twentieth century. In this book, we will be reviewing the history of the philosophy of religion since 1955, concentrating on the problems, doctrines and figures making up the tradition of analytic philosophy of religion dominant during that period in Britain and the United States.[1] Although my primary concern will be with the history of this tradition in the philosophy of religion, I will also be defending two historical claims about the general development and progress of the philosophical research and discussion composing this tradition. First, I will be charting the obvious trend from a nearly universal consensus in favour of atheism among the central figures in analytic philosophy of religion in the 1950's to the dominance of theistic philosophers of religion by the turn of the 21st century. Secondly, I shall be arguing that there has been a paradigm shift in the way that discussion of the philosophy of religion has been undertaken in the last fifty years from a largely deductivist perspective to a more inductivist one and then, ultimately, to a Post-Deductivist perspective. This change parallels a similar trend in the epistemology in the same period but seems to have developed largely independently of that trend, or at any rate does not rely directly upon it.[2]

I shall begin by filling in some of the historical background, beginning with the late nineteenth century developments in the Catholic Church that led to the rise of the neo-Thomist movement and which, I will argue, initiated the modern deductivist paradigm and its model for conceiving and discussing the central issues in the philosophy of religion such as the existence of God and the problem of evil. I shall then turn to the origins of analytic philosophy and of the early analytic philosophers of religion who quite naturally adopted the deductivist paradigm and used it to make the formidable case for atheism that seemed all but unchallengeable in the 1950's.

---

1 For a history of Anglophone philosophy of religion prior to this period, see Sell (1974); for a comprehensive history of twentieth century philosophy of religion see Long (2000).
2 The parallel is evident in Plantinga (1993a).

However, I will then argue that, in response to Nelson Pike's refutation of the deductive argument from evil in the 1960's, the analytic atheists inadvertently initiated the new, inductivist paradigm that, over the next twenty years, transformed both the standards of argument and the very way in which problems in the philosophy of religion were conceived by philosophers. I will then chart the development of the revival of theism in the philosophy of religion, concentrating on the two main approaches to a contemporary philosophical defence of theism: the inductivist approach of Richard Swinburne and the Post-Deductivist approach of Alvin Plantinga.

This, as it turns out, is quite a story to tell and by no means will I be able to tell all of it. Since there is so much relevant material, I have opted for breadth rather than depth and conceive of the book as a kind of handbook that will provide sufficient acquaintance with the material for students and other non-specialists while serving as a guide and platform for further, more sophisticated research in the field or with regard to special topics that readers may feel inclined and competent to pursue. Although I will occasionally offer my own arguments or assessments of the current debate in the various topics I will be discussing, this is a work of scholarship rather than creative philosophy. My intention is to present the philosophical work of others rather than to contribute to the ongoing debate, something I hope to do on another occasion. I will be well pleased if the reader goes away with the (hopefully correct) impression that he or she knows the lay of land in this fascinating and increasingly sophisticated branch of philosophical inquiry. I shall be even more satisfied if the reader is then motivated to investigate the relevant problems and texts more fully. To begin with, however, I shall assume that the reader is approaching these questions for the very first time and proceed accordingly. Let us begin, then, with the preliminaries.

What is the Philosophy of Religion?

The philosophy of religion is the branch of philosophy that deals with the central, substantive claims of religion from the rational point of view, such as the existence and nature of God, the nature and function of religious language and the justification for religious belief. Because it is a branch of philosophical investigation, the philosophy of religion ideally begins from an external and neutral rational perspective on the substantive, metaphysical claims of religion and proposes to evaluate and assess those claims from that perspective. The philosopher of religion, regardless of his antecedent religious commitments (or lack of them) is bound by the philosopher's general commitment to the objective and impartial examination of these substantive claims from the rational point of view. As such, the philosopher of religion is not permitted to privilege any sources of religious belief or religious authorities in such a way as to take their truth for granted or place them beyond the limits of rational investigation unless one is prepared to justify these exclusions on purely rational grounds. While such claims are appropriate and weighty in theological contexts, they are not appropriate in philosophy of religion. It avails nothing, from the rational point of view, that a particular claim is well-attested in the Scriptures or promulgated by institutionally recognized religious authorities. Only analyses and arguments that can be formulated and justified using our common human reason are appropriate in a philosophical discussion.

The analytic philosophy of religion, the tradition with which we will be most concerned in this book, sees the role of reason in the analysis and evaluation of the substantive claims of religion as having three essential aspects. First, there is conceptual analysis, in which philosophers attempt to provide an account of the substantive meaning of a particular term, one intended to provide a clear and perspicuous theoretical account of the referent of that term. This can be done formally, by offering an analysis of a term intended to constitute a theoretical definition of that term, or informally in terms of the ordinary usage of the term and the linguistic intuitions evoked by these reflections. Thus, one may attempt to analyze the term "God" in the hopes of arriving at a theoretical conception of God consisting in a set of essential properties uniquely belonging to the referent of that term, something that can pass muster as a definition of that term and thus state the necessary and sufficient conditions for anything to count as God. Alternatively, one may study and reflect on the way the term "God" is used by religious believers and its function in religious discourse, including ritual and prayer, in order to gain insight into the meaning of "God" and to grasp the "cash value" of that term within a certain mode of discourse. As we shall see, these different analyses of the concept of God, such as those offered by classical theists, by evangelical protestant thinkers, process panentheists and Wittgensteinians, result in different, competing and perhaps even to some extent incommensurable conceptions of God with important implications for what one claims about the existence and nature of God.

Secondly, analytic philosophers of religion engage in the clarification of claims, putatively substantive propositions about God, such as the claims that God exists, that God is love, that God is omnipotent and omniscient and so on. Here philosophers proceed largely by an examination of the intuitions evoked by questions or objections intended to test the implications of a claim. So, suppose we consider that claim that

God is omnipotent. Since "omnipotent" means "all-powerful", one might suppose that to say God is omnipotent is equivalent to saying that God can do just anything at all. But it doesn't take much reflection to suggest that such an interpretation of "God is omnipotent" is puzzling, to say the least. For example, can God make square circles? Can God change the past, bringing it about that something that happened yesterday should never have occurred at all? Nor is this merely a matter of what is intrinsically possible, for there appear to be some things that God, conceived of as a perfect being, is incapable of doing or bringing about that are well within the power of ordinary human beings such as ourselves. For example, I can sin or destroy myself, but it hardly seems correct to say that God could do these things, since God is usually thought to be both morally perfect and necessarily existent. Although some atheistic philosophers of religion have attempted to use such considerations to prove that the concept of God is somehow incoherent, the great majority of contemporary philosophers of religion regard puzzles such as these as challenges to clarify the concept of God rather than abandon it.

At the beginning of the second half of the twentieth century, there was a widespread conviction among philosophers in the English-speaking world that analysis of the sort sketched above would prove sufficient by itself to resolve (or, it was hoped, to dissolve) all distinctively philosophical questions in such a way as to eliminate the need for any form of substantive philosophical theorizing. This view is no longer in the ascendant. Contemporary philosophers are still offering competing analyses that amount to different substantive theoretical accounts of the putative realities those analyses are intended to describe or capture. Further, since philosophical theories are not directly and straightforwardly testable by observation or experiment in the way that scientific theories are, philosophers attempt to build a case for their views by offering rational arguments for those views, objections to the views and arguments of others and responses to the objections presented against their own views. As such, rational argument is very much the life-blood of philosophical discourse and this leads to the third major task of the philosopher of religion; the evaluation of reasons and arguments for and against specific philosophical positions. Thus, theistic philosophers will generally use one or more of the traditional philosophical arguments – the ontological, cosmological or teleological arguments – to justify belief in God. Other philosophers will offer objections to those arguments and exponents of these arguments will endeavour to reply to those objections.

In what follows, we will see many examples of each of the foregoing, with a decided preference for the latter. The tremendous growth of discussion in the philosophy of religion, especially with the rise of analytic philosophy of religion beginning in the 1950's, has led to an equally impressive increase in the number of competing views within the discipline. In accordance with my stated plan, I will attempt to acquaint the reader with most of the main positions that have been held and defended in this burgeoning field in the last fifty or so years. Those who are content with a broad overview will, I hope, be satisfied and those wishing a more sophisticated treatment of these figures and issues given a solid foundation to pursue further studies.

FAITH AND REASON

The philosophical virtues of rationality, objectivity, impartiality and intellectual charity are easier to attain in some branches of philosophical inquiry than in others. Few who investigate the intricacies of advanced logic, the philosophy of mathematics or the philosophy of language are likely to have strong pre-philosophical commitments prior to the examination of the questions and theories that arise in these areas of inquiry. This is not so where the philosophy of religion is concerned. Religion, unlike mathematics or linguistics, is a matter of common human concern and in many areas – including metaphysics, cosmology, ethics and even politics – living religion competes with philosophy for the role of *biou kubernetes* or "helmsman of life." For this reason, one rarely comes to the philosophy of religion without strong opinions either for or against religious belief, usually derived from one's prevailing culture and early childhood training. This, in turn, hampers our ability to engage the issues, theories and arguments in the true spirit of philosophical inquiry, which requires that we put aside our feelings and opinions and restrict ourselves only to what can be discussed and defended from the perspective of neutral reason. For both religious and irreligious people alike, it is very easy to beg the question by assuming that certain favoured views are obvious ("science disproves religion")[1] or beyond philosophical questioning ("the Bible is the word of God"). Indeed, many come to the philosophy of religion with their minds already made up, looking either merely for confirmation of the views that they antecedently hold or material that might be useful for apologetic purposes; in neither case do they approach the issues in a properly philosophical spirit, one specified by the ideal of philosophical inquiry.

At the same time, the issues canvassed in the philosophy of religion are hardly

---

[1] For examples of this sort of thing, see the selections from Dawkins and Dennett in Martin and Bernard (2003) pages 430–31 and the essay by John Worrall in Peterson and Van Arragon (2004) pages 59–72.

trivial or insignificant; by any reckoning, they possess significant importance for what we believe about the most fundamental questions the human mind can contemplate and equally important implications for how we live. While no one likes or wants to be perceived to be a fanatical dogmatist either for or against religious belief, a person who could approach the questions discussed by philosophers of religion with an objectivity born of cultivated, passionless indifference or unconcern for how these questions are ultimately decided seems hardly to understand what is at stake. Indeed, if the day ever comes in which people can genuinely discuss their views about religion dispassionately and without any personal stake in the outcome of those discussions, the day will also have arrived when there is no longer any reason to discuss them. The decision for or against religion involves whole-hearted, passionate commitment involving and effecting one's whole being and it is only appropriate, then, that it should evoke strong feelings. Because of this, the first problem that faces the prospective student of the philosophy of religion is the problem of faith and reason.

As this problem is generally framed and discussed, it is a problem solely for the believer who decides to engage in the philosophical discussion of religion. It is often suggested, for example, that religious believers cannot be *truly* philosophical discussion partners because their antecedent religious commitments make it impossible for them to follow the argument where reason demands it to go when that argument goes against those pre-philosophical beliefs. However, we must not beg the question here by assuming that reason will inevitably lead us away from religious belief. The philosopher's commitment to reason is to the use of our native intellectual powers, themselves neutral with respect to substantive theoretical views, to investigate those intellectual questions that it lies beyond the power of the natural sciences to answer, recognizing that these powers may be limited or even ultimately inadequate to that task. The philosopher's commitment to reason must not be confused with the view that only someone who renounces any source of belief other than discursive reason counts as rational or reasonable. Clearly, a dogmatic atheist who refuses to admit that the argument has gone against him or her on some point in the philosophy of religion is not a whit more rational (nor more truly philosophical) for being a rationalist in this sense.

The question I have in mind here is one that is more general than that problem as it is often discussed in the literature. Essentially, it concerns the proper balance between one's antecedent, often strongly–held pre-philosophical beliefs on the one hand and the results of philosophical inquiry on the other. Does sincere and genuine engagement in the enterprise of philosophical inquiry demand that we check all of our previous beliefs at the door and be prepared to call everything into question, as some philosophers (e.g., Descartes) have maintained? Does a commitment to rationality or reasonableness require that we always follow the argument wherever it happens to lead? Or, on the other hand, it is necessary, reasonable or both to take some of our beliefs to be privileged on account of their apparent obviousness or centrality to the worldview we happen to find ourselves in possession of and only to be altered upon reflection that seems more obvious still? This is a general methodological or metaphilosophical question, one that arises in other areas of philosophy such as metaphysics and ethics as well. However, it seems to be most acutely felt in the philosophy of religion and that, after all, is our subject here.

The question of faith and reason has evoked three traditional responses from philosophers of religion. The first of these, which affirms both the sweeping nature of philosophical investigation and the necessity of submitting our will to believe in religious matters to the yoke of rational argument, can be called *rationalism*; this view generalized maintains this view concerning all beliefs whatsoever, maintaining that in every area of inquiry, reason and reason alone should be the guide to belief. On this view, faith and reason are inevitably opposed to one another and reason trumps the claims of faith, so that no appeal to faith can have standing as true or likely to be true. Either the claims of faith can be justified by appeal to reason, in which case faith as such is superfluous and unnecessary, or they cannot be so justified, in which case they are not permissible objects of belief. For the first rule of the ethics of belief is that we should apportion our belief to the evidence and follow the argument wherever it leads; we should neither believe beyond the evidence nor resist its apparent implications. Those who do are wilfully irrational, being in violation of their fundamental epistemic and doxastic obligations, even if those beliefs are held only at a personal level. Those who are prepared to act on those beliefs, living by them and interact with others in accordance with their dictates are worse still, being nothing less than the enemies of truth and freedom. A typical exponent of this form of rationalism was the American Absolute Idealist philosopher Brand Blanshard (1892–1987)[1] who was for many years Sterling Professor of Philosophy at Yale. Blanshard was both a rationalist in philosophy, believing that discursive reason, founded in *a priori* first principles was the sole source of philosophical truth, and a "rationalist" in the popular, nineteenth century sense in which it is a synonym for "freethinker", i.e. a person sceptical about the claims of religion. For Blanshard, anyone who affirms any claim on the basis of authority or embraces any belief on the basis of faith independently

---

1 See especially Blanshard (1974), pages 400–433.

of rational justification is a potential Torquemada and an enemy of human progress. Only those who allow reason to be their guide and reject all religious authority meet the minimum conditions for full membership in the community of rational inquirers; everyone else, regardless of his or her contributions to scholarship, is less than fully committed to the ideal of truth, being willing to follow the dictates of reason only as long as they do not conflict with their faith–commitments. Of course, for Blanshard no such person can possibly have standing as a philosopher, for whom the love of truth must outweigh all.

Not all exponents of rationalism in the philosophy of religion have embraced the extreme version of rationalism sketched above or regarded themselves as the enemies of religious belief. John Locke, for example, was a stout critic of "enthusiasm" with a strong tendency toward rationalism.[1] Locke even gives a religious justification for his rationalism concerning all religious positions other than those common to all Protestants; God has given us reason to guide us to the truth and even putative divine revelations have to pass muster before the bar of reason. Indeed, many contemporary theologians have gone out of their way to endorse the rationalistic approach to interpreting the Scriptures and traditional Christian doctrine.[2]

Contrasting to the rationalist position, there is the position known as fideism, which asserts that faith is a superior source of knowledge to reason and there have been a number grounds proposed for embracing fideism. Sceptical fideists, for example, have argued from the weakness and fallibility of human reason as demonstrated in the inconclusiveness and lack of progress in the philosophical investigation of reality to the claim that there is no good reason to suppose that there is any prospect of our ever discovering the truth about things. As such, if each of us has nothing more to depend on than our own, individual reason (which is limited, fallible, historically conditioned and so on) serving as the final court of appeal with regard to what is real and what human happiness consists in, we have little reason to suppose that there is any realistic chance that we will arrive at anything approaching the truth about reality. Even the apparently solid claims of modern natural science have been questioned by the followers of Kuhn and the exponents of anti-realism in the philosophy of science. Recently, a new sort of fideist, whose views are rooted in the Post-Modernist critique of "neutral" reason, has appeared. For example, Nicholas Wolterstorff (1931 –), himself retired Noah Porter Professor of Philosophy at Yale, has defended a posi-

---

1 See Wolterstorff (1996) pages 1–12 and 118–133.
2 In this regard we might mention Tillich, Bultmann, Maurice Wiles and Donald Gustafson; see the essays by Wiles and Gustafson in Tracy (1994) pages 13–29 and 63–74.

tion that closely approximates fideism in his monograph *Reason within the Bounds of Religion*.[1] According to Wolterstorff, the classical rationalist (like Blanshard) stakes his all on the possibility that there is some comprehensive philosophical system that is based on something certain and indubitable and from which the entire system of knowledge can be deduced by means of rules of inference that are themselves certain and indubitable. But the history of philosophy has put paid to this idea; we possess neither indubitable first principles nor incorrigible foundations in experience upon which to base such a system or rather, to the extent that we have these things, they are insufficient to justify even a fraction of our everyday beliefs. Since I cannot know with certainty or prove by a deductive argument even a belief as simple and mundane as that I had breakfast this morning is rationally justified, to accept it must a violation of our sacred doxastic obligation to decline any belief for which I cannot give adequate proof or justification. Thus, if we accept the rationalist position concerning rationally justified belief, the stock of our available (because epistemically justified) beliefs will shrink to nothing. Rationalism, then, proves to be untenable and commitment to rationalism itself, ironically, a kind of faith-commitment that cannot be made without carrying us beyond the limits of what we can prove or justify by reason.

Wolterstorff does not direct his critique solely to rationalism, however. He argues just as strenuously against any version of Foundationalism, any attempt to privilege any single perspective or point of view as normative for intellectual inquiry generally and this even includes the Christian scriptures themselves. Wolterstorff thus embraces a kind of Post-modernism according to which the practice of theoretical inquiry is foundationless and for which no stereotypical procedure or "method" can be proscribed in advance. Instead, theorizing has to begin from where one happens to be and admit the influence of one's culturally and temporally conditioned starting–point or "control beliefs", concerning the truth of which there is no guarantee and from which there is no neutral perspective against which they can be compared and adjusted to the truth *simpliciter*. As such, all inquiry operates from "the inside out" and involves interplay between the control beliefs that serve as the starting–point for that inquiry and the impact that research and investigation have on those beliefs. In line with this, authentic Christian commitment impels, indeed requires, that Christians bring the Biblical perspective to every aspect of their lives, including intellectual inquiry and, if one is a philosopher, to philosophy as well. The same will be true, according to Wolterstorff, of the sincere, believing Buddhist.[2] However, one's control–beliefs

---

1 Wolterstorff (1976; 2nd ed. 1984) pages 28–55.
2 Wolterstorff (1976), second edition (1984), page 11.

are not necessarily (and do not typically function as) rigid dogmas that must be tenaciously defended in the teeth of the results of inquiry. Instead, there is a dialectic here: sometimes, the control beliefs are modified or reinterpreted in the light of the results of inquiry (as in the case of Copernicanism or Darwinian evolution) and in others the results of inquiry have to be questioned or reinterpreted. Nor are there any rigid rules or procedures that can be used to decide which of these responses we make; each situation of conflict is unique and has to be decided, if possible, by the consensus of the inquirers reflecting sincerely on the facts before them. Although non-methodical and too uncomfortably "seat of the pants" to satisfy most philosophers, it hardly follows that such a procedure ought to be stigmatized as "irrational" on those grounds alone.

One characteristic of post-modernist fideism, as reflected in the title of Wolterstorff's monograph, is shared with classical rationalism: it refuses to recognize separate realms or autonomous competences for faith on the one hand and reason on the other. Just as Blanshard wants to treat discursive reason as the only true source of knowledge, Wolterstorff wants to see authentic Christian religious commitment as providing the overriding control-beliefs that guide the Christian's research in and contributions to intellectual inquiry. The mainstream position in the history of the faith/reason dispute, however, is characterized by its rejection of exclusive claims of this sort. According to the view we might call *convergentism*, the realms of faith and reason are largely autonomous (though partially overlapping) and characterized by appropriately different standards of justification, modes of argument and methods of inquiry. This view, associated historically with Catholic theology[1] and especially with the view of Thomas Aquinas[2], has generally held that the relation between faith and reason is complex, but that any genuine conflict between what the true religion teaches and the sound results of intellectual inquiry in the natural sciences is impossible. As Aquinas puts it, in opposition to the fideists of his day, there is but one God and one wholly self-consistent truth about the world that God has created. As such, there can be no ultimate or irresolvable conflict between faith on the one hand and reason on the other. There are *apparent* conflicts, of course, but according to a convergentist that is all they are; the apparent conflict can always ultimately be resolved by showing either that the data of faith or the data of reason have been misinterpreted or their implications incorrectly understood. As such, there is an element of fideism

---

1 This is still the official position of the Catholic Church; see the *Catechism of the Catholic Church* (1994), Section 159 and the citations referenced in Denzinger (31st edition, 1954) systematic index page 10 and Dupuis and Neuner (Seventh edition, 2001) pages 35–36.

2 On Aquinas's position, see the selection from the *Summa Contra Gentiles* in Martin and Bernard, pages 255–7. For a critique of Catholic/Thomist teaching, see Blanshard (1974) pages 23–118.

here, since we have to believe beyond what we can prove. At the same time, however, the autonomy of reason, so precious to the rationalist, is appropriately preserved. The realm of faith is the realm of religious doctrine and practice, designed to show us how to get to Heaven, whereas the realm of reason is the realm of philosophy and natural science which largely concerns the truths about this world. The methods appropriate to each realm are largely autonomous and inapplicable in the other, so that the results of theological inquiry are beholden neither to those of the scientist nor to be used to resolve purely empirical questions. By the same token, the scientist ought to stick to his last and not attempt to dictate to the theologian.

There is an area of partial overlap, of course, and it is here that the problems arise. The Christian faith asserts substantive claims about the nature of the world and, although for the most part the results of dogmatic theological inquiry are insulated from any sort of philosophical or scientific inquiry, there are areas, such as the origin and nature of the world, the nature of the human soul and salvation history where apparent divergence between what theologians maintain on the one hand and philosophers and scientists maintain on the other may occur. Such cases have to be decided on a case by case basis. Aquinas himself, for example, engaged in two such disputes during his lifetime. The first was over the eternity of the world and the second over the nature of the agent intellect as understood by Averroes; these cases are instructive for our purpose here. Aquinas was both a committed Aristotelian and a Christian theologian, a combination that many of his contemporaries doubted was possible. In the first case, Aquinas walked a delicate line between rationalism and fideism by arguing that reason could not decide the question, there being no conclusive proof either for the eternity of the universe or for its having a discrete beginning in time as taught by *Genesis*. As such, it is correct and proper to affirm the teachings of the faith on this point.[1] In the case of the Averroist controversy, Aquinas argued that the view that there is a single agent intellect for all men is neither the view of Aristotle (as the Averroists maintained) nor philosophically sound,[2] once again dissolving the appearance of conflict between Christian theology and the philosophy of Aristotle. In later times, Catholic respect for the autonomy of reason, inspired by Aquinas, led in the end to the acceptance both of Copernicanism and the fact of evolution, though many of the claims made by Darwinists are still disputed and rejected by the Church and Catholics are still required to believe many things that Darwinists reject, such as

---

1 See Aquinas (1965), Volume II, Chapters 31–38
2 See the *Treatise on the Unicity of the Intellect* in Aquinas (1968)

that there was an original pair of human beings.[1] In addition, as we shall see, it also led to the distinctive view that some (though by no means all) of the propositions that are properly the object of faith are also simultaneously demonstrable or otherwise justifiable by reason, so that reason can actually reinforce our faith. The Catholic confidence in natural theology can be traced to this basis and is especially applicable to the central question of the philosophy of religion: Does God exist?

DEDUCTIVISM AND INDUCTIVISM: TWO APPROACHES TO THE PHILOSOPHY OF RELIGION

In *Dialogues Concerning Natural Religion*,[2] Hume distinguishes two strategies for the philosophical defence of theism. The first of these, which he associates with the "rigid, inflexible dogmatism" of Demea, is traditionally known as the program of natural theology. According to this approach, for which Hume's model was probably Samuel Clarke's *Demonstration of the Being and Attributes of God*,[3] God's existence is to be proved *a priori* and with certainty by a deductive proof (a version of the cosmological argument) beginning from self-evident first premises and intended to be rationally compelling to all who examine it, regardless of their antecedent beliefs. Since God is transcendent and incomprehensible to us, our conception of the Deity can only be acquired by conceptual analysis of the notion of God as a perfect being, the content of which is largely negative rather than positive. The second strategy, associated with Cleanthes and loosely based on the position and strategy presupposed by Joseph Butler in his *Analogy of Religion*,[4] is the program of natural religion referred to in the title of Hume's book. On this approach, probability is, and always ought to be, the guide to our substantive beliefs. Both the evidence for God's existence and our knowledge of his nature are the product of an inductive strategy in which argument by analogy plays a central role. This strategy employs a version of the teleological argument to argue that God's existence is highly probable relative to its major competitor (that the orderly universe we see around us was the product of chance) and that we rightly attribute to God the same properties, different in degree rather than kind, that we would attribute to human designers, thus arriving at conception of God with positive content.

Hume, of course, pits these two views against each other and clearly hopes that he

---

[1] For a Catholic perspective on evolution, see Ratzinger (1986, English translation 1990), especially pages 41–50. In 2005 Josef Ratzinger succeeded Pope John Paul II as Pope Benedict XVI.
[2] See Popkin's edition of Hume's *Dialogues,* Hume (1980) page 2.
[3] See Clarke (1998) pages 3–33.
[4] Butler (1736); reprinted in facsimile by Kessinger Publishing (no date).

has shown that neither strategy can succeed in providing either a successful proof for God's existence or any knowledge whatsoever of God's nature. We will have occasion later to consider these Humean criticisms. Here I only want to note that the two strategies briefly outlined in the last paragraph can be generalized in such a way as to constitute two distinct paradigms in which the issues that arise in the philosophy of religion can be discussed and which I call the Deductivist and Inductivist paradigms respectively. According to Deductivism, the subject matter of the philosophy of religion consists largely in *a priori* analyses of the concept of God and the evaluation of deductive arguments for and against the existence of God. In some cases, these are combined – as in the case of the Ontological Argument, by means of which God's existence is deduced from a particular *a priori* conception of God captured in the definition of God as "the being a greater than which none other can be conceived." Within the Deductivist paradigm, philosophical discussion centres around the various proofs for God's existence and whether or not these proofs will pass muster as valid and sound demonstrations of God's existence. Theistic philosophers operating within its ambit will generally defend one or more of these arguments, reconstructing them as formal proofs and defending them against objections, whereas atheistic philosophers will critique these proofs and offer deductive disproofs for God's existence, urging that the concept of God is self-contradictory or logically incompatible with the existence of evil, for example.

Philosophers operating within the Inductivist paradigm, however, generally reject the sorts of self-imposed limitations that Deductivists take for granted. Philosophers of this sort are much more likely to raise the question of the reasonableness of religious belief or belief in God and to treat belief within the context of an ethics of belief, asking such questions as "Is belief in God permissible given our understanding of our doxastic obligations?" When discussing the reasons for belief, Inductivists are likely to rest content with probability in lieu of provability and be willing to adopt *a posteriori*, even quasi-scientific approaches to gathering and assessing the reasons for belief in God. Theistic Inductivists will generally argue that it is reasonable to believe that God exists or that God's existence is probable relative to some chosen standard for reasonableness or probability, while atheistic Inductivists will argue that it is neither reasonable to believe nor probable that God exists, often by reference to the same standards but just as often by reference to a competing set of standards regarded as more fair or adequate than those proposed by the theist.

The distinction between these two views is hardly a sharp one, and we will find figures that are both difficult to classify in terms of it and others who straddle both sides of the fence, either at different points in their careers or all at once. Nevertheless, I shall argue that the history of the philosophy of religion in the latter half of the twentieth century is largely the story of the shift from one dominant perspective or paradigm to the other. More specifically, I shall argue that over time the concerns of the Inductivist paradigm largely displace those of the Deductivist one in which the problems of the philosophy of religion were most often couched in the 1950's. Further, I shall argue that this happened quite naturally as the dialogue between theist and atheist philosophers developed in accordance with its own natural dynamic quite independently of the prior commitments of the discussants and that this development has lead to the current situation in the philosophy of religion. Before moving on to the defence of this thesis, however, let us become acquainted with the primary combatants in the field and the issues about which they contend. This will be the subject of the next chapter.

Chapter One

Theism and Atheism

As far back as we go in the history of western religion, we find pronounced scepticism among Greek intellectuals concerning traditional polytheistic folk religion. Already in Xenophanes, a younger contemporary of Thales, we find a critique of the claims made by Homer and Hesiod concerning the Olympian gods, one apparently made with impunity.[1] By no means, however, is Xenophanes merely a critic of religion: on the contrary, he proposes his own account of the nature of the deity that consists in a kind of materialistic pantheism.[2] In this, he is at one with the rest of the pre-Socratic thinkers, each of whom attempts to reduce the complexity and plurality of nature to an explanatory scheme in which some ultimate principle or set of principles generates and governs the physical world.[3] In many of these schemes, such as that of Anaximander, one finds something approaching the theistic God.

Even so, it is arguable that none of the Greek philosophers ever managed to arrive at the notion of a personal God of the sort that is familiar to most of us from monotheistic religion.[4] Plato, in postulating his realm of hierarchically–ordered forms topping out in the Form of the Good that can be grasped only in a kind of mystical experience, perhaps comes closest, unless we reckon Aristotle's attribution of consciousness to his deity ("God is thought thinking itself") to be an advance over Plato's conception. Regardless, Plato's theory of forms was almost immediately jettisoned by the Academy after his death and Aristotle's god remains a mere physical postulate, the first cause of motion in the universe. Even the Stoics, who managed to arrive at the notion of a deity who was in some sense rational, benevolent and providential still

---

1 See Gerson's discussion of Xenophanes in Gerson (1990) pages 15–19
2 Gerson (1990) pages 16–17.
3 Gerson (1990) pages 18–19.
4 As is so argued by Giovanni Reale in Reale (1986), Volume I; Reale maintains that the Greek philosophers were never able to achieve the notion of God as an immaterial spirit existing independently of the physical universe as its creator.

conceived of God in materialist pantheist terms, a god whom the emperor Claudius supposedly dismissed as something like a Great Pumpkin.[1]

However much the ancient philosophers may have paved the way for it, there is no reason to suppose that the Greeks would ever have arrived at the notion of the theistic God if left to their own devices; it seems to have been the unique contribution of monotheistic religion, specifically of the Jewish and Christian faiths, to western civilization. Indeed, when the neo-Platonists attempted to craft a religious system based on Plato and Aristotle capable of competing with Christianity, they opted for an impersonal absolute, the One, as their surrogate for the theistic God, one which proved incapable either of breathing new life into the old religion or of capturing the Hellenistic imagination and winning it back from Christ. At the same time, Jewish and Christian intellectuals were in many cases willing to adopt and employ elements of Greek thought in the philosophical articulation of their theological ideas, invoking the traditions that Pythagoras and Plato were themselves taught by Moses.[2] The philosophical position known as theism – long the dominant conception of God in the West – is the product of this largely happy marriage and helps to explain both the content and the preoccupations of western philosophers of religion down to the present day. Whenever western philosophers argue about the existence and nature of God, it is the theistic God about which they argue. But what then is theism?

THE ELEMENTS OF THEISM

Theism is a complex topic that is well worth book length treatment on its own. Here, however, considerations of space require that we deal with it somewhat summary fashion. First, I shall outline the basic elements of theism by contrast to other views about the nature of deity. Then I shall present the mainstream interpretation of that conception of God, known as Classical Theism or Perfect God theology. I shall then briefly consider some contemporary criticisms of and surrogates for, the classical view. Finally, I shall consider three alternative views that have some following in contemporary philosophy of religion: finite God theory, moderate scriptural anthropomorphism and Process Panentheism.

---

1 This story is the origin of the title of Lucian's satire *The Pumpkinification of Claudius* written on the occasion of that emperor's deification.
2 The story is repeated in both pagan and Christian sources from the early centuries CE; see, e.g. Guthrie (1992) p. 60.

Theism: A Basic Sketch

In this section I will identify the basic elements of theism by contrast to opposing views, thus arriving at a list of standard claims asserted by the great majority of theists, regardless of how they are interpreted.[1]

> First, as opposed to *polytheism*, theists maintain the existence of a single God, a supreme being incorporating all the powers and functions polytheists divide among the various gods and spirits worshipped in traditional folk–religions.
>
> Secondly, as opposed to *anthropomorphic materialism* (e.g., Hobbes), theists maintain that God is a spirit who neither has a body nor is subject to or constrained by the laws of nature governing the physical universe.
>
> Thirdly, as opposed to belief in the neo-Platonic *One* or the Hegelian *Absolute*, theists maintain that God is a personal being, one possessing intellect, will and the power of free agency.
>
> Fourthly, as opposed to Leibnizian *necessitarianism*,[2] theists maintain that God created the physical universe through a free act, such that both that universe and everything in it need not have existed and could have been different than it is.
>
> Fifthly, as opposed to both Plato's *Timaeus* and neo-Platonism, theists maintain that God created the universe *ex nihilo* neither relying on anything pre-existent (such as eternal matter) nor emanating it from His own substance (creation *ex deo*).
>
> Sixthly, as opposed to Pantheism and *Panentheism*, God transcends the universe He has created, exists separately from it and is in no way dependent on that universe either for His existence or His nature.
>
> Seventhly, as opposed to *Deism*, God is not only the creator and designer of the physical universe, but also a providential God who has an ongoing concern for and relation to that universe involving occasional but significant direct divine interventions in its operation.

Although not a standard thesis of theism as such, since nearly all theists are adherents of one or another of the monotheistic faiths, the seventh point above underwrites the possibility that God could perform miracles and communicate with us through special revelations given by means of prophets or inspired writings, a possibility that the majority of theists will claim has been realized in fact in human history.

---

1 For a more complete account, see Owen (1971) *passim*.

2 According to Leibniz, all of God's choices are ruled by necessity insofar as God must always choose only the best alternative; thus, God only creates – and does so by necessity of nature – if it is better to do so than not; this Leibniz takes to be compatible with the logical contingency of God s decision to create. On this point, see Adams (1994) pages 36–42.

Subscription to the foregoing points is practically *de rigueur* for theists, though of course exceptions can always be found. However, theists differ about how best to understand or interpret these various claims and, as one might expect, there is a range of options here. At one end of the spectrum there are the views of theists who are most influenced by traditional Greek philosophy and who thus tend to emphasize the uniqueness, transcendence and self-sufficiency of the theistic God, embracing what is nowadays referred to as *Classical Theism*. At the other end of the spectrum, consisting of theists who are suspicious of Greek philosophy and its potential for distorting the nature of the God revealed in the monotheistic scriptures such as the Bible and the Holy Qu'ran, there are what we might call *moderate scriptural anthropomorphists*, who deny that God possesses many of the properties attributed to Him by Classical Theists. Between these two extremes lie a number of intermediate views, all of which represent different degrees of commitment to the full-blown classical conception of God. Since classical theism has always been, and largely remains, the mainstream view of God, we will begin there and advance by degrees to the more attenuated positions in the field today.

CLASSICAL THEISM

Classical theism, also known as Anselmian theism or Perfect God theology,[1] arose at the period when the influence of Greek philosophy was greatest among the early Church Fathers and in which Greek ideas were proving most useful in the resolution of the doctrinal disputes over the Trinity and the relation between the two natures in the incarnate God–man, Jesus Christ. Classical theism represents a "high" conception of God that tends to exalt His nature and emphasize its superiority to and difference from that of any creature, including our own. In the Latin west, the principle and most influential exponent of this view was Augustine of Hippo (354–431 CE), who credited the writings of the "Platonists" (probably Plotinus) with having removed some of the intellectual difficulties that hindered his acceptance of the Christian faith. On the one hand, Augustine acquired a sufficiently Platonic, high conception of God from neo-Platonism that emphasized God's transcendence both of creatures and literal human depiction in words or images. At the same time, tempered by a Christian conviction that God was providential, both acquainted with particulars and continually involved with His creation, Augustine rejected the neo-Platonic account of God

---

1 These characterizations are most closely associated with the writings of T. V. Morris, formerly of Notre Dame. See Morris (1989) and Morris (1991).

as "beyond being," beyond personhood and too exalted to even be aware of the paltry world of creation. The result of these two perspectives is the classical theist conception of God.

In his *De Doctrina Christiana*,[1] Augustine observes that a universal fact about the history of religion is that people always worship whatever it is that is the highest and best thing they can conceive of. No matter how people's conceptions of God differ from time to time and place to place, the concept of God as the best and highest thing conceivable in principle remains a common core notion, a sort of Kantian regulative idea that people fill out in different ways in accordance with what they are capable of conceiving at those times. Centuries later, Anselm of Canterbury will use this insight to arrive at his famous definition of God as the being a greater than which none other can be conceived. Although Augustine has not yet arrived at this definition of God, he is already attempting to articulate its core elements more than six centuries before Anselm, an articulation that Anselm will in turn accept more or less as Augustine presented it.

Augustine rejects the neo-Platonic One, an impersonal absolute characterized as beyond being and personhood, in favour of the notion of God as a perfect being. For Augustine, following Plato, the mark of perfection is immutability or incapacity to change. For this reason, Augustine adopts immutability as the ruling theme in his articulation of the divine nature. Thus, for Augustine, God is immutable, impassable, unique in nature, one in substance, timelessly eternal, utterly simple and infinite in the sense of unlimited. Further, God is utterly independent of creatures and in no way dependent upon them. God has no accidental properties and no real relations to creatures; instead, any relational properties we attribute to God, such as being prayed to by Augustine or being Lord of last year's corn harvest are real only in relation to creatures due to changes occurring in them, not in God. Since God is immutable, impassable and eternal, He neither comes into nor goes out of existence nor is even capable of doing so. As such, God is a necessary being both in the sense of being radically independent of everything other than Himself and by existing *a se*, containing within Himself the explanation or reason for His existence.[2]

Despite being immutable, God is nevertheless a personal being who possesses intellect, rational will and the power of agency. Indeed, God not only possesses these characteristics, but possesses and exercises them in the most perfect way possible. God is the source of all being other than Himself and the first cause of all change

---

1 Book I, section 7; see Augustine (1997) p. 11.
2 See Anderson (1965).

occurring in the realm of mutable being. Since intellect and rational will presuppose the possession of knowledge, we must say that God is *omniscient* or all-knowing, i.e. possesses perfect knowledge. In a like manner, since the exercise of agency requires power, we must attribute power to God commensurate to His status as perfect being, hence describe Him as *omnipotent*. In the exercise of his agency, God is the creator, designer and conserver of all things other than Himself. From the observation of the world around us the wisdom, power and goodness of God are evident to our natural reason and even pagan philosophers such as the Platonists and Stoics find it undeniable. Finally, since God's act of creation (which requires no pre-existent material and involves no change in God Himself) is a free act, one that God need not have done and is not required in order to acquire any good for Himself that He did not already possess, it follows that creation is a gratuitous act of love for and intended for the benefit of the created. God is thus *omnibenevolent* or all-loving as well.

In Anselm of Canterbury, we find the foregoing analysis reduced to a definition of sorts: *God is the being a greater than which none other can be conceived.*[1] God is not simply the most perfect being that happens to exist; He is the most perfect being in principle, unsurpassable even by Himself. Further, the being of which God is the supreme exemplar is participable by creatures, who form a "great chain of being" admitting a seemingly infinite series of gradations between absolute non-existence and the supreme degree of existence enjoyed by God and thus of different degrees of resemblance between God and creatures. For Anselm, then, being or existence itself is a *degreed* property, of which other properties are merely aspects and which tops out in the conception of a being whose being is inseparable from it even in thought. It is on this basis that Anselm mounts his famous Ontological Argument for God's existence.

While Thomas Aquinas rejects Anselm's Ontological Argument, he agrees with Anselm that God is a perfect being. Indeed, according to Aquinas, God is Being, Truth and Goodness Itself whereas other beings exist, are true and are good only by their degreed participation in God's Being. Aquinas attempts to articulate this idea in a two primary ways, both of which are influenced by his Aristotelianism. First of all, using the Aristotelian potency/act analysis of change, Aquinas argues that God is *pure act*, i.e. act without potency, the total, complete and exhaustive expression of the act of existence. This makes God different in kind from creatures, which possess both potency and act and are thus subject to change, development and decay, but which nevertheless innately strive to perfect themselves to the degree possible within

---

1 *Proslogion* II; see the translation in Deane (1962) pages 7–10.

the limitations of both nature and circumstance. Secondly, and in the opinion of his followers more profoundly, Aquinas uses his doctrine of the real distinction between essence and existence to argue that God is different in kind from creatures while nevertheless still the highest and best expression of what creatures themselves are striving to become. In creatures, says Aquinas, the act of existence that realizes essence and the essence that informs and structures that act have the character of being merely arbitrarily juxtaposed; neither is the principle, explanation or natural expression of the other. In God, however, the act of existence receives its full and exhaustive realization and thus God possesses the essence proper to that unique being. In God's case, then, and in His case alone, the act of existence is the principle of essence and its natural expression so that in God there is no distinction between essence and existence. Aquinas expresses this analysis in the form of a slogan: In God, existence and essence are identical, so that to be God is to be the being whose essence is to exist.

VARIANT VERSIONS OF CLASSICAL THEISM

Let the foregoing sketch of full-blown classical theism of the sort associated with mediaeval philosophy be called "High Theism." Needless to say, there are many theists, even among those who would call themselves classical theists, who decline one or more elements of the High Theist account of God's nature. For example, many contemporary theists find the notion of God as the being whose essence is to exist tied to a metaphysics of being that is outmoded and obscure. If God's essence is to exist, they ask, is God nothing but an undifferentiated, qualityless act of existing? If so, how could God as so described be the personal God of monotheistic faith? In general, contemporary metaphysicians would rather do without any notion of being whatsoever or any notion of existence other than that expressed by the existential quantifier and so have little sympathy with any philosophy that makes the analysis of being a central metaphysical task.

More generally, many modern theistic philosophers reject Augustinian "High Theism" on the grounds that it is more Platonic than Christian. In particular, the notions of immutability, impassability, timeless eternity and simplicity are singled out as both paradoxical in themselves and seemingly superfluous to the proper understanding of God.[1] If God is immutable and impassable, how can He be the cause of anything other than Himself or act in any way, since it seems that this would require

---

1 See Craig and Moreland (2002), who affirm that God, rather than being simple, has distinct properties and is a temporal being with temporal thought–processes, and so on; see pages 524–27.

change in God. Further, how could an immutable and impassable God answer prayer, perform miracles or become incarnate in Jesus Christ? Indeed, how could such a God be providential in the ordinary sense that religious believers have generally thought Him to be? How could a timelessly eternal God be related to the temporal order of the created world and could such a God know what time it is now? If God is utterly simple and without parts of any kind, then how are we to understand the divine attributes? If each of those attributes is identical with God's simple essence or nature, then each will have to be identical with the other; yet God's power, knowledge, goodness, mercy and so on are intuitively distinct from one another. In most contexts, difficulties of this sort would simply be a challenge to philosophers to provide an analysis that removes the apparent paradox. In the case of these attributes, however, the majority of contemporary theistic philosophers have found the best course to be to simply jettison these attributes as superfluous Greek accretions on the more religiously central concept of God shared by all monotheists and articulated by theistic philosophers.

What is generally retained is the notion that God is a perfect being, conceived of on Anselmian lines as a being that possesses all perfections, i.e. the in principle highest degree of all great–making properties that come in degrees. God is thus conceived of as possessing an essence consisting of a set of distinct and independently conceivable/analysable divine attributes, the three most importance of which are omnipotence, omniscience and omnibenevolence (sometimes called "moral perfection"). Some contemporary theistic philosophers add necessary existence to this list as one of God's "essential properties", but others (as we shall see) do not. On this account, we investigate the divine nature by considering our intuitions and offering thought–experiments intended to clarify the concepts of omnipotence, omniscience and omnibenevolence. However, even within this tradition we find further deviations from the position generally held by classical theists.

While even the highest of High Theists have generally wanted to place some intrinsic limits on divine power (e.g., God cannot change the laws of logic or the *a priori* truths of mathematics, create square circles or a stone so heavy He can't move it) they have wanted to keep these to a minimum. However, contemporary critics of omnipotence, such as Peter Geach (1917–), have argued that there are many things that it is logically possible for an agent to do that God cannot do, such as destroy Himself, commit sin and order us to hate him.[1] He concludes that the notion of omnipotence simply amounts to the vacuous claim that God can do whatever God can do and plumps instead for the notion that God is "almighty" instead, according to which one can assert God has

---

1 See Geach (1977), pages 1–39.

power enough to control the course of events and keep His promises to believers without requiring a specific analysis of the limits on that power.

By the same token, it has generally been maintained by classical theists that God's omniscience extends to the future as well as to the present and the past. However, both Geach and Richard Swinburne[1] (among others) have rejected this classic analysis of omniscience by maintaining that God's knowledge, while extending to everything that can be known at any particular time, does not extend to the future, on the grounds that since the future does not yet exist, there is nothing to be known about it. In particular, Geach maintains that the almighty God does not need to know what the future will be like in order to control the future in such a way as to keep His promises or achieve His ends; instead, like a Grandmaster playing a novice at chess, He depends on His superior skill and expertise to defeat the plans of every opponent, progressively reducing the options available to them until they are forced to concede defeat. More recently, the group known as the Open Theists[2] have denied the compatibility of the classical notion of divine omniscience with freedom of the will and on those grounds denied that God is omniscient.

There seems to be general agreement among all theistic philosophers that God is omnibenevolent or morally perfect, though this hardly seems consistent with the tradition, which would have looked askance at such terms. Both mediaeval and Reformational theology reject the idea that there is any moral law existing independently of God by which He could be bound or to which He must conform. In general, the classical tradition in theology maintained that God has no natural obligations to creatures and can be bound to perform with regard to them, if at all, only by His own free choice, the guarantee of which is God's steadfastness – He will do as He has promised. Neither is it generally taken for granted that God directly desires and actively pursues the good of finite persons. Quite the contrary, both late mediaeval and Reformation theology assume that God will save only a few humans from the eternal punishment of Hell and those He does save will be saved for no reason having anything to do with them. Such a being hardly bears description as "omnibenevolent." Still, even in this tradition God is described as possessing moral predicates, such as being loving, just and merciful and regardless of how wrathful God may be toward sinners, no one wants to describe God as malevolent. However, the contemporary conception of God as omnibenevolent has been little analyzed by theistic phi-

---

1 See Swinburne (1977) pages 158–72.
2 See Hasker (1989), the essay and responses by Clark Pinnock in Basinger and Basinger (1986) and the essays by Pinnock, Randall Basinger, Richard Rice and Bruce Reichenbach in Pinnock (1989).

losophers and even less attempt has been made to relate this conception to traditional ideas about God's relation to creatures. However, since discussion of these topics is ongoing and we will be returning to them later, let us stop at this point and consider some alternative conceptions of God that have contributed to those discussions.

ALTERNATIVES TO CLASSICAL THEISM

Classical Theism is not the only view in the field, though it certainly deserves to be called the mainstream position among contemporary philosophers of religion, however they may disagree about the details. Not all philosophers of religion, however, accept this conception. Some theistic philosophers of the Protestant tradition, for example, are generally suspicious of the influence of pagan philosophy in Christian theology and emphasize the differences between God as depicted in traditional theology – especially in Catholic tradition – and the God revealed in the Scriptures. Echoing the words of Tertullian they ask "What has Athens to do with Jerusalem?" The God of the Bible is shown to be a passionate being whose on–going relationship with his chosen people/covenant communities is full of ups and downs, who changes His mind and plans and improvises like someone who has to roll with the punches. The God of Abraham, Isaac and Joseph is nothing at all like the God of the Philosophers, yet it is this God and not that other who is the God of living religion and to whom monotheists are committed by both faith and religious tradition. Further, it is that faith, as informed by scripture and the religious traditions of the community that ought to be normative for the believer rather than the speculations of philosophical theologians. Although this view has no name, we might call it *moderate scriptural anthropomorphism*.[1]

While only Hobbes and in our time the Latter Day Saints go so far as to claim that God is a material, embodied being many more theistic philosophers adopt a Cleanthean perspective on the divine intellect and will. God is said to have a set of distinct, discrete essential properties that are inseparable from His nature. Further, the divine intellect is a mind like a human mind, containing many distinct concepts and discursive processes (such as inference) by means of which God entertains and makes the plans that He then enacts using His will. On the view that the future is "open" and not determined in advance, God then modifies and adjusts his plans to take into account changing circumstances, sometimes even abandoning one scheme to enact another, as in the view that "salvation history" consists in a series of covenants by

---

1 See Wolterstorff in Morris (1988) pages 196–137 and in Tomberlin (1991) 531–52.

means of which God attempts to establish a relationship with the human race. God can thus be understood in categories analogous to those we use to understand the thoughts and behaviour of any rational being, as different in degree but not kind from ourselves.

The primary argument in favour of such a view, besides its fidelity to scriptural depictions of God and religious tradition, is the difficulty in making sense of the classical view. It will be claimed that the classical view, by incorporating Greek philosophical ideas into theology, created many unnecessary paradoxes and difficulties that can be dispensed with simply by adopting the "plain anthropomorphism" of the scriptures. However, there is little consensus on how far we can or should go in the direction of anthropomorphizing God. Neither is such a view devoid of problems in its own right. As Hume points out, if God is internally complex and analogous to a human being, oughtn't we to conclude that God is a finite, contingent being like we are in need of a cause or designer in his own right – and, if so, what does the appeal to God actually accomplish so far as explaining the existence or design of the physical universe is concerned?

Finite God theism is another variant on theism, one that sacrifices even the central properties of omnipotence and omniscience in order to arrive at a conception of God that is both intellectually and spiritually satisfactory. Partly motivated as a response to the problem of evil, finite God theism is most closely associated with the nineteenth century movement known as personal idealism or *Personalism*, a view that proclaims that reality consists of a network of individual minds or souls rather than (as in the Hegelian tradition) an all-encompassing impersonal absolute. In the school known as Boston Personalism,[1] this view is articulated by postulating a theistic God who, however, is not completely in control of the world-process and is dependent on us for help in securing the triumph of good over evil in the world. God is thus dependent on our cooperation to accomplish his goals for the created world and human beings a more exalted place in the universe than the one usually assigned to them in perfect being theology.

Although not a form of theism *per se*, the *process panentheism* of Alfred North Whitehead and Charles Hartshorne[2] has also been taken seriously as a competitor to the classical theist conception of God in American universities and divinity schools. According to Hartshorne, who did the most to popularize and articulate the view,

---

1 The best known contemporary exponent of Boston Personalism is Peter A. Bertocci (1925–); see his (1970).
2 See Whitehead (1929) and Hartshorne (1970).

God and the world are co-eternal and mutually dependent on one another. More than this, God is *anima mundi*, the soul of the world and related to the physical cosmos as the human soul is related to the human body. Conceived of in this way, God has a dipolar nature. God's consequent nature is the divine ideal which God asymptotically approaches over time as a consequence of the cosmic process by means of which divine self-development takes place. At any given time, however, God's nature is as yet incomplete, only partially realized and thus limited in his effective control over the physical universe, thus fails to be omnipotent or omniscient. God thus brings into existence subordinate spiritual beings such as us in order to help Him in the process of ordering the world and establishing a universal community of peace and love. God thus remains omnibenevolent in Hartshorne's system, albeit only in intention rather than in fact.

Rejecting the classical notion of perfection, Hartshorne emphasizes the real relatedness of God to creation, His interaction with it and the ever-changing character of the divine being. Indeed, Hartshorne insists that it is better for God to be wholly immanent, intimately related to and affected by every aspect of the physical universe than it is for God to be transcendent and at best indirectly related to that universe in a manner that does not compromise His immutability. In Hartshorne we once again find the charges that classical theism is religiously unsatisfactory inasmuch as it makes God too distant from and indifferent to us to be a genuine object of religious devotion or spiritual intimacy. By the same token, since God needs us in order to accomplish His ends, our choices take on a cosmic significance that far exceeds anything that they can possess in classical theism. Be this as it may, however, it remains that classical theism of at least the minimal sort is the main focus of discussion, so we shall leave this brief survey of the competing conceptions to consider the major alternative to theism discussed by philosophers of religion, i.e., atheism.

ATHEISM

Etymologically, "atheism" includes everyone who is not a theist as above described, which would include the adherents of all non-monotheistic religions as well as unbelievers. Indeed, we find that sometimes the term has been used to describe pagans and idolaters, even though they affirm the existence of spiritual beings. In contemporary philosophy of religion, however, the term "atheism" has a more restricted sense than this and does not refer to adherents of non-theistic faiths. At the same time, while all atheists reject theism, the position known as atheism in the contemporary philosophy of religion generally encompasses more than just this, since atheists in this sense reject all religious belief of whatever sort and eschew all supernatural claims. Modern atheism is almost always part of a larger worldview, which is sometimes nowadays called *metaphysical naturalism*, of which the following are characteristic theses:

1. There exists only the universe that is present to us in sense-experience and studied by the natural sciences; there is no supernatural reality of any sort.
2. The existence of the universe is a surd fact neither needing nor admitting of any further explanation.
3. Matter is the ultimate reality and every phenomenon is ultimately reducible without remainder to matter and explicable in terms of its properties, states and processes occurring within nature and studied by natural science.
4. The preferred materialist ontology is *physicalism*, according to which the fundamental laws governing matter and material processes ultimately reducible to and expressible in the ontology required by the fundamental natural science, physics.
5. The laws of physics govern all phenomena at the macroscopic level, including human thought and behaviour; all phenomena, then, including human acts, are explicable in terms of efficient causes and are thus physically necessary.

Of course, not all atheists endorse every one of the foregoing claims. For example, *emergent naturalists*[1] (sometimes called *non-reductive materialists*)[2] maintain that matter is the ultimate reality and source of everything that exists but that some realities, such as conscious mind, have powers and properties neither governed by nor reducible to those of physical systems. However, just as classical theism of some sort is the mainstream view among theists, so too is metaphysical naturalism the mainstream view among atheists on the whole.

POSITIVE AND NEGATIVE ATHEISM

Since the 1950's, many atheists have distinguished two forms of atheism: positive and negative.[3] Positive atheism is the affirmation of God's non-existence, taking the form of assent to the claim "God does not exist." Negative atheism is merely the non-

---

1 See Hook (1991) pages 202–6 and the selections by Roy Wood Sellars and Dewey, Hook and Nagel in Ryder (1994), pages 79–120.
2 This includes John Searle and Thomas Nagel; see Searle (1992).
3 See Flew (1966) pages 13–23 and Martin (1990) page 26, 281–84, 463–4.

affirmation of God's existence, taking the form of refusal to assent to the claim that "God exists." Unlike the agnostic, who neither assents to nor denies the existence of God but suspends judgment on the question, the negative atheist simply declines belief in God on the ground that there is insufficient evidence for God's existence and not on the basis of positive proof of His non-existence.

The position of the negative atheist vis-à-vis God's existence is analogous to that of the sceptic concerning the existence of UFO's, Sasquatch or the Loch Ness monster. On the one hand, the evidence for the existence of these entities is far from compelling; on the other hand, the failure over time of dedicated to Ufologists and monster hunters to produce significant hard evidence for their existence, evidence that ought to be available if they did, tips the scales in favour of sceptical doubt about their existence. Given this situation, the appropriate response is not suspension of judgment with regard to the existence of such beings but rather disbelief justified by the Negative Evidence Principle:

> NEP: It is reasonable to decline any claim for which a concerted effort fails to provide positive evidence of the sort we would reasonably expect to find if we inquired.

The same, says negative atheism, applies to the claim "God exists." The failure of theists to provide any solid proof or evidence for God's existence justifies scepticism about the existence of God.

This naturally suggests a two-pronged atheistic critique of the claims of theism. The first part, negative atheism, attempts to show that there are no good reasons of any sort for believing that God exists. The second part, positive atheism, attempts to provide good reasons and evidence for denying that God exists. Of course, we are not at the point where we can yet judge whether an atheist of either sort can make out his or her case. However, it is appropriate to discuss this distinction here because of the role it plays in the *burden of proof problem* in the philosophy of religion, to which we now turn.

Religious Commitment and the Ethics of Belief

In his oft–referred to but rarely read essay "The Ethics of Belief,"[1] the English neo-Positivist W. K. Clifford attacks religious belief on ethical grounds, essentially claiming that to the extent that religious belief is based on a faith–commitment rather than

---

1 See Clifford (1999) pages 70–96.

on scientific evidence it is a stolen pleasure and essentially in violation of our basic doxastic obligations, the first and greatest of which is that "it is always and everywhere wrong to hold any belief without adequate evidence." It emerges in the course of the essay that the primary reason for this is that indulging in such beliefs may have bad social consequences; in particular, even one's merely personal religious commitments may retard or delay the progress of the human race. Clifford's essay represents the sea–change in the attitude of intellectuals toward religion in general and personal religious belief in particular that has its roots in the Enlightenment. Religion is now in the dock and needs to prove its innocence in the eyes of educated persons who regard it much more likely to be a source of evil than of good in the world.

In his much more often read essay "The Will to Believe"[1] William James defends the propriety of religious belief without evidence, at least in certain conditions. Although James has been accused of being unfair to Clifford[2] – and this claim has sometimes been backed up argument[3] – my reading of these essays does not confirm this accusation. It seems to me that James certainly understands and fairly represents the gist of Clifford's position and makes a serious response to it from the point of view of his own pragmatism; how successful it may be is another matter. In essence, James maintains that Clifford's view is too conservative to be useful in the pursuit of theoretical truth or the discovery of the human good and is likely to retard, rather than promote human progress. When applied to the theoretical context – obviously of importance to a scientific man like Clifford – the strategy of Clifford's essay privileges avoidance of error over the discovery of truth to such a degree that many useful hypotheses would have to be foregone and many truths left undiscovered. The discovery of theoretical truth requires risk of error as one of its pre-conditions and one of the advantages of the scientific method is that it gives us a rational way to manage that risk. Clifford's moral abstemiousness concerning belief contradicts his practice as a working scientist, where we are often called upon to adopt an hypothesis in order to "try it on for size."

It does not follow, of course, that James licenses a wholesale right to believe whatever one wants whenever one wants. James places a number of strictures on the exercise of the will to believe that greatly reduces the scope of this practice by setting the conditions for doxastic risk–management. These conditions include:

> 1. Reason must not antecedently decide the issue. (James does not countenance

---

1 See James (1979), pages 13–33.
2 See the editor's introduction to Clifford (1999), page xxii.
3 See the articles by Hollinger and Rorty in Putnam (1997), pages 69–102.

believing contrary to the available evidence, at least in standard cases.)
2. The option in question must be a genuine option, i.e.
   (a) *living*, i.e. have some intrinsic plausibility or attraction
   (b) *forced*, i.e. one for which suspension of belief is tantamount to the rejection of it, and
   (c) *momentous*, i.e. involve the potential gain/loss of a significant good.

Given that all of these conditions are met, James argues that it is permissible for us to believe whatever it is that our "passional nature" prompts us to believe in an experimental fashion, "trying it on for size" in the hope/expectation of significant benefit to ourselves and others.

Just as Clifford does, James applies his analysis to the context of practical questions of living as well as that of theoretical inquiry, and it is here that we find James's defence of religious belief. Clifford, though not completely unsympathetic to religion, was an agnostic on essentially Huxleyan grounds so James does not need to argue in this context that reason does not resolve the issue concerning God's existence. Nor does anything Clifford says suggest that conditions 2a–2c above are not met. The only question is whether or not there is a legitimate practical good that justifies a morally responsible passional adherence to religion. James suggests that there is, both in "The Will to Believe" and in another essay written around the same time "The Moral Philosopher and the Moral Life."

Essentially, this great good is the support that sincere religious belief gives to the moral life specifically and to the strenuous life in general. The religious believer, he tells us, has the confident expectation that, in pursuing the life of personal moral striving and of contributing human social progress he or she is on the side that "throws the last stone"[1] – victory is assured if only we will do our part. Furthermore, says James, it is not even necessary for the success of this project that the beliefs in question be true in the correspondence sense! Some beliefs are self-fulfilling in that there is a strong causal connection between their being believed and their becoming true. Thus, if one believes that one can do something (such as jump a mountain chasm) it is much more likely that one can do it than if one has doubts about whether or not one can; indeed, that one fully believe that this is so may well make the difference between whether or not one will succeed at the task. By the same token if religious believers, convinced that their actions will usher in a better world on the strength of a divine promise, strive under the aegis of those beliefs to secure that end, this greatly increases the probability that the goal will be achieved quite independently of whether there is a God. In

---

1 See 'The Moral Philosopher and the Moral Life' in James (1979), pages 159–62.

this case, at least, believing in God may well be efficacious regardless of whether it is true in the correspondence sense and that will justify adherence to it so long as the possibility that there is a God remains theoretically open for us.

The dispute between James and Clifford is, of course, only the opening salvo in the debate over the rationality of belief in God one that continues to intensify in the twentieth century. Let us next consider another challenge to the rational permissibility of religious belief, this one known as the Presumption of Atheism.

THE PRESUMPTION OF ATHEISM

In the mid–twentieth century, a number of atheistic philosophers of religion mounted a new strategy against the propriety of religious belief known as the Presumption of Atheism. Essentially, this is seen as the consequence of a standard and seemingly plausible view about the role of burden of proof in discussion in the philosophy of religion, one that theistic philosophers will eventually challenge. Antony Flew is the philosopher most closely associated with this position. In his essay "The Presumption of Atheism"[1] he lays out the presumption, the arguments for it and its consequences for religious belief. Flew takes it for granted that a belief is rational only if it is grounded in some way, i.e. justified by sufficient proof or evidence to make it true or very likely to be true. In the debate between the theist and the negative atheist (or *nontheist*), however, it is the theist who makes the positive claim and thus, in accordance with the principle first enunciated by Stratonicus of Lampsachus, which Flew calls the Stratonician Principle, the *onus probandi* is clearly on the theist. The nontheist, however, makes no positive claim, not even that God does not exist and thus has no need to prove anything; it is sufficient for the non-theist to carry the day that he or she show that there is no good evidence for the existence of God. The failure of the theist to make out his case leaves belief in God without rational support and thus beneath the credence of a rational person.

Thus, in abeyance of a successful philosophical defence of theism, monotheistic religious belief is hoist with the same petard, in accordance with the following reasoning:

    1. Monotheism cannot be true unless theism is true.
    2. There is no reason to believe that theism is true.
    3. Therefore, there is no reason to believe that monotheism is true.

Given that it is irrational to believe any substantive theoretical claim without ade-

---

1 In Flew (1976), pages 13–30.

quate proof or evidence and that the central substantive theoretical claim of theism lacks that proof or evidence, the same will hold for religious belief as well, since it depends for its rational provenance on the truth of theism. So, given the nature of the burden of proof in the discussion of God's existence, the philosophical defence of theism becomes a matter of life and death for religious belief. Supposing (as most philosophers at mid–century did) that the burden of proof cannot be carried, to persist in religious belief is to be guilty of wilful irrationality and, once again, to be in violation of one's basic doxastic obligations. By the same token, agnosticism is also ruled out by the same argument; given the lack of evidence for God's existence and the NEP, it makes no more sense to be an agnostic about this issue than it is for one to be an agnostic about UFO's, Sasquatch or the Loch Ness monster.

The application of Flew's strategy is less clear–cut that it first appears. For one thing, it seems open to the following sort of parody argument. Just as nearly all theists are monotheists as well, so too are all negative atheists also positive atheists as well. Now, we can imagine a form of theism – call it "negative theism" or *nonatheism* consisting of all those people who do not affirm atheism. Now, in the debate between the positive atheist and the nonatheist, it is clearly the positive atheist who makes the positive substantive claim that the nonatheist simply declines without affirming anything. As such, in the debate between the positive atheist and the nonatheist, the burden of proof is clearly on the positive atheist such that the failure of the positive atheist to make his or her case leaves positive atheism without rational support and thus beneath the credence of a rational person, in which reason requires that we embrace the default position in the debate, i.e. nonatheism. To this we may add the observation that nontheism and nonatheism are sub–contraries: both can't be false but both could be true. The latter would be the case if neither the theist nor the positive atheist were able to make out a case for their positions. Of course, the union of these two views would be agnosticism, i.e. suspension of judgment about the existence of God by neither affirming nor denying God's existence. The upshot of all of this appears to be the following: either the theist carries the burden of proof, or the (positive) atheist does, or neither does. If either side carries the burden, it wins the debate. If neither does, then agnosticism is the default position. The supposed presumption of atheism, then, disappears and leaves everything as we thought it was before Flew made his suggestion.

We see from this that the real debate is not between theists and negative atheism, or between positive atheists and negative theists, but instead between theists and positive atheists. It is this debate that we will consider in the chapters to follow.

Chapter Two

Neo-Thomism and the Rise of Analysis

In 1871, Pope Pius IX called the First Vatican Council in Rome in order to respond to the modernist "crisis" within the Catholic Church. Among the many modern errors to be condemned were the twin threats of rationalism and semi–rationalism, views that maintained that the truths of faith could be grasped and proven by reason alone without the need for revelation or even, if initially knowable only through revelation, subsequently demonstrable by reason. At the same time, the council also condemned the errors of fideism and traditionalism, according to which knowledge of the truths of faith is to be found solely in the Scriptures and the tradition of the Church. As part of the rejection of this position, the following was established as one of the dogmas of the Catholic Church:

> If anyone says that the one, true God, our Creator and Lord, cannot be known with certainty with the natural light of human reason through the things that are created, let him be anathema.[1]

Thus, according to Vatican I, one of the truths of faith that can be known with certainty by unaided reason is that God exists. Although the Latin text of this canon excludes the word *demonstratio* ("proof") it nevertheless clearly teaches that God's existence can be shown to be true on neutral grounds sufficient to convince all sincere and rational inquirers.

Vatican I did not go on to provide such a proof nor even indicate in broad outlines how such a proof should go. When *Pio Nono* died in 1878 after serving the longest reign in the history of the papacy, the College of Cardinals decided to choose an interim pope to replace him and settled on 68 year–old Giuseppe Pecci, whom it was expected would reign for a few years at most. In fact the new pope, Leo XIII (as Pecci styled himself) would reign for a quarter century and prove to be as progressive as

---

1 See Denzinger (31st edition, 1954) section 1806 and Dupuis and Neuner (Seventh Edition, 2001) section 115/3026.

Pius had proved to be reactionary. His encyclicals would become the basis for what is now known as Catholic social teaching and his fascination with *rerum novarum* ("new things") would lead to his being the first pope to have his image recorded on film, the first pope to have his voice recorded on a wax cylinder and the first pope to ride in an automobile – all of these when he was in his nineties! However, Leo's contribution to our subject here consists in his first encyclical, *Aeterni Patris* (1879), in which he mandated that henceforth the teaching of philosophy and theology in all Catholic universities and seminaries should be based on the teachings of St. Thomas Aquinas. This launched the movement known to contemporary historians as neo-Thomism, intended as the positive complement to the condemnations of Vatican I and destined to dominate Catholic thought for the next eighty-five years.

Catholic theologians and philosophers were quick to heed Leo's call and soon a burgeoning neo-Thomist movement was under way, complete with rival schools of interpretation. While Leo's successor, St. Pius X, reigned only ten years (1903–13) he was extremely busy reinforcing the legacy of his immediate predecessors. In particular, he mandated that the basic principles of the new Thomist orthodoxy should be codified so that limits could be placed on what could count as an authentically Catholic philosophical position. The result was the document published in 1914 by the Congregation of Studies in Rome that became known as the "24 Theses of Thomism."[1] Although neo-Thomism would continue to develop as a living movement, the "24 theses" became the groundwork for the scholastic manual tradition known as "textbook Thomism" that would be used to train generations of Catholic seminarians and college students and would become identified with Thomism itself among many intellectuals. Since "textbook Thomism" is neo-Thomism for our purposes here, we will concentrate on the basic elements of this system, taking the "24 theses" as our guide.

NEO-THOMISM: BASIC ELEMENTS

Neo-Thomism is a decidedly anti-modern philosophy but it does not ignore the modern tradition in philosophy. Instead, it desires to engage the modern tradition, demonstrate its shortcomings and supersede it using the updated categories of mediaeval thought. While Thomists worked at preparing critical editions, producing translations and commentaries to the works of Thomas, they also produced textbooks and critical studies intended to clarify and update Aquinas's ideas, often in relation to

---

1 See the article 'The 24 Theses of Thomism' in Sahakian (1968) pages 316–19.

contemporary philosophical problems and movements. Appearing as it did during the heyday of Idealism in the English-speaking world, the neo-Thomists tended to take neo-Kantian and Idealist philosophy as their stalking horse.

The neo-Thomists generally rejected the notion, prevalent since the time of Descartes, that epistemology is first philosophy and the problem of the egocentric predicament is the starting point for philosophical reflection. Thomism is a form of realism that maintains that metaphysics, conceived of as the science of being *qua* being, is first philosophy. It is being, not the contents of one's own mind, that is the first object of the intellect. Although the neo-Thomists did have a theory concerning the mechanics of cognition, they were externalists in epistemology concerned to explain how knowledge is possible but not concerned to combat scepticism, which they dismiss as the product of dispensable Cartesian assumptions and as ultimately self-refuting along Aristotelian lines. Philosophy, then, begins with metaphysics or the philosophy of being.

That metaphysics, of course, is the metaphysics of Aristotle as derived primarily from the *Categories* and understood in accordance with the doctrine of the *De Ente et Essentia* of Aquinas. The fundamental existents are individual, particular things or *beings*, some of which are also *substances*. In each being, there are the twin principles of *existence* (that by which things are) and *essence* (that by which things are what they are.) In finite beings, existence and essence, while inseparable in being, are nevertheless really distinct; neither is the principle of the other nor are they aspects of or grounded in something more fundamental than themselves. As such, every finite being is a composite being at its very core.

Many particular things are also substances and possess both essential and accidental properties classifiable according to Aristotle's categories, the most important of which are the categories of quantity, quality and relation. By the same token, any particular that is more than an aggregate of material particles is a composite of form and matter, relative terms that refer to that which structures a substance and governs its behaviour on the one hand and that which receives form and is structured by it. Form is, in fact, essence conceived of as concrete and immanent in a particular thing as its nature. In finite, temporal beings form as nature is the source of spontaneous behaviour and immanent development in that thing (the fall of a rock, the growth of an animal) as well as the principle determining that thing's powers and liabilities in relation to other beings. Change, then, whether of the immanent variety or as the consequence of external affection, is the actualization of potency in that thing for which form as nature is the ultimate explanatory principle. While each substance possesses many forms corresponding to its individual properties, it is *substantial form* (= concrete essence or nature as found in actually existing things) that is primary both in being and explanation and thus the object of scientific inquiry.

Due to their being composite and finite, all observable things are subject to *change*, to both generation and corruption (coming–to–be and passing–away) and to change of state or property. In all such cases, we are inevitably led to postulate an external cause of change, at the very least a generator who has brought that being into existence or one that produces the external conditions necessary for the immanent exercise of a thing's inherent natural powers. Finite things, then, are non-self-explanatory and thus need an external cause in order to account for any change they undergo, even those that are the consequence of that thing's inherent, natural powers. Further, nothing can change itself, since this would require that it both be in potency and act at the same time in the same respect, which is a self-contradiction. Even in the case of spontaneous and immanent change, nature expresses itself in an environment that permits that expression, where it acts as the cause by imposing form on pre-existing matter; neither the presence of that form to begin with, nor its unity with matter nor of the presence of its enabling conditions is accounted for in such cases. Science, then, is the search for the causes of things and a complete account is arrived at only when the effect is seen as arising necessarily from the causal nexus that produces it. This search for causes can have no final terminus except in a cause that is somehow self-explanatory.

For Thomists, this cause is the theistic God, understood from the point of view of Aristotelian metaphysics as an *infinite* or unlimited being. Central to this conception is the claim that there is no real distinction between essence and existence in God; God's essence is to exist. This claim is notoriously hard to explicate, but one way of attempting to conceive this is to say that the divine essence or nature is the essence that belongs to existence itself when fully realized or actualized in a concrete entity. God is thus being itself (i.e. enjoys the highest in principle mode of being) rather than a being characterized by an essence that arbitrarily limits one's existence and capacities. Such a being will be *pure act*, i.e. fully and completely realized and actualized as well as such to realize all the potentiality inherent in existence as such in the highest and most complete way. This mode of being excludes both the need and the possibility of change; as such, God is immutable, impassable, immortal and timelessly eternal. God is also utterly simple, lacking parts of any kind. Although we attribute various perfections to God, we must understand that in this case all these terms refer, not to discrete or separable divine attributes, but instead to the entire divine essence as apprehended from a particular point of view by analogy to creatures. In the divine nature, all of these "properties" converge or coalesce into a single act of fully realized existence with which they are all substantially (not logically) identical.

REGINALD GARRIGOU–LAGRANGE AND THE FIVE WAYS

The neo-Thomists followed their eponymous master in insisting that the only valid and sound demonstrations of God's existence were arguments beginning from facts evident to the senses and proceeding by syllogistic inference to the conclusion that God exists. In his *Summa Theologiae*, Aquinas had presented five such arguments.[1] Each Thomist textbook attempted to reconstruct these arguments, either individually or in some unified version, as a valid and sound deductive proof of God's existence from some–self evident fact about the world. Among these reconstructions, the most thorough and sophisticated was that undertaken by the French Dominican theologian Reginald Garrigou-LaGrange (1883–1964) in his two-volume *God: His Existence and Nature*,[2] originally published in 1909 and translated into English in 1934. In this book, Garrigou affirms that God's existence can be proven by reason alone without relying on faith or any other disputable claim from self-evident first principles by means of a syllogistic argument. Although Garrigou defends each of the traditional five ways separately, he also reconstructs the core of the cosmological argument as a valid and sound deductive proof, as follows:

> The world necessarily demands a primary extrinsic cause.
> Now we call the primary extrinsic cause of the world God.
> Therefore, God exists.[3]

The proof of the first premise we can briefly summarize as follows. First of all, the notion of a contingent being existing without any cause or reason is impossible. By definition, a contingent being is one that exists but need not have existed and thus needs an extrinsic cause other than itself in order to exist, being by nature "indifferent to existence." To suppose that such a contingent being exists without such a cause, then, is to suppose that it exists without one of the necessary conditions for its existence having been met, which is impossible, like a square existing without one of its

---

1 In *Summa Theologiae* I, I Art. 1, Quaestio 2; see Aquinas (1969) Volume II, pages 4–17.
2 Translated by Dom Bede Rose and published in two volumes by Herder and Herder; hereafter, Garrigou (1934).
3 Garrigou (1934), p. 225. Garrigou does not include this argument in his exposition of the formal proofs for God's existence.

sides. Therefore, every contingent being requires an extrinsic cause for its existence; this proves the Principle of Sufficient Reason by an indirect proof from the principle of non-contradiction. But the world is a contingent being, one that need not have existed. Therefore, by the PSR, the world needs a cause for its existence and only an extrinsic cause will do. The world cannot be cause of itself, since this would require that the world exist prior to itself in order to bring itself into existence and be both in potency and act in the same respect at the same time, both of which are self-contradictory and impossible. Neither can the world consist of or have been caused by a series of causes all of which were contingent. Given that none of the members of the series need have existed and that the series is nothing more than merely the collection of its members, neither need the series have existed. In that case the entire series would be contingent as well and be such as to lack an explanation for its existence: one could still sensibly ask the question "Why is there such a series at all rather than not?" and to answer that each member of the series is caused by one of the other members would simply beg the question, since this answer already presupposes, hence cannot explain, the existence of the series in the first place.

This extrinsic cause must therefore be something other than the world itself existing independently of it. Furthermore, this being would have to be non-contingent, such as to exist without requiring a cause for its existence since, as we have seen, even an infinite series of contingent beings would fail to be self-explanatory. But only a being of the sort represented by the theistic God could possibly be such a being, one in whom there is no distinction between essence and existence and who is therefore an immutable, timelessly eternal pure act simultaneously realizing all the potentiality inherent in the act of existence to the highest possible degree in principle. Therefore, Garrigou concludes, the God of the philosophers exists. Further, given that God has defined Himself in *Exodus* 3:14 as being itself – *He Who Is* – the God of the philosophers is plausibly taken to the be the God of Abraham, Isaac and Joseph as well once the dispensable anthropomorphisms of the Bible are removed. Thus, the proof concludes not to a merely theoretical entity, but one that is identical to the God of living monotheistic faith.

This will do for a sketch of the deductivist natural theology typical of mainstream neo-Thomism in the first decades of the Twentieth Century. We will return to it later, but now it is time to introduce the philosophical movement that, by taking neo-Thomism as its stalking horse, produced contemporary philosophy of religion.

The Beginnings of Analytic Philosophy

The philosophical movement now called analytic philosophy emerged in England early in the twentieth century and was largely the product of two Cambridge philosophers, G. E. Moore (1871–1958) and Bertrand Russell (1872–1970). Indeed, the two main traditions within analytic philosophy can be directly traced to the work of these two men. The first tradition, which became known as ordinary language philosophy, originated in the philosophy of Moore, who began as part of the neo-Realist reaction against the then–dominant Hegelian philosophy and wrote the first classic of analytic philosophy, *Principia Ethica*, published in 1903. The second, which roots philosophical analysis in modern symbolic logic, arose out of the pioneering work, inspired by Peano and Frege, that resulted in Russell and Whitehead's *Principia Mathematica*, published in three volumes from 1910–1913. In this latter form, it would become dominant in the United States later in the century. The Austro–English philosopher Ludwig Wittgenstein, perhaps the most influential philosopher in the English-speaking world in the mid– and late twentieth century, would play a pivotal role in the development of both traditions.

Although these two traditions in analytic philosophy have had many permutations and expressions, so that analytic philosophy is less a school than a sort of movement, there are several dominant themes that we can associate with analysis as a whole. I will now attempt to summarize them.

Systematization vs. Specialization

When Moore and Russell were beginning their careers at the turn of the twentieth century, the standard picture of the philosopher's task, arising from the then dominant Idealist tradition, was to provide an overall, systematic theory of the nature of things capable of integrating all aspects of reality, including natural science, in a single, very general scheme of things or worldview called a *system*. Philosophy, then, was regarded as an overarching discipline capable of explaining everything and providing the fundamental principles for every other discipline. Analytic philosophers challenged this notion, maintaining that philosophy was simply one discipline among others and by no means the most important one either. Rather, the philosopher was a specialist devoted to a particular set of problems and a certain set of techniques designed to deal with those problems without regard to the results attained in other disciplines; by the same token, philosophy was thought to have few if any implications for other disciplines.[1] At the same time that such disciplines as cosmology and psychology were declaring their autonomy from philosophy, philosophers in the Moorean tradition were attempting to salvage something for the philosopher (and the philosopher alone) to do as a means of justifying his existence.

Preoccupation with Language

Another main theme of analytic philosophy is its preoccupation with questions concerning language. Although philosophers have always been interested in language, the analysis of concepts, the clarification of claims and the evaluation of arguments, the analytic philosophers made these activities central to the philosophical enterprise. Indeed, in some cases, they regarded this to be the sole concern of the philosopher. However, analytic philosophers were neither interested in philology, traditional grammar and rhetoric nor in empirical linguistic studies; their own approach to language involved a set of questions that were thought to be independent of any of these disciplines. One expression of this concern with language was a set of general questions about language – concerning sense, reference and linguistic meaning – that came to be the subject matter of the branch of philosophical inquiry known as the Philosophy of Language, regarded by many of its practitioners as first philosophy in the way that earlier ages had regarded metaphysics or epistemology as the key philosophical endeavour. A second, more widespread expression of this idea was that many of the particular questions traditionally discussed by philosophers could be resolved (or, more typically, dissolved) using the techniques of philosophical analysis and so finally be put to rest. According to the logical atomists, for example, formal logic would help us clear up the traditional problems of metaphysics by giving us formal analyses of notions like existence and – through the exposition of the logical forms of basic sentences – provide us both with the basic structure of language and the outline of the basic structure of the world captured by language. According to the Logical Positivists, a perfected empiricist language would eliminate the ambiguity and vagueness inherent in ordinary language and thus provide an instrument adequate to the needs of modern science. According to the Oxford philosophers, close attention to the nuances of ordinary language would serve to dispel the confusions that lead philosophers to imagine that there are any such things as distinctly philosophical problems or questions at all. Indeed, in the latter two cases, analytic philosophy becomes a kind of

---

1 This was especially the case with regard to what became known as Oxford philosophy as exemplified by Ryle and Austin; see Urmson (1960) 165–87 and Soames (2003), Volume 2, Parts II and III, especially chapters 3, 4, and 8.

anti-philosophy, intended primarily to attack the conceit of traditional philosophers to somehow compete with natural science in describing or explaining the world.

Logic as the Primary Tool of Analysis

The term "logic" often appears in the writings of analytic philosophers of both persuasions, though the two traditions within analysis tend to use this term in widely divergent ways. In the tradition stemming from Russell, logic refers to modern symbolic or "mathematical" logic that treats logic as a formal discipline rather than as an organon or method for intellectual inquiry. Nevertheless, the techniques of contemporary symbolic logic – including modal logic – have been regarded by many philosophers as powerful tools for the analysis of implications and arguments. Indeed, in the second decade of the twentieth century, Russell and the young Wittgenstein attempted to use this logic as the foundation for a new systematic philosophy known as Logical Atomism, in which the new formal logic would be used to exhibit the logical forms of all sentences and thus provide a general picture of the nature of reality, complete with a fundamental ontology. Although interest in this project faded fairly quickly, the influence of formal logic remains significant to the present day.

In the writings of those in the Moorean tradition, "logic" (or sometimes "grammar") is used to refer to something inherent in ordinary language but not capable of being modelled by or represented as a formal system. The logic of ordinary language is not some sort of system, set of rules or general worldview (beyond the pre-philosophical commitments of "common sense", which hardly counts for Moore as a theory of anything) that can be theoretically articulated. Rather, it is something to be appreciated *in situ* as applying to particular terms or forms of expression meticulously studied in their typical, everyday contexts and may be as particular as the term or expression itself. In this context, logic refers to a loosely organized set of analytic techniques that are distinguished by their flexibility and sensitivity to nuance rather than anything like a strict methodology. Indeed, among those "ordinary language philosophers" who embraced the deflationary project of debunking philosophy in general, these techniques were likened to a kind of therapy the purpose of which was to free philosophers from the delusions that led them to take traditional philosophical questions seriously and thus as particular as the subjects to which they were to be applied. Less radical linguistic analysts treated these techniques as having "the first word" in philosophical investigation, as providing the primary data for philosophical consideration, the careful review and consideration of which would help philosophers avoid the myopia arising from the consideration of a small number of stock examples and thus theories reflecting this limited perspective.

TECHNIQUE VS. SUBSTANCE

In analytic philosophy as largely practiced in the first eight decades of the movement, the emphasis on technique led to a tendency to conceive of the philosopher's task as wholly analytical rather than substantive. Whereas earlier philosophers thought that philosophy was the search for substantive truth and wisdom, analytic philosophers tended to conceive of philosophy as defined in terms of the techniques of analysis and clarification. One popular conception of the philosopher's task involved the notion that philosophy is a "second-order" discipline that reflects on the results of the special sciences and other disciplines and that deals with questions that those disciplines are not capable of dealing with using their own particular modes and techniques of investigation but which takes the results of those other disciplines as given and non-revisable in the face of philosophical investigation. On this conception, philosophy leaves everything as it is and makes no contributions to substantive knowledge, dealing with idling questions of no direct concern to scientists, mathematicians, historians and others involved in the acquisition of substantive knowledge. Another way of conceiving of the task of the philosopher, the "underlaborer" view, suggests that the philosopher does contribute to the growth of knowledge, not by discovering anything new, but by using the techniques of analysis to "clear the ground" by eliminating confusions and errors that may retard the growth of scientific knowledge and by clarifying the techniques and methods used by scientists and others by making them fully explicit through formalizing them in the language of symbolic logic or some special-purpose language for which that logic would provide the basic syntax. This view was especially popular among those in the Logical Positivist camp.

The conception of philosophy as largely exhausted by technique means that, in contrast to earlier times, philosophers cannot be counted on to be the source of worldviews or, to use Stephen Pepper's phrase, *world hypotheses*. Having abrogated the role of offering general theories about the nature of things, our substantive beliefs have to be derived from elsewhere, from a source regarded as wholly autonomous from philosophy itself and regarded as beyond philosophical critique. For most contemporary philosophers, as for most contemporary intellectuals, this source is natural science, especially physics. However, late in the twentieth century, some philosophers have been willing to countenance religion as such a source as well, a fact that we will return to later.

Stages in the Development of Analytic Philosophy

Although there are as many individual expressions of analytic philosophy as there are analytic philosophers, there are dominant trends in the history of the analytic tradition. Analytic philosophy spawned a number of successive movements that may be viewed as stages in the development of the analytic tradition up to the present. This development is one in which analytic philosophy becomes increasingly less substantive, more methodological and eventually more of a style of doing philosophy than anything else. Throughout, analytic philosophers retain the emphasis on logic and philosophical grammar, conceptual analysis, clarification of claims and evaluation of arguments using the techniques of deductive and inductive logic and so are identifiable as a tradition; however, it is no longer possible to identify analytic philosophy with any sort of common substantive view or position. Instead, contemporary analytic philosophers occupy a full range of positions on the substantive questions of philosophy.

The first stage in the development of analytic philosophy, flowing directly from Russell and Whitehead's *Principia*, was the short-lived movement known as *Logical Atomism*.[1] Logical Atomism finds its expression in the writings of the early Wittgenstein, especially in his *Tractatus Logico-Philosophicus* (1921) and Russell's *Lectures in Logical Atomism* (1920). Wittgenstein and Russell, proceeding on what was later excoriated by Wittgenstein himself as the "picture theory of language", agreed with Aristotle that the primary function of language is to describe or depict the world. However, whereas Aristotle based his logic and metaphysics on the surface grammar of ordinary language, Russell and the early Wittgenstein believed that the new mathematical logic would allow us to "surface" the deep logical structure disguised by ordinary speech and thus limn the world at its true joints. Central to this project was the notion of *logical form*, which was to be had by translating ordinary language propositions into the symbolism of the *Principia* and from which both the fundamental ontology and the basic structure of the world could be discerned and read off. Although Logical Atomism had some notable early successes – Russell's treatment of negative existentials has become a canonical part of logical theory[2] – seemingly insuperable problems quickly developed. The failure of the logicist program in mathematics and the discovery of Gödel's theorem put paid to the Logical Atomist program, although the school associated with Tarski continued to work on

---

1 See Soames (2003), Volume I, especially Chapters 8, 9 and 10.
2 See Soames (2003), Volume I, pages 93–101.

similar ideas for many decades after Wittgenstein abandoned it. Nevertheless, Logical Atomism represents the sole attempt to erect a new, substantive philosophy on the foundation of the New Logic.

In 1919, small groups of scientists and philosophers, inspired by the work of Ernst Mach, Relativity Theory and the New Logic began to meet in Berlin and Vienna. The most famous of these groups, the Vienna Circle, produced the next major movement in analytic philosophy, *Logical Positivism*. From its inception, the Vienna Circle rejected the claims and methods of classical philosophy, insisting that only the natural sciences, especially physics, are sources of substantive knowledge about reality. Combining Mach's "Empirio-Criticism" with scientism, early Positivists such as Moritz Schlick attempted to find a general criterion for distinguishing genuine scientific claims from the spurious, pseudo–claims made by systematic philosophers. They found it in the doctrine known as *verificationism*.[1] According to this doctrine, there are only two kinds of statements, analytic statements, true in virtue of their meaning alone and synthetic statements, true in virtue of correspondence to the world. Only synthetic statements give us factual, substantive knowledge about reality and all such statements are contingent; as such, they can be justified, if at all, only in terms of sense experience. On this platform, Schlick proposed the Verifiability Criterion for Meaningfulness of synthetic propositions: a statement is meaningful only if it is capable in principle of verification or falsification by reference to sense-experience. Any statement, like that of a traditional metaphysician, which is not potentially testable in experience is rejected, not as false, but as simply meaningless, as not making any substantive claim at all.

The elimination of traditional metaphysics did not exhaust the ambitions of the Vienna Circle, however. Eager to prove useful to modern science, Positivists such as Neurath and Carnap undertook to construct a new, artificial empiricist language that would aid natural science by providing a perfectly clear and perspicuous idiom in which to formulate and test scientific hypotheses. Beginning from so-called "protocol sentences" (e.g. "Beer here now") and using the New Logic, it was hoped that all of the approved parts of ordinary language could ultimately be translated into and systematically organized in the language of science. Hand in hand with this, the major figures in European positivism gave tremendous impetus to an emerging new study, the Philosophy of Science and hoped to unify science by accomplishing the logical reduction of all of the special sciences to physics, which became known as the physi-

---

1 On the Vienna Circle and the origins of positivism, see Blanshard (1969), pages 105–119 and Soames (2003), Volume I, pages 257–60.

calist program. With the rise of Nazism in Europe, the Logical Positivists were forced to flee the Continent; most of them found immediate employment in universities in the English-speaking world, where they carried on these projects and influenced generations of British and American philosophy students.

However, it was a home–grown positivist who popularized Verificationism and gave it the orientation that it would become associated with in England and the U.S., i.e. as a form of anti-philosophy. In 1936, a young English philosopher, A. J. Ayer (1910–1989) published *Language, Truth and Logic*,[1] a kind of positivist manifesto intended to affect a revolution in philosophy. Ayer had little interest in symbolic logic, physicalism, natural science or the dream of a perfect empiricist language. Instead, he saw the Verifiability Principle primarily as a weapon against not just metaphysics and systematic philosophy but against traditional ideas and mores generally. Ayer did not hesitate to draw the apparent implications of verificationism for cherished popular beliefs: not just metaphysics, but ethics, aesthetics and theology must go by the board, condemned as meaningless by the verifiability criterion. Morality, beauty and religion are all merely cherished illusions, based in nothing more that subjective feelings of approval and disapproval projected on and canonized as properties of persons, actions and things and with no basis whatsoever in reality. However much some people may be disturbed by this fact, it remains that the claims or morality and religion are less than false; they are merely and literally nonsensical. As such, they need not be refuted, merely identified and exposed as being beneath the credence of any rational person.

In this straightforward form, Logical Positivism evoked a strong reaction, even among philosophers. Now identified solely with the doctrine of verificationism, attacks on positivism were quickly mounted. It was argued that the Verifiability Principle was self-refuting, since meaningless according to its own standard, being neither analytically true nor testable in principle in sense-experience.[2] Counterexamples to the principle, i.e. apparently meaningful claims capable of being neither confirmed nor falsified by sense experience ("There is a star somewhere that never burns out") seemed to abound. More seriously, there were large classes of statements, e.g. negative existentials, which seemed to escape the net of the principle or could be accommodated to it only by *ad hoc* additions to the principle.[3] In the end, it was deemed that

---

1 Ayer (1936)

2 This was originally argued in Berlin (1934) and repeated many times; it took, despite valiant attempts by the Positivists to evade this objection.

3 For a full rundown of the difficulties here, see Blanshard (1969) pp. 189–248 and Soames (2003), Volume I, pp. 271–99. For a latter–day defense of verificationism see Nielsen (1971) pages

the principle was too artificial as amended to command serious consideration on its merits. At the same time, despite some notable successes, such as the Hempel/Nagel Model for Scientific Explanation and the reduction of the laws of chemistry to physics, the positive programs associated with Logical Positivism proved impossible to carry out in practice and eventually were abandoned.[1] By 1950, Logical Positivism was a spent force ripe for replacement.

In the U.S., post-Positivist analytic philosophers like Goodman and Quine continued to develop analytic philosophy along the earlier lines set down by Carnap in a manner that became increasingly relativistic, sceptical and focussed on the technical problems of the philosophy of language. In England, and later in the U.S. as well, a new movement called *ordinary language philosophy*, inspired by the work of the later Wittgenstein, arose to fill the gap. G. E. Moore was the original fountainhead of this movement: his own method of philosophical analysis, anti-philosophical to the core, took as its guiding idea that there are no genuine philosophical problems, as can be demonstrated by close attention to the implications of ordinary speech. At the same time, Moore regarded ordinary language, though by no means theoretical in construction or aim, as expressive of what he called the common–sense view of the world and thus implicitly committed to certain substantive claims, such as the claims that the external world exists independently of my perception of it and has existed for more than five minutes. However, he did not regard these claims as theoretical in any way, so when he set about to "defend" these beliefs, not through traditional philosophical arguments, but rather through examples and appeals to intuition.[2]

Although heavily influenced by Moore, Wittgenstein (1889–1951) was generally contemptuous of Moore's version of the "philosophy of common sense" and his account of its ontological commitments to e.g., non-natural supervenient properties of goodness and beauty and proofs of the external world. Instead, Wittgenstein developed Moore's approach by drawing its apparently radical conclusions. Having freed himself from the "picture theory of language" in the early 1930's, Wittgenstein returned to Cambridge after an absence of nearly ten years to begin lecturing from a new perspective. Wittgenstein's new perspective, which became the foundation for

---

65–71 and Martin (1990) pages 40–78; for a response to Martin's view, see Alston's essay in Copan and Moser (2001) pages 17–32.

1 By 1950, Nagel himself had rejected the Positivism as inadequate to the needs of modern science; see Pap and Edwards (1957), page 462. Thus, he is willing to concede that religious claims are meaningful; despite this, he still maintains that they are all false.

2 On Moore's Common Sense Realism, see Soames (2003), Volume I, pages 3–33 and Klemke (2000) pages 115–205.

Ordinary Language philosophy, rejected the notion that language has as its sole or even primary aim the description of reality or that it exists as a medium for conveying information about the world. While never denying that language does these things, Wittgenstein denied that there was any one role or function for language that would permit a general theory about it. Further, he rejected the notion that the use of language, especially ordinary language, carried with it any substantive ontological or epistemological commitments. Language consists of a series of rules, like the rules for a game, that govern what counts as licit or illicit, intelligible or nonsensical speech in whatever context those rules apply. These rules are not conventional in the sense that they were made up, instituted or agreed on by those who use the language; however, they are the products of natural history and thus contingent and could have been different than they are, like the laws of nature themselves. Even so, like the laws of nature themselves, they govern us with a kind of natural necessity not amenable to reflective apprehension or change. To the extent that we can talk about the meaning of a word or a phrase at all, that meaning is exhausted by an inventory of its uses in the various contexts in which it can intelligibly function. What ordinary language analysis reveals that is that ordinary language has no substantive commitments whatsoever, not even to Moore's "common sense" ontology.

The urge to philosophize about being, knowledge, truth and so on arises from the philosopher's misunderstanding of ordinary language, resulting most often from hasty generalization from a few stock examples misconstrued to suggest that ordinary language, embodying some sort of substantive but hard-to-justify ontological or epistemological commitment, commits us to views that give rise to imponderable problems. So, for example, A. J. Ayer argues that our ordinary view of the world commits us to the existence of "sense-data" that constitute the immediate objects of conscious awareness and thus generates the problem of the external world.[1] The way out of this is not to embrace the philosopher's folly, but instead attempt to dispel the illusion by a closer look at what we actually say so as to reveal that the philosopher has got it wrong. So, J. L. Austin (1913–1961) in *Sense and Sensibilia* argues that neither Ayer's arguments nor anything that we might plausibly say in everyday life commits us to a belief in "sense-data", "the external world" or anything else that might be used as a platform to generate a general epistemological problem from the facts of perception.[2] Once this is accomplished, one realizes that ordinary language is quite in order as it is and requires no advanced help from the philosopher. Indeed,

---

1 Ayer (1940) as interpreted by Austin (1955) pages 6–32.
2 Austin (1955) pages 84–102.

philosophers in this tradition, beginning with Wittgenstein himself, often compared ordinary language analysis to a kind of therapy designed to free the philosopher from the blinkered view of the world that causes him or her to raise philosophical problems in the first place and realize that all such problems are really just pseudo-problems arising from linguistic confusions.

Ordinary language philosophy was losing influence by the 1980's, primarily because, by its very nature, it had no positive program and so exhausted itself in a negative critique of philosophy the only practical conclusion to which was to exit from the field and do something else. This does not mean that analytic philosophy came to an end, however. Instead, in the last twenty–five years analytic philosophy, now reduced simply to a set of techniques no longer associated with any particular philosophical program or perspective, found flexible application across the board in every branch of philosophical inquiry, including metaphysics, epistemology, philosophy of mind and the philosophy of religion. Even adherents of once competing traditions were eager and in many cases willing to adopt the analytic perspective in order to apply it to the articulation of their own worldviews: thus, we began to hear of "Analytic Marxism" and "Analytic Thomism." In this pluralistic context, analytic philosophy is no longer necessarily associated with any particular philosophical tradition or school, nor can all analytic philosophers be dismissed as "logical positivists." In contemporary philosophy of religion all of the major figures would best be described as analytic philosophers, regardless of whether or not they believe in God. Early on, however, this was hardly the case.

Analysis and Neo-Thomism: Early Encounters

At the time that analytic philosophy was first being applied to questions in the philosophy of religion, the movement was strongly associated with the philosophical critique of religion along broadly positivist lines. In the next chapter, we will consider the major lines of attack initiated by the first generation of analytic philosophers against theism. Here I want to briefly consider how the battle–lines were initially drawn by reference to neo-Thomism, at that time the only well-established school of theistic philosophy and thus a natural target for their critique. Not surprisingly, the analytic school quite naturally and eagerly embraced the deductivist paradigm in which neo-Thomist natural theology was couched. Not only did analytic philosophers see an opportunity to exercise their logical acumen; the neo-Thomist commitment to rational argument made them a much more accessible target than Protestant theologians like

Barth, Brunner and Tillich who eschewed rational argument and took refuge in an existentially motivated leap of faith, thus excluding themselves from serious consideration in the eyes of the analysts. Even more than this, it appeared to put theists at a serious disadvantage in the debate, since it seemed sufficient to refute theism to simply show that the neo-Thomists could not make good on their claims to be able to provide apodictic proofs for God's existence. Analytic atheists quickly established a strong presumptive case for negative atheism on the basis of such a critique.

Early Encounters: Russell, Copleston and Ayer

Russell and Moore, the founders of analytic philosophy, were both known for their indifference – even hostility – to religion. Moore, though raised in a religious household, lost his faith at an early age[1] and seems never to have been troubled by religious questions again in his life; his only essay on the topic, from early in his career, is a critique of the classic arguments for God's existence.[2] Russell, though attracted to Hegelianism in his youth, came under Moore's influence at Cambridge and soon embraced his neo-Realism; he later became a notable critic of religious belief in such books as *Why I am not a Christian*.[3] Moore can best be described as a negative atheist, who stops short of making any positive assertion about whether God exists; Russell was by his own admission an agnostic, but one with a decided preference for atheism.

Two radio debates from the late 1940's illustrate a pair of early skirmishes between analytic philosophers and a noted exponent of neo-Thomism. In 1948 Russell and Frederick Copleston, S. J. (1907–1990) later noted for his nine–volume history of western philosophy, debated the existence of God on the BBC Third Programme.[4] The next year, Ayer and Copleston debated logical positivism and its implications for the topic of religious language.[5] In both debates, issues and arguments were scouted that would become staples of the philosophy of religion for several decades. In both cases, the analytic philosophers challenged the Thomistic argument from contingency by attacking the meaningfulness of the appeal to God as an explanation for the existence of the world. Both Russell and Ayer made the claim that the question "What is

---

1 See Moore's autobiography in Schilpp (1941) pages 10–12.
2 See Moore (1901); for an account of Moore s views on religious topics, see Klemke (2001) pages 415–33.
3 Russell (1957); see especially pages 3–23.
4 A published transcript of the debate (apparently rewritten by Russell after the broadcast) can be found in Pap and Edwards (1957) pages 473–90.
5 Also in Pap and Edwards (1957), pages 726–56.

the cause of the world?" is a different sort of question from the question "What is the cause of X, where X is a particular event in the world?" The second has an answer, at least in principle, in terms of something else that exists in the world, whereas the first requires that we go beyond the world in order to find an answer for it. Both Russell and Ayer are loath to make this inference, though for different reasons. According to Russell, the inference to God as a necessary being is meaningless, because necessity is a feature of propositions, not of things. According to Ayer, talk of God is meaningless because unverifiable by reference to sense experience. To both charges, Copleston responds that, since talk of God, though different in various ways from ordinary language, nevertheless appears to be meaningful, that any criterion for meaningfulness that denies the claim to that effect is highly questionable and likely to be an expression of a pre-philosophical preference or perhaps even of dogmatism. Subsequent analytic philosophers, such as Paul Edwards and Antony Flew, themselves coming out of the positivist tradition, would sharpen these criticisms in the decade to come.

CRITIQUE OF THE COSMOLOGICAL ARGUMENT

Following the example of their eponymous master, the neo-Thomists had made the cosmological argument their primary (though not sole) argument for God's existence and the only argument that was capable of passing muster as a deductively sound proof for God's existence. It is no surprise, then, that the first generation of atheistic analytic philosophers applied their considerable logical acumen to the critique of the by-now standard textbook presentations of the argument to found in scholastic textbooks.[1] The criticism themselves were most often retreads of the Hume's arguments against Demea's version of the cosmological argument as presented in the *Dialogues*, although presented in a much more sophisticated manner. Typical of these early critiques were the arguments offered by Paul Edwards (1922–2004) in the U.S. and Ronald Hepburn (1926–) in the U.K.

Edwards presents what was then the standard analytic critique of the Thomistic cosmological argument deriving from Hume.[2] First of all, even if the argument proves the existence of a first mover or a necessary being, that does not prove that the theistic

---

[1] Although histories of Thomism in the twentieth century tend to highlight such figures as Gilson, Maritain and Marechal, these figures had almost no impact on Anglo–American philosophy and their works are rarely commented on. Instead, it is textbook Thomism, as described above that draws the brunt of their attack, the most common targets being Joyce (1922) and Phillips (1948).

[2] Edwards, 'The Cosmological Argument' in Burrill (1964), pages 101–123; originally published in the *Rationalist*, 1959.

God – the God of living religion – exists. Secondly, however, there are strong reasons for supposing that the argument does not work, because it cannot exclude the possibility that the universe consists of an infinite series of dependent, contingent beings each of which is caused to exist by another member of the series. Aquinas simply begs the question when he asserts that if the first cause is removed, so too are all the secondary causes as well, since what the proponent of the infinite regress is denying is not the existence of any of the causes in the series, only that any one of them is a first or primary cause of the rest. Nor does the attempt to distinguish between a series of temporally–extended causes (*causae in fieri*) and one in which the causes act simultaneously with their effects (*causae in esse*) make any difference. In both cases, if each cause in the series has a sufficient cause for its existence, then there is no incoherence or impossibility in the existence of that series. Further, if one asks why the infinite series exists rather than not, it will be replied that since the series is nothing more than the sum of its members, the fact that each member of the series has a cause also explains why the series exists. In a memorable example, Edwards argues that the presence of six Eskimos on a New York street corner is fully accounted for by the conjunction of the explanations for each of them individually being there. Having explained why each is present, the further question as to why they are all present becomes otiose. Finally, the appeal to the Principle of Sufficient Reason as a ground for inferring to a necessary being ultimately leads the Thomist into absurdity. If every existent thing needs a cause then so does God; to suppose that God is somehow "cause of himself" is very likely incoherent. On the other hand, if we are to avoid an infinite regress here, we are ultimately going to have to admit that something exists simply as a brute fact. If that is so, why not suppose that the physical universe is that thing?

Hepburn[1] makes a similar critique from the point of view of postivistically-tinged Ordinary Language philosophy. The Thomist claims that the cosmological argument as present in the first three of the five ways is an empirical argument, one that begins from plainly observable facts such as that things move or come into and go out of existence. However, the motor of each of these proofs turns out to be the PSR. The PSR is not an empirical claim, says Hepburn, because it cannot be tested in experience: it is neither confirmable nor falsifiable, since our failure to discern a cause for some event does not prove that it does not have one. At the same time, the only alternative is that the PSR is a logical truth; but, as we now know, all such truths are mere tautologies. The Thomist seems to want to have his cake and eat it too, treating the PSR in some contexts as if it were a substantive claim, in others as if it were a truth of

---

1 See Hepburn (1956) pages 155–85.

reason: but there are no significant tautologies. As such, the cosmological argument in all its forms is stillborn. Furthermore, it is not clear that it makes sense to even ask the question "What is the cause of the universe?" The notion of cause has a clear application to particular events from within the universe, but what would it mean to say that the universe as a whole has a cause, any more than to say that it has a top or a bottom, a boundary, speed or direction? Words such as "cause", suggests Hepburn, lose their meaning when taken from their natural context.

Hepburn then turns to the distinction, crucial to the argument, between necessary and contingent beings. According to Hepburn, we have another case where terms are being used outside their natural context, being applied to beings rather than propositions, or rather, to the notion of existence as applied to beings. Once again, however, it is not clear that such terms can be coupled. For "existence" is not the name of property that comes in degrees or varieties and that beings possess along with their other characteristics; to the contrary, "exists" applies to a being a whole and merely expresses the fact that a thing of such-and-such a description is real or actual. Thus, to the extent that the cosmological argument requires that we infer from the existence of finite or contingent beings to an infinite or non-contingent being, it rests on a linguistic confusion that dissipates upon analysis. To the suggestion that the five ways are not literal arguments but merely intended to evoke an intuitive awareness of the unique "cosmological relation" obtaining between God and creation, Hepburn responds by suggesting that, while this strategy evades the logical difficulties inherent in taking the arguments literally, it ultimately fails because it robs the notion of "cause" in the phrase "First Cause" of any expressible meaning. It thus begins by speaking of God as if He were a cause in the ordinary sense as a means of evoking a particular way of seeing the world, only to change the meaning of that term in application to God at a later stage in the dialectic, thus undermining the very intuition that the argument was intended to evoke. Hepburn concludes by dismissing the senses of wonder, dependence and of the evanescence of life as platforms for a theistic "intuition of God" as resting on contentious misconstruals of ordinary expressions for persuasive effect.

Of course, these criticisms did not go without response from the theistic side. Philosophers such as Ninian Smart[1](1927–1991) and Peter Geach[2](1917–), for example, came to the defence of the Five Ways. However, the next major event in the career of the Thomistic cosmological argument was affected by Anthony Kenny (1926-) in his book-length discussion of Aquinas's proofs.

---

1 Smart (1962)
2 See Geach's essay on Aquinas in Geach and Anscombe (1963) pages 109–17.

Anthony Kenny: The Five Ways

In 1965, the Second Vatican Council concluded in Rome and ushered in a new age of openness in the Catholic Church. One of the first victims of this new spirit of reform was neo-Thomism. Although still the "official" theologian of the Catholic Church, Catholic intellectuals (and, in particular, Catholic theologians) fled Aquinas like the plague and began to imbibe a wide range of increasingly heterodox figures and traditions with apparent impunity.[1] Ironically, this led to a renewed interest in Aquinas among non-Catholics and a greater appreciation of Aquinas as thinker once he was no longer being read and interpreted through Counter-Reformation eyes. Although neo-Thomism has not disappeared, its current influence is greatly diminished and may even be described as neglible both within Catholicism and outside of it.

In 1969, Anthony Kenny (now Sir Anthony, b. 1931), a former Jesuit priest who had been educated in Rome, published *The Five Ways*, regarded at the time as a devastating and unanswerable critique of Aquinas's arguments for God's existence. Unlike other critics of the Thomistic approach, Kenny takes the perspective of a historian of philosophy, arguing that Aquinas's arguments are firmly embedded in a discredited Aristotelian physics that was inadequate in its day and is totally superseded today. Although the beginning premises of the first three ways look like empirical claims that can be confirmed by casual sense observation ("Some things are in motion", "There is an order of efficient causes", "Contingent beings exist") these claims are in fact thoroughly "theory-laden", a fact that is disguised to us since the Five Ways occur at the beginning of the *Summa Theologiae* and appear to be immediately accessible to us. In fact, the Summa was written for what we would today call graduate students in theology, and who in Thomas's time would have already been thoroughly grounded in philosophy, including Aristotelian physics. Kenny proposes to lay out the background and theoretical commitments of the Five Ways in order to discredit them. For our purposes here it will be enough to consider his demolition of the First Way, which I will summarize and simplify. Readers are encouraged to read Kenny's own thorough and careful presentation of this critique in his own text.[2]

The first way begins from our observation of *motus* or change; this includes qualitative (as when something changes colour), quantitative (as when something grows or diminishes in size) and local motion (i.e., change of place). According to Aristotle, change involves the actualization of potency, either through the operation of a thing's

---

1 For example, the preface to Owens (1993), pages vii–viii demonstrating how quickly neo-Thomism became old hat.
2 Kenny (1969) pages 6–23.

nature (as when an animal feeds and grows) or through the influence of an external cause that induces a change in that thing which nature alone would not produce in the ordinary course of events (as when my wastebasket becomes dented because I kick it.) Applied to the case of local motion (Kenny's chosen stalking horse), this means that there are two sorts of motion: *natural* and *violent* (or unnatural). Natural motion is either up or down, and dictated by the elemental composition of a body, so that things composed of heavy elements (earth and water) tend to fall toward the centre of the universe whereas those composed of light elements (air and fire) rise toward the limits of the celestial sphere. The terminus of natural motion is rest and all bodies seek this state and remain in it unless disturbed, as when an obstacle to natural motion is removed. Violent motion is motion contrary to nature in which an object at rest is made to move neither up or down but horizontally. Since this motion is unnatural, a body tends to resist it because its nature dictates that it devolve to its former state of rest. Therefore, according to the Aristotelian analysis, violent motion requires the constant application of an external cause in order to produce it. This is summarized in the scholastic principle that becomes one of the premises of the First Way: *omne quod movetur, ab alio movetur*, i.e. "whatever is being moved is being moved by another." Since violent motion is contrary to nature, a thing's nature cannot produce it; it must therefore be induced in that thing by an external cause and the operation of that cause must be continuous with the production of the effect or it will cease. Thus, as an example of something's being moved, Aquinas offers the case of a ball being moved by a stick which in turn is being pushed by someone's hand. The ball moves because it is pushed by the stick, which is in turn pushed by the hand which is in turn directed by the person's soul, an Aristotelian "self-mover." If any of these causes is removed, the ball will immediately cease to move because it can move in this fashion only if it is being moved by something else.

On this analysis, one reasonably concludes to the existence of an Unmoved Mover upon the observation of violent local motion in the world. Given the *quod movetur* principle, every series of moved movers needs to terminate in something that is a principle of motion without being in motion itself; otherwise, nothing will be in motion, which is contrary to observation. However, this will follow only if it is the case both that the *quod movetur* principle is true and that there cannot be an infinite series of moved movers operating simultaneously to produce the motions we observe. However, says Kenny, neither of these claims is in fact true. The *quod movetur* principle admits obvious counterexamples that "could have been observed in any medieval kitchen": a ball rolling across the floor is a classic case of violent motion, yet nevertheless a case in which something is in motion without being moved by an external force operating simultaneously with that motion. Further, the modern physical conceptions of gravity and inertia, which treat motion and rest as nothing more than persistent states of a body, abolishes the distinction between natural and violent motion and thus dispenses with the need to explain why a body set in motion remains in motion. Finally, as if in response to those neo-Thomists who are willing to admit the pragmatic usefulness of the concept of inertia at the "empirical" level of physical analysis but insist that the *quod movetur* principle still applies at some deeper, metaphysical level of analysis, Kenny offers a thorough critique of Aristotle's philosophical arguments for that principle. In a like manner, Kenny examines the Aristotelian arguments against the possibility of an infinite series of simultaneously operating moved movers and finds them wanting as well. The First Way, then, shows itself to be hopelessly dependent upon Aristotelian physical theory and incapable of surviving the paradigm shift to the new physics.

This does not mean, of course, that interest in the philosophical works of Aquinas has disappeared in the years between Vatican II and the present. Quite the contrary, once Aquinas was no longer the "official" philosopher of the Catholic Church, secular philosophers began to read his works with a new eye and to find merit in his writings. Nor has neo-Thomism altogether disappeared; even today we can find defenders of the Thomistic cosmological argument and, in the Catholic world, pockets of resistance to Post-Vatican II theology.[1] At the same time, neo-Thomism can hardly be said to be as prominent or as hopeful as it appeared to be when Leo XIII initiated the movement at the end of the nineteenth century. Analytic philosophy of religion may have cut its teeth on the critique of neo-Thomism but it soon began to develop a life of its own in accordance with its own internal dynamic. To that part of the story we now turn.

---

1 See the series of volumes entitled *Thomistic Papers* published the Center for Thomistic Studies at University of St. Thomas in Houston since 1984. For more on Post-Vatican II Thomism, see: John (1966), Hudson and Moran (1991), Clarke (2001) and McInerny (2006). James F. Ross of the University of Pennsylvania, a philosopher with roots in the scholastic tradition, has also engaged the analytic tradition: see Ross (1976). However, he is more properly designated a Scotist than a Thomist. It is also to be noted that a number of non-Catholic philosophers have been influenced by Thomism, including John Wild (see Wild 1956), Mortimer Adler (see Adler 1982) and Henry Veatch (see the essay by Veatch in Kennedy (1988)).

Chapter Three

The Problem of Religious Language

Given the preoccupation of analytic philosophers with language and the theory of meaning, it is not surprising that the meaning of "God-talk" as it was called moved in to centre stage in the philosophy of religion of the 1950's. The immediate impetus was, of course, the earlier challenge offered by Logical Positivism. Although official adherence to positivism has largely ceased by the mid–'50's of the last century many crypto-positivists, having repackaged themselves as Wittgensteinians or "empiricists" in the philosophy of language continued to hope that a way might be found to undercut the possibility of any return to natural theology. In the end, this effort failed, though not because the problem itself was somehow solved. Although both theists and atheists debated the problem from every conceivable angle, in the end little progress was made and philosophers went on to discuss other, more substantive questions. For about a decade, however, discussion of the problem of God-talk was a central concern of philosophers of religion and no historical account of its development can skip over this episode despite its having led to a dead end. Should this issue ever surface again as a major subject of discussion, undoubtedly those interested in this issue will return to the positions entertained and developed by the figures we will be reviewing here.

The Thomistic Theory of Analogical Predication

Speculation about the meaning of God-talk was not new with analytic philosophers, of course. Since the early middle ages, philosophers and theologians had discussed the problem of whether and how we can use human language, derived from everyday sense-experience, to talk of an infinite, transcendent God. The neo-Platonic tradition, which stressed the incomprehensibility of the One, had claimed that no term employed in ordinary language, not even the term "one" itself, is able to express any positive conception of the ultimate reality. The influence of neo-Platonism found its way into the writings of the Pseudo–Dionysius,[1] the unknown fifth century Christian mystic whose teachings about the divine names became normative for mediaeval thinkers until the dawn of the fourteenth century and which still largely inform Eastern Orthodox "apophatic" theology today. According to Pseudo–Dionysius, God cannot be known except through mystical union, which is ineffable in human language; there is no "natural" knowledge of God's nature or essence available to us through our natural powers. Hence, human language is utterly inadequate to convey any positive information about God since we have no positively meaningful concept of God. Therefore, when we use human language about God, what we say about God has to be understood *negatively* rather than positively, or rather, as negating even in the act of describing. This process, described by later writers as the way of *negation* and *eminence*, first asserts all positive perfections of God, then denies that God possesses those perfection in the manner in which we find them in creatures, then asserts them of God in a way different from and higher than they exist in creatures. Later on, these perfections were also said to exist in God *virtually* as well as eminently, as the power to cause the existence of those perfections in other things in the limited fashion in which we experience them. This *via negativa* was endorsed by many subsequent mediaeval thinkers, especially those noted for orthodoxy and piety, but became especially associated with the teachings of Moses Maimonides.[2]

For Aquinas and other late mediaeval Aristotelians, however, the *via negativa* falls short of providing us with enough of a concept of God to justify the many positive attributions we make to God and the distinctions we make among the predicates we apply to Him. After all, the way of negation and eminence allows us to attribute being, goodness, wisdom, mercy and so on to God virtually as the cause, due to his power to cause their existence in creatures but it also allows us to say that God is a rock or a lion in the same way, since the natures of those things likewise pre-exist virtually and eminently in God who is their cause. Surely, however, when we say that God is wise we mean something more than that wisdom as we experience it in ourselves pre-exists in God insofar as He is its cause. In some appropriate sense, we want to say that to be wise or good is said of God *as such*, as referring to something that exists as part of God's essence or nature, whereas to be a lion or to be angry (insofar as this is constituted by a bodily–based feeling) is not said of God in this way but is to be cashed out in terms of God's relation to creatures.

The theory of analogical predication is Thomas's solution to this difficulty. Although

---
1 See Pseudo–Dionysius (1987), pages 47–131.
2 On Maimonides, see the article by Seymour Feldman in Buijs (1998), pages 267–83.

tricked out (and sometimes presented) as though it were a linguistic or grammatical doctrine, nothing like modern formal logic or philosophy of language existed in the thirteenth century, nor were the strong distinctions between metaphysics, epistemology and so on that we recognize today as yet available to Aquinas. For Thomas and other mediaeval thinkers, *reality* as it exists independently of mind ("being") is the first object of the intellect, not words, concepts or subjective states of consciousness, all of which are simply media through which the real is made present in and to the knowing subject. *Concepts* or "ideas" are derived from our encounter with external realities in sense-perception by means of which the essences or natures of things come to exist in our minds as objects of thought; the *ideational contents of concepts*, then, are the things themselves as apprehended and thus *known* by the intellect. In turn, *words* when used as signs of things or *terms* express the contents of concepts, which are their *meanings* and are ultimately referred to, because constituted by, the natures or essences of things. Given this picture of how knowledge and language work, there is no utility in attempting to discuss questions of meaning and reference, truth and knowledge, objectivity and intentionality independently of metaphysics, since they are by their very nature referred to the real and have no status or import independently of it. Metaphysics is and remains first philosophy and thus, from the Thomistic point of view, philosophers like Descartes, Kant or Russell and Wittgenstein, who begin from consciousness, from the possibility of knowledge, formal logic or some account of the nature of language have already taken a fatal misstep. It remains, then, for the Thomist to explain the possibility of God-talk in terms of the very structure of reality itself, one that encompasses but at the same time cuts across grammar, logic, epistemology and the philosophy of language. This, of course, is very old fashioned; however, attempts to reconstruct the theory in less sweeping terms appear inevitably to distort it, so I will present it as its proponents generally preferred to present it.[1]

Presentations of the doctrine of analogical predication typically begin with a classification of three kinds of terms: univocal, equivocal and analogical. However, in line with the foregoing, we must note that these three kinds of terms are intended to correspond to three different types of concepts representing three different ways in which things can be known (i.e. present to the intellect) in virtue of three different ways in which the realities represented by those concepts are related to each other

---

1 Here I will be following the accounts presented in Garrigou–LaGrange (1909, English translation 1934) pages 205–32 and Joyce (1922) pages 236–75. In both accounts, it is analogical *knowledge* of God, rather than analogical predication as such, that takes centre stage. I have adjusted their account to make it more linguistic and thus familiar to philosophers trained in the analytic tradition.

independently of the mind. A term is used *univocally* when it is applied in identically the same sense to two different individuals, as when we describe both Peter and Paul as human beings. Here the term "human being" applies to Peter and Paul both in its full and proper sense and to both men in exactly the same way; so far as being human goes, Peter and Paul are indistinguishable from one another on account of their exact similarity in nature. Of course, they are separate human beings and thus different instances of that specific nature ("humanity"); however, their being different individuals is constituted independently of the common nature they share and thus does not enter into meaning of the common concept that applies to them both in virtue of that fact. By contrast, a term is used *equivocally* whenever, even if the words used are homonyms, they are used in entirely separate senses of things that share nothing in common with one another. Thus, the word "bank" used to describe the side of a riverbed and the word "bank" used to describe a financial institution are completely equivocal uses of that word, which expresses separate concepts in each of its uses due to the fact that the things to which the terms apply share nothing in common that can form the basis for a common conceptual content for the word to express. In this case, the fact that we use the same word (considered as a series of phonemes or combination of letters) is merely a linguistic accident of no philosophical significance.

According to the exponents of analogical predication, the foregoing classes of terms are not exhaustive. There is a third class of terms that are neither equivocal nor univocal, but used in *different* but *related* senses, or *analogically*. These analogous terms express analogous concepts formed by through our apprehension of analogous relations between things and thus constituting analogous knowledge of things. The difficulty, of course, is in making any sense of these notions and at this point the tradition is largely silent. Here we can but follow the presentation of the exponents of this doctrine and see what light emerges. The next step in the standard presentation is to classify the kinds of analogous terms.

One way in which terms can be analogous is known as analogy of *attribution* (or *proportion*). In this form of analogy, a set of concepts, all of which are expressed adjectivally using the same predicate, are applied to each of the subjects in a different way, but in such a way that the meanings of all of them are "cashed out" by reference to the full and proper sense of the term that applies in only one of those uses. Thus, the adjective "healthy" can be used in a literal sense of a human being, of medicine, of the complexion, of exercise and of the air. However, in only the first of these cases is the term used *formally* of the subject, in the full and proper sense attribution of a property to a subject. Only the human being has bodily health as an attribute or property inhering in him or her as a subject. "Healthy" as used in the other cases refers not to an inherent property of the subject, but rather the manner in which that subject is related to health as it exists in the "prime analogate", i.e. the subject to which the terms applies in the full and proper or formal sense. So, medicine is healthy as restorative of lost health, a complexion is healthy as the external sign or symptom of health, exercise is healthy as a means of maintaining bodily health and the air is healthy insofar as breathing that air is not known to be deleterious to the health of a normal person. These "secondary analogates" are all different in meaning reflecting the different ways in which the subjects to which the term is applied are differently related to health as it exists in the prime analogate. The use of the term as it applies formally in the case of the prime analogate thus provides the *focal meaning* to which the meaning of that term as applied to the secondary analogates is inevitably referred when we characterize the content of the corresponding concept.

Analogy of attribution perhaps illustrates the class of analogous terms or concepts, but it has limited application in theological contexts. In analogy of attribution, only the prime analogate possesses the referent of its analogous term formally, whereas in the case of the secondary analogates the term can be applied only relationally. However, in the case of divine and creaturely perfections, we cannot avoid using the term applied to the putative "secondary analogates" formally; wisdom is wisdom, whether it is applied to God or creatures. Thus, either we must admit some similarity between the two forms of wisdom (in which case the terms will be used univocally and the difference between God and creature will be merely one of degree and not of kind) or we will end by using the term formally only of creatures and relationally of the putative "prime analogate", which will carry us only so far as the claim that God is wise in a virtual sense, as the cause of wisdom in creatures. On either of these alternatives, no progress has been made.

At this point, exponents of analogical predication take refuge in what amounts to a doctrine of *intrinsically analogous terms*, terms that while applied both literally and formally to each class of subject to which they can be properly attributed have different concrete meanings or correspond to different conceptual contents in each case. Traditional neo-Thomists such as Garrigou–LaGrange and G. H. Joyce, for example, point to the "transcendental notions" of late mediaeval philosophy as one class of intrinsically analogous terms. These transcendental notions are really transcategorical or "transgeneric" terms that apply across kinds and are not classifiable in terms of Aristotle's ten categories. There are six such notions that are usually recognized in the traditional presentation of these terms: thing, being, one, true, good and beautiful.

According to the traditional doctrine, these terms are universally applicable across kinds despite obvious differences in that to which they are applied. Whatever can be an object of thought, talked about, described or can be quite literally referred to as a thing: an idea, an atom, a part of a chair, a human being or an angel. Yet clearly what it means to be a thing differs from case to case; not even the notion of "distinct individuality" captures the common meaning of the term, since a part of a chair that is not a proper part (like an arm or a leg) is still a thing even though it is not an individual. Whatever is a thing is likewise a being, something that exists; by the same token, what it means for something to exist differs from case to case: a substance, a property, an idea, a university, the labour movement, the number 2 and so on all exist but clearly there is at best a Wittgensteinian "family resemblance" between existence as participated in by all these diverse types of things. Again, each kind of thing has better or worse examples exemplifying its essence or nature, according to some standard appropriate to that kind and divergent from others, defying any attempt to reduce what it means for something to be good to any sort of simple common quality exemplified by each kind of thing. Further, as the old Ray Stevens song has it, "everything is beautiful, in its own way." This is good Thomistic doctrine and expresses the idea that beauty is a transcendental concept that applies across categories and genera. The beauty of a beautiful table–setting at dinner is clearly different from the beauty of a mathematical equation; even if we describe them both as beautiful due to their elegance and simplicity, what "elegance" and "simplicity" amount to in each case bids fair to be something irreducibly different.

Another class of analogous terms are those that name *pure perfections*, those whose concepts contain no inherent limitations, despite being derived from our experience of finite beings. Attributes such as being, goodness, power, knowledge, consciousness, freedom and so on are pure perfections, attributes that come in degrees and change their quality as they change their altitude.[1] Since these perfections lie upon a unidirectional continuum, they are all plausibly regarded as modes of the same reality; yet as they are concretely realized in specific kinds of being, they come close to being so diverse as to share no characteristics in common whatsoever. For example, years ago Thomas Nagel argued in his paper "What is it like to be a Bat?"[2] that, given our best scientific guesses about what bat–consciousness is like, it is very likely incommensurable to our own and thus not imaginable for us. Even so, we do not stint to attribute this qualitatively different form of consciousness to bats and

---

1 To paraphrase Farrer (1943) page 45.
2 Nagel (1979) pages 165–80.

even to talk about and study it. For example, we say that bats are aware of the world around them using "bat sonar" just as we are aware of the world around us using our more familiar sense–modalities, and so we are: but again, the notion of "being aware" is equally an analogous term, having no sense for us that can be abstracted from its various concrete instances. The best we can say is that bats have some way of being aware of the world through "bat–sonar" that is phenomenologically closed to us but which occupies the same place and performs the same role in a bat's life as our characteristic sense–modalities occupy and perform in our own.

To take this tack is to arrive at the Thomistic account of *analogy of proper proportionality*, according to which attributes that are formally predicated of various subjects differ materially from one another in such a way that there is no common conceptual content to provide a specifiable common "sense" that could usefully be abstracted from those concepts and stated as such. However, despite this fact, the terms used are not mere homonyms; there is a similarity between the cases consisting in their similarity of relation to or function within their subjects. Thus, we might characterize our claims about what it is like to be bat in the following way:

> Bat sonar is to bat consciousness AS (e.g.) vision is to human consciousness

That is to say, bat sonar serves the same role in the production of the phenomenological content of bat-consciousness of the objects present in the bat's immediate environment as any one of our variegated sense–modalities does in producing the phenomenological content our human consciousness of our immediate environment. We can neither experience bat sonar nor imagine what it is like to be a bat; it does not follow that we can say nothing true about bat sonar or bat- consciousness, since we can place bat sonar functionally in relation to something in the bat (consciousness) that we directly experience in ourselves. Further, the claim here is that the notions involved here are irreducibly analogical. Even if we assert that the notion of consciousness as "awareness of reality" is a common element of meaning, we will be seemingly be defeated by the reflection that what "awareness" refers to in the cases of a bat or a man takes its concrete meaning from its characteristic phenomenological contents, so that "awareness" itself refers to two quite different things in each case.

Applied to the theological case the claim is that, in attributing to God those pure perfections that we are aware of in limited forms in the case of creatures, what we are doing is making the same sort of functional and relational claims about those perfections as they exist in God as we do in our own case. So, for example:

> Divine wisdom is to God's nature AS human wisdom is to human nature

According to this scheme, in attributing wisdom to God we claiming that, in God, there is something formally present that corresponds to what we call wisdom in ourselves due to its serving the same role in the divine mind that human wisdom does in our own. Wisdom is a pure perfection portending apprehension of the real and is not intrinsically limited by definition or its reality as such. In the human case, of course, it is limited by its very nature because human nature is a limited nature; but a kind of wisdom that exceeds our own, not just in degree but in kind, is not inconceivable in principle to us and using the method of negation and eminence we are able to get closure on the idea of a being whose wisdom is perfect wisdom, wisdom of a sort unsurpassable even by God Himself. So, human knowledge is limited in scope and depth, largely indirect and conjectural, mediated by the senses and the operations of discursive inference, conditioned by space, time and circumstance and dependent on something outside of ourselves lying beyond the control of our wills. None of these circumstances, of course, is merely contingently related to our human nature; each of them is a pre-condition for it in such a way that the characteristically human form of knowledge is inseparable from them. At the same time, the very dynamism of our intellect, which has as its goal above all else the acquisition of wisdom, sees in these ineliminable natural limitations on human knowledge a series of barriers to full and complete participation in the perfection of wisdom and thus even the fullest degree of human wisdom as an intrinsic frustration of the innate aspiration to know. As such, we are led to conceive, by way of negation, of a nature not so limited that does realize the ideal of perfect wisdom, perfect possession of all knowledge in the highest and best possible way. Such a nature would be one whose knowledge was comprehensive in breadth and depth, direct and intuitive, derived from a consciousness that is omnipresent and timelessly eternal and which is cause of what it knows, so that it knows all things other than itself, whether possible or actual, through an act of self-contemplation that is identical with God's very essence, hence not really distinct from God's other attributes. We, of course, cannot imagine what it is like to be God in respect to the divine wisdom any more than we can imagine what it is like to be a bat with regard to the phenomenology of bat sense-perception. However, this does not seem to be an insuperable bar to our claiming to have enough of a conception of what this is like in relation to our own case that we are able to think – and thus speak – meaningfully about it.

This will have to do as a basic statement of the theory. In fact, beyond this fairly simple presentation, the doctrine of analogy bristles with technical difficulties and not even the Thomistic tradition is united in its interpretation of the theory.[1] In addition, notable alternate traditions within scholasticism itself, such as Scotism and Ockhamism, reject the analogical theory. Casting our net wider, we find that Christian mystics in the tradition of the *via negativa* reject the doctrine of analogy on the grounds that it is anthropomorphic and thus degrades God to the level of creatures. On the other hand, we find Christians in the Protestant tradition rejecting the doctrine on just the opposite ground, i.e. that it represents a conception of God closer to that of Greek philosophy than to the way that God is described in the Bible and that the clear implication of the biblical witness is that God differs from us only in degree, not in kind. This is the perspective of what I earlier called moderate scriptural anthropomorphism.

Among analytic philosophers, the standard objections to the Thomistic theory of analogy are generally variations on a theme, clustered around a rejection of the notion of intrinsically analogous concepts. Similarity in meaning, it is argued, requires at least partial sameness in meaning and hence an element of univocity in the terms we use to describe both God and human beings.[2] As such, there can be no intrinsically analogical terms; any proposed examples of such terms can always be analysed in such a way that their meaning is partly univocal and partly equivocal, so that the appearance of irreducible analogy is eliminated. Thus, the analytic philosopher proposes a dilemma for the Thomist: either the terms used of God and of creatures are at least partly univocal, so that there is enough commonality of meaning to constitute them as related in meaning, or they are not, in which case they share no common meaning and are thus purely equivocal. Given the first horn of the dilemma, our knowledge of God must be accounted for in some way other than merely by means of His relation to creatures and we are owed some account of how direct knowledge of such an allegedly transcendent being is possible. Given the second, religious language is clearly meaningless, since the common terms we apply to God on the one hand and creatures on the other turn out to be homonymous. The Thomistic attempt to have one's cake and eat it too – a wholly transcendent God and meaningful God-talk – turns out to be impossible after all.

This is not the place to attempt to characterize the ongoing discussion of this

---

1 Among the many books by twentieth–century Catholic authors we may mention Luytens (1964), Mondin (1968) and McInerny (1961), (1968) and (1994). More recently, James F. Ross of the University of Pennsylvania has come to the aid of the theory of analogy despite his Scotistic leanings; see Ross (1981).

2 See Hepburn (1956); for typical criticisms of the doctrine of analogical predication see Ferre (1961) *passim* and Gutting (1982) pages 50–78.

theory and the many issues and problems it raises. Suffice it to say that the doctrine of analogy has remained largely a distinctive teaching of the Thomist tradition and being largely rejected by philosophers outside of that tradition has not, therefore, played a major role in the discussion of the meaningfulness of God-talk as it has been discussed by the analytic tradition. It is this discussion, with its roots in the positivistic critique of religious language, to which we now turn.

Talk of God in the Analytic Tradition

In the course of his famous essay "Gods",[1] the Wittgensteinian philosopher John Wisdom uses a now–famous parable to suggest that the modern dispute between theists and atheists amounts in the end to no dispute at all, or at least no dispute that concerns any matter of fact to which any further experience could possibly be relevant. A dispute can begin as a factual, substantive dispute that has real implications for experience but degenerate over time into a fruitless dispute that cannot be resolved by any possible observation or experiment. In Wisdom's story, two people return after some time to their long–neglected garden only to find that, contrary to expectations, it and its plants show signs of having been tended by someone in their absence. One of the persons in question forms the hypothesis that a gardener has been taking care of the garden, while the other supposes that the appearance of being tended is merely the product of chance. Careful inquiries reveal that no one has been seen taking care of the garden and all attempts to catch such a gardener at work fail to yield any results. Each of the persons involved agrees about all the facts and neither expects, at this point, that any further facts are relevant to the dispute. Nevertheless, each continues to maintain the opposite point of view: one man continues to believe that an invisible, undetectable gardener exists and works in the garden to keep it up to the degree that we would not expect it to appear "kept up" if the garden were altogether untended; the other denies that there is any gardener and chalks up the appearance of being attended to chance while pointing to those aspects of the garden which give the appearance of not having been tended to.

Wisdom does not dismiss this dispute as meaningless or merely the result of some sort of confusion on the part of the disputants so that it is simply to be abandoned as fruitless. Nor does he suppose that the disputants will cease to attempt to persuade one another by different means, each intending to induce in the other a realization to which the other is currently blind. Still, Wisdom claims, in each case the grounds for

---

1 Wisdom (1963) pages 149–68; originally published in 1946.

the opposing beliefs are different from the reasons given for them and more fundamental than they are. Further, while they are associated with strong feelings, they are more than the feelings they evoke. In some sense, they involve a total picture of the world that can only be expressed and appreciated in an aesthetic way, and to which poetry, rather than rational argument, is the only appropriate entrée. In the case of the religious believer, the ground and final refuge of faith is the experience of oneness with God (or Christ), an experience that the unbeliever lacks and does not credit. For Wisdom, this explains both the significance of the dispute, its continuance and its intractability; he does not offer any resolution to the dispute, since that is not the job of philosophy as he conceives it, but merely to account for the appearances.

Other philosophers, of course, are bound to resist this analysis of the dispute between theists and atheists, maintaining that the issue between them can be resolved by some rational means. Even if rational argument cannot serve the turn, perhaps the tools of modern linguistic analysis can do so. This conviction animated the first generation of analytic philosophers of religion as they attempted to refute theism. The fruits of their researches, in the 1950's and '60's, led to the debate over the meaningfulness of religious language, one with its roots in the earlier positivist critique of God-talk but freed from the dogma of verificationism. It was initiated in the famous 1955 collection *New Essays in Philosophical Theology* and if any document can claim to be the founding document of analytic philosophy of religion, it is surely Antony Flew's 900–word essay, "Theology and Falsification".[1]

THE "THEOLOGY AND FALSIFICATION" DEBATE

Flew begins from Wisdom's parable, but takes it in a different direction. What really happened in the dispute over the gardener? According to Flew, we began with a perfectly straightforward hypothesis about the garden: the apparently kept–up features of the garden were to be explained in terms of the action of a gardener of the ordinary sort, asserted by one party to the dispute and denied by the other. The claim in question is perfectly clear as is the evidence relevant to testing it. However, as the hypothesis in question continues to fail every attempt to confirm it, its exponent continues to modify the hypothesis in order to prevent it from being falsified as a result. In the end, we arrive at the hypothesis of an invisible, undetectable gardener whose activity is so subtle that the only evidence for its occurrence is the evidence that suggests that hypothesis in the first place. The exponent of the gardener hypothesis presented the

---

1 Flew (1955), pages 99–100.

hypothesis as though it was a straightforward, substantive empirical claim that could be tested in experience; upon examination, however, it becomes a claim to which no empirical evidence is relevant at all – and, it turns out, never was. As such, its status as a substantive, factual claim is now in doubt as well since precisely what made the original hypothesis seem intelligible and substantive was its testable consequences, all of which have now disappeared.

Flew maintains that something like this happens in the case of religious belief as well. Theists claim to believe in an omnipotent, omniscient, providential God who loves us and has a plan for the world. At first glance, this appears to be a substantive, factual claim that is in principle testable in experience. At the same time, there is much about our experience of the world (e.g. the existence of both natural and moral evil) that apparently contradicts these claims. In response, we find the theist modifying his claims about divine love and providence in order to accommodate these contrary observations. God's love is not like our love, His ways are not our ways and we are not privy to the details of God's plan, and so on. In the face of the all too palpable evidence that God, if there is one, is derelict or indifferent to our sufferings and needs, we are advised to have faith. At this point, however, it is not clear that these claims are even genuine claims, nor that their central notions, e.g. love, have any substantive meaning, since "God love us" seems to be compatible with the observation of any state of affairs whatsoever. Flew's ultimate aim is to put a dilemma to the theist: Either we interpret the claim "God loves us" substantively, in which case it will be falsified by what we observe about the world, or we interpret that claim in such a way that it is no longer substantive and may well be meaningless. Theism thus dies the "death of a thousand qualifications", giving up its substantive content by an imperceptibly slow process that allows the illusion of substantiveness to continue after all significant content has been evacuated from its characteristic religious claims – at least until an analytic philosopher comes along and reveals the fraud!

Early Responses to Flew

In the same issue of *University* in which Flew's piece originally appeared, two commentators made responses to Flew on behalf of theism and these were joined by a third in *New Essays in Philosophical Theology*. R. M. Hare (1921–2004)[1], soon to become a leading 20th-century moral philosopher, counters Flew's parable with one of his own. An insane man is convinced that all Oxford dons are out to get him and

---
1 Flew (1955), pages 99–103.

remains adamant that this is the case regardless of how much evidence to the contrary is produced, while we dismiss his fears as irrational. Although one might naively suppose that the dispute between the insane man and ourselves is over the evidence, according to Hare this is not so. The insane man's delusion results in his having a certain *controlling belief* or *blik* which is prior to the evidence and leads him to interpret that evidence in a certain way, whereas we have a contrary blik that leads us to interpret that evidence differently. Thus, in the face of evidence to the effect that there are friendly, innocuous dons that mean him no harm, the lunatic responds that those dons are simply trying to put him off his guard so that he can be done away with: he simply *knows* that the dons are out to get him. We, on the other hand, simply *know* that they are not and so take the apparent innocuous and friendly behaviour of the dons in question at face value. Flew's mistake, says Hare, is in assuming that theism or Christianity is a kind of hypothesis intended to explain something and in principle testable by evidence. In fact, however, religious beliefs are *bliks* and, for religious people, constitute the overall framework for what counts as a credible hypothesis or as evidence in the first place. This does not rule out the possibility that one position may be correct and the other false, even though the issue cannot be decided on the basis of evidence: the lunatic has an insane blik, whereas we have a sane one – and that makes all the difference. By the same token, the Christian's blik may be the correct one even though there may be no way to convince the determined atheist of that fact.

Oxford philosophical theologian Basil Mitchell (1917–)[1] was the next to enter the lists and offers his own parable to illuminate the believer's position. Suppose, says Mitchell, that you are a revolutionary fighting against an oppressive regime, and one night you are introduced to someone who claims that he is the leader of the revolution who outlines to you his plan for bringing down the oppressor. On the basis of that individual's personal charisma and apparent wisdom as you experience it in that encounter, you pledge your allegiance both to himself and to his movement. Before leaving, however, the stranger warns you that, in order to carry the revolution to a successful conclusion, he will sometimes have to do or say things that appear to be contrary to the aims of the revolution and asks for your continued trust and faith, both in him as leader and in the revolutionary movement he leads. The path of faith, however, is not easy; one hears and sees things that make one doubt that one has made the right decision. Nevertheless, the evidence does not overwhelm one's conviction of the stranger's sincerity and sagacity and so one persists and continues to work for

---

1 Flew (1955), pages 103–5.

the success of the revolution.

Mitchell's parallel to the plight of the religious believer is patent. The believer encounters God or Christ in religious experience, prayer and worship and is induced to both believe His word and live according to His will. At the same time, the existence of apparently gratuitous evils, etc., creates a crisis for faith since they provide *prima facie* evidence against the claims of Christian teaching. It is not true, says Mitchell, that the believer does not recognize that there is evidence against theism and Christianity; if this were not so, there could not be for him a crisis of faith. To the extent, then, that the facts to which the atheist points are seen to count against the claims of faith, they are so far forth meaningful because recognized as being in danger of falsification. At this point, however, the believer, like the revolutionary falls back on faith and refuses to let that evidence count *decisively* against belief, holding to the possibility that what seems to be the case prima facie will not turn out to be so *ultima facie*.

Flew is not persuaded, of course, and briefly responds to his critics, thus creating the possibility of a fruitful dialectic arising from the *University* discussion. However, the discussants did not continue to elaborate their views. Let us then turn to a further development of the issues arising from Flew's "Theology and Falsification."

CROMBIE AND RAMSEY: THE DISCLOSURE MODEL OF GOD-TALK

Although not part of the original *University* discussion, Flew's *New Essays in Philosophical Theology* contains an untitled paper by Plato scholar I. M. Crombie[1] inspired by that discussion and devoted to the same issues. Crombie, writing in defence of the cognitive value of religious belief, provides his own account of the origins and purposes of religious speech, insisting that it can be cognitively significant even if it cannot meet the analytic philosopher's standards of clarity, rigor and empirical testability. Religious claims have the form of factual statements (not expressions of feeling or performance) and so, claims Crombie, they are. However, they arise in an unusual way and have a different function from other factual statements. The "logical mother" of religious language resides in those general features of reality as we ordinarily experience them that naturally suggest (and which we instinctively interpret as testifying to) the existence of God to us and lead us to speak in general or vague generic terms about our experience from a religious point of view. While the

---

1 Flew (1955) pages 109–130; see also his more extended discussion in Mitchell (1957) pages 1–50. Crombie, in turn, notes his indebtedness to Austin Farrer (1904–68); see Farrer (1943) and (1948).

attempts to articulate these traditional evidences as rational arguments have failed, it nevertheless remains that our experience of the contingency of the universe, its order and beauty, the depths of love between persons and so on naturally evoke a religious response to reality that we might call "natural theism." (Although Crombie does not mention this, even Hume seems to have admitted this phenomenon.)[1] The "logical father" of religious belief and the talk that expresses it, at least in the Christian faith, is that set of events that give doctrinal content to religious belief allowing us to flesh out "bare theism" in the form of a full-blown system of religion. Religious language also has a "nurse", in the form of the ongoing experience of the believing community that continues to encounter the divine in prayer, worship and living the Christian life. Religious belief, and the language that expresses it, arises at the confluence of these three sources within the believer's experience.

However, because of the uniqueness of the object of religious apprehension and worship, in order to talk at all the believer has to use language in an unconventional way. The only language available to him or her is ordinary language, which was crafted for quite another purpose. It is not surprising, then, that religious language looks out of order when viewed from the perspective of the logic of ordinary speech as understood by the analytic philosopher, whether in the Russellian or the Moorean tradition. The believer can only respond that the words he or she uses seem to him or her the best words available to express what is being talked about in such a way as to communicate how the believer experiences and feels compelled to interpret the world. Further, the religious person communicates what he or she means, not by asserting discrete propositions, but instead attempting to *induce* in others the religious point of view, using religious language in such a way as to make it possible for the unbeliever to "get the point" and see what (by experiencing for him- or herself *how*) the believer sees, just as in Wisdom's example one viewer of a painting may try to get another to focus on various aspects of a painting being viewed in order to induce the experience of that painting's beauty, which the second viewer claims not to see. For Crombie, religious language neither expresses an hypothesis about the way the world is to be tested by its observable consequences nor the product of some sort of cosmological inference; instead, it is the articulation of an intuitive apprehension of a reality mediated by the created world for which ordinary language is inadequate to express straightforwardly but, if properly understood, capable of communicating to those who do not yet explicitly enjoy that apprehension, though they may do so inchoately. Thus, success in "inducing" the proper intuition is not marked by a response like "I am persuaded by your argument"

---

1 Hume (1980) pages 77–9; the *Dialogues* were originally published in 1777.

or "My experience confirms your predictions" but rather "Now I get it! I couldn't see it before but now I do and it's as obvious as the nose on my face!"

Working in the same line some years later, Ian Ramsey, then Nolloth Professor at Oxford and later Bishop of Durham, developed a sophisticated version of this view, combining what might be called the *disclosure model of God-talk* with a sophisticated account of how religious language communicates the believer's experience of the world from the religious perspective. To some extent, Ramsey's account reflects the then–popular tendency to treat scientific theories, especially those of great generality, as non-literal but nevertheless descriptive "models" of transcendent physical realities that are structurally isomorphic to the realities being described without necessarily resembling them in their material aspects.[1] A mathematical model in quantum physics, for example, represents the statistical behaviour of unobservable subatomic particles (photons, electrons, neutrinos, quarks and so on) as mathematical relationships in which the things themselves and their properties are represented by variables in equations. In a like manner, a scale model of the solar system or of the DNA molecule made out of plastic and wood uses some of those bits of plastic and wood to represent stars, planets, moons and asteroids or the four basic types of amino acids and the manner after which they form polypeptide chains in the DNA molecule. Through understanding the equations or examining the wood and plastic bits I am thereby able to grasp whatever reality it is that is being represented by those models without the necessity of being able to directly confront them in experience. According to Ramsey, the metaphysician, the theologian and the religious believer are doing something similar in their fields, with the exception that the models they construct are expressive of an apprehension that, while mediated by sensible particulars are not in any obvious way testable in experience.

Ramsey argues that natural science, while rooted in sense-experience, treats sense-experience as a *disclosure* phenomenon, at one and the same time the presence in and to consciousness of something that nevertheless presents itself as existing independently of (and in that sense *transcendent* to) consciousness. It is only because of this that descriptive language possesses *objective reference* (what other philosophers call intentionality.) If we focus simply on the subjective, mind-dependent sense-data and recast perceptual claims accordingly (e.g. "It is as though I were presently seeing a tree") we achieve epistemic certainty but are now no longer able to successfully refer to anything existing apart from the mind. Science, however, is not

---

[1] This view is most closely associated with the writings of Mary Hesse; see Hesse (1965); see also Emmet (1948) and Barbour (1974).

about sense-data and the hypotheses it formulates, though testable in sense-experience, are about independently existing external objects that affect us in and by means of sense-experience.[1]

Further, awareness of a (putatively) extramental object carries with it awareness of the subject, the self or "I" which is notoriously elusive.[2] Indeed, precisely because it is *subject*, it can never itself become an object for itself. Whenever I attempt to capture the self by means of a reflective act, I form a new reflective act that takes my previous conscious act as its content and which, in turn, fails to be contained in that act. Still, my failure to make the self an object reveals to me two facts about the self: first, that the self is constituted by a particular kind of activity, i.e. reflectivity and that the self-conscious subject is by that very fact a *self-transcending* subject; in this way, both the notion of *activity* (what neo-Thomists like Austin Farrer call *existence*) and of *transcendence* acquire empirical grounding in an episode of self-disclosure.

In the same way, our common, everyday experience of other persons is also a disclosure phenomenon.[3] We do not first intuit sense-data, infer from sense-data to the existence of an external body causing those sense-data and then merely interpret the flat, uninterpreted movements of that body as constituting actions caused by an otherwise hidden inner self or mind on the basis of analogy. Quite the contrary, we see those bodily movements as already *expressive* of and the "mentality" behind them as *disclosed in and through* the behaviour of which we are aware, as once again both transcendent to and yet immanent in observable "behaviour" which are never normally experienced as merely bodily movements with a merely external relation to a hidden cause. Rather, while transcendent in its being, mind or self is immanent in its external expression by means of the activity by which it is produced. It is only due to this that external behaviour can be experienced by us as *action* in the first place. It is on the basis of disclosures such as these that data for metaphysical model-making is to be found.[4]

Experience of God follows the same pattern.[5] In our everyday experience there are moments of *cosmic disclosure* such that we ineluctably take some ubiquitous feature of that experience to be the effects of the immanent activity of a transcendent personal agent expressive of His nature and will. To express our apprehension of this agent we use the language of personhood and agency, cause and effect but, because

---

1 See Ramsey (1964) *passim* and Ramsey (1974) pages 143–176.
2 Ramsey (1974) pages 17–31.
3 Ramsey (1974) pages 164–72.
4 See Ramsey's essay in Steinkraus (1966) and Ramsey (1961) pages 153–77.
5 Ramsey (1964) pages 47–71 and Ramsey (1957) 11–89.

the agent apprehended is unique, we vary in our use of these terms in a way suitable to express our recognition of this fact. The terms in question become *models* drawn from experience rather than literal descriptions and are *qualified* by adjectives and adverbs intended to convey the uniqueness of what is disclosed in and through our experience. Thus, talk of God consists of *qualified models* that at one and the same time apply a descriptive predicate to God but qualify it in such a way as to prevent misunderstanding. Thus, God is the *First* Cause, the *Unmoved* Mover, and Creator *ex nihilo*, etc. Cosmic disclosures, however, are not limited to the models forming the foundations for traditional philosophical theology. To the contrary, Ramsey is most comfortable when dealing with the *authorized* models of God derived from the Scriptures consisting in the interpretation of the various metaphors and images used to describe God, His actions and His relationship with His chosen people of both the Old and the New dispensations.[1] Not all of these, Ramsey notes, are personal models and many (such as J. A. T. Robinson, a follower of Tillich) prefer impersonal models of God as "beyond being", "beyond personhood" and as "the ground of being" and "object of ultimate concern." While expressing his preference for personal models of deity, Ramsey does not deny the usefulness of impersonal models as well.

Nielsen, Hick and Eschatological Verification

The attempts of Ramsey and others (such as the English philosophers H. H. Farmer[2] and H. D. Lewis[3]) to defend the cognitive meaningfulness of religious language while denying that it is subject to scientific methods of verification or falsification receives short shrift at the hands of Kai Nielsen, a prominent atheistic philosopher of religion of a decidedly positivistic bent. In his essay "Linguistic Philosophy and Beliefs",[4] Nielsen defends contemporary analytic philosophy against the charges of triviality, overspecialization and the abrogation of the philosopher's traditional role as a source of wisdom about the nature of things and about how to live. To those philosophers (like Copleston) who claim that there is an "intuition of being" that grounds the pretensions of traditional metaphysicians, Nielsen bluntly responds that whatever about such claims can be justified by appeal to the facts can be shown to have no metaphysical implications at all and that, where anything more than that may be suggested that nothing needs to be explained except some "quite interesting facts about the psychol-

---

1 See Ramsey (1957) 90–186, Ramsey (1965) and Ramsey (1973).
2 See Farmer (1947)
3 See Lewis (1962)
4 See Gill (1966) pages 52–72.

ogy of certain people." No doubt he would respond to Crombie and Ramsey in the same way. The role of the analytic philosopher, a modern academic specialist who claims no universal extent or provenance for his researches, is rather to root out and expose the linguistic confusions that lead people to puzzle over and to seek metaphysical answers to questions like "Why is there something rather than nothing?", "What is the meaning of life?" and "What must I do be happy?" This is no mere matter of showing that from the formal viewpoint that these questions are technically meaningless, but more than this – as Wittgenstein's image of the philosopher as therapist suggests – to relieve us of the deluded perspective on things that makes us think that these questions matter in the first place. The implications for everyday beliefs – metaphysical, religious and moral – are clear and represent the philosopher's major contribution toward influencing public opinion in a positive way. This may not be what traditional philosophers or modern existentialists (and those influenced by them) may want to hear, but the fact that they want to hear something else is part of the problem to which linguistic philosophy is the answer.

Still, not all philosophers of religion have been willing to concede that the demand for experiential confirmation cannot be met at some level. In his 1964 book *Faith and Knowledge*,[1] John Hick (1925–), after having reviewed the parables of Wisdom and Flew, offers his own parable in favour of the view he calls *eschatological verification*. Imagine two travellers along a road that both of them are forced to travel. One of the travellers believes that the road leads to the Celestial City and that the road is designed in such a fashion as to conduct us there in a manner that will make it possible for us to best appreciate its delights. The other denies this and regards the trip as a purposeless ramble heading nowhere in particular, the pleasant stretches of which are to be enjoyed and the rough patches endured for lack of an alternative in the interim before the trip ends in nothingness. Both are compelled to make the journey, neither can turn aside; the issue between them cannot be decided by appeal to the facts. Nevertheless, if the first traveller is correct, when the Celestial City is reached his belief about the trip will have been verified in experience and thus confirmed eschatologically, by an experience or set of experiences that happens after death. His claim cannot be falsified, since if death is the end of everything then no one can know this fact; still, the fact that some experience is in principle relevant to the assessment of religious claims, this is sufficient to hold those claims to be meaningful.

Nielsen disagrees,[2] claiming that these putative post-death experiences, having

---

1 See Hick (1957, second edition 1964) pages 169–99.
2 Nielsen (1971) pages 65–67.

been described in religious terms, beg the question with regard to the meaningfulness of religious language. However, if these experiences are described in neutral terms (i.e. "seems" language) then the religious person is in the same position as a realist *vis-à-vis* a phenomenalist about external objects; the realist insists that his sense-experiences are of independently existing external objects whereas the phenomenalist rejects this metaphysical commitment and insists on interpreting sense-experience as consisting solely of recurrent patterns of sense-data. Since no experience can decide between these descriptions, they are in fact logically equivalent and the difference between them amounts to a merely verbal difference: the realist can in fact *mean* no more that what the phenomenalist does, though he intends to claim something further and mistakenly thinks that he can do so. So too, the atheist can claim that while he is having *putative* experiences of an afterlife of the sort predicted by theism, he can simply decline to interpret them supernaturalistically and instead suppose that the natural world is simply more complex than it appears to be and that these experiences are produced by a purely natural process. On this ground, says Nielsen, one can argue that no experience of any sort could ever conclusively verify any claim about God.

The natural retort to this sort of claim is that if this is appropriate standard for empirical confirmation, then empirical evidence can never justify any substantive belief at all, including the religious sceptic's belief about what natural processes are likely to produce. Further, this seems to be an awfully high price to pay to avoid the possibility of eschatological verification of religious claims and contrary to our best practices both in science and of common sense. Only someone dogmatically committed to the claim that religious language is meaningless would find it plausible. However, since we will be looking into the subject of empirical confirmation later in this volume, we will defer further discussion of this issue here. Instead, let us look the further development of problem of God-talk in the 1960's and 70's.

NON-COGNITIVIST APPROACHES TO RELIGIOUS LANGUAGE

For whatever reason, theologians during this period largely abandoned traditional accounts of the meaning of God-talk in favour of non-cognitive accounts of religious language. Apparently convinced by the Logical Positivists that any literal construal of God-talk was impossible, theologians progressively evacuated religious language of any substantive content and were joined in this task by some philosophers as well. Instead, "sophisticated" theists developed accounts of God-talk intended to salvage some sort of credibility for their discipline in the eyes of their non-believing colleagues, though without much success in this endeavour.

EXISTENTIALIST ACCOUNTS OF RELIGIOUS LANGUAGE

For the Lutheran theologian Karl Barth,[1] the very project of Christian apologetics and natural theology is wrong–headed and impious. From the Reformational Christian point of view, the effects of original sin are so pronounced and pervasive that the unregenerate soul is quite blind to the presence of God in the world. Only those who have received the gift of faith can see the world aright and the change wrought by that grace is so profound that the believer and the unbeliever live in different worlds. For the believer, who clearly perceives the reality of God through the eyes of faith, no proofs for God's existence are needed; for those without faith, no such proofs are possible. Religious language, then, is cognitively meaningless *for the unbeliever* and it is as useless to attempt to explain its meaning to him as it is to describe the experience of redness to one who is congenitally blind – one's descriptions can never attain any sort of literalness for him nor is there any way to bridge the gap between these two incommensurable perspectives. Only the gift of God's grace and subsequent conversion can make it possible for an unbeliever to understand the truth of the Christian message: Anselm's *fides quarens intellectum* entails that living faith *precedes* understanding rather than merely informing the theologian's project as a personal commitment.[2]

Taking Barth's position in juxtaposition to Nielsen's (which refuses to countenance any religious claims whatever unless they can be expressed in non-religious terms) it's just one dogmatism against another. However, this has not prevented other theologians from attempting to articulate some sort of meaning for religious claims that is accessible and meaningful from some sort of neutral perspective. The existentialist theologians Paul Tillich[3] and Rudolf Bultmann,[4] both of whom enjoyed some currency in the English-speaking world, followed in the footsteps of Hegel and Feuerbach by proclaiming that all religious language is symbolic and mythical, even that language that previous theologians have used to make dogmatic pronouncements about God; in this sense, "God exists" is no more literally true of God than is "God is a lion" or "The Lord is my shepherd." The ultimate religious object ("God") cannot

---

1 Barth (1961) pages 29–86; see especially pages 38–51; for a critique of Barth, see Blanshard (1974) pages 288–322.
2 So Barth argues in Barth (1962) *passim*.
3 Tillich (1951) pages 235–41; see also Tillich's contribution to Hook (1965) pages 1–23 and 232–45.
4 See e.g. Bultmann (1984).

be literally captured or described in any words due to its utter transcendence of the world as we experience it; it always lies beyond our words as something to which our language inadequately points.

In Tillich's case, God becomes a kind of neo-Platonic One, so utterly transcendent that He can only be described as beyond being, beyond personhood and so beyond all non-metaphorical ("mythical") description. Although Tillich prefers to replace metaphors of height ("beyond") with those of *depth* (God is the "ground of being"), Tillich's God is so completely distinct from the world that even to call God the creator of the universe in the standard sense in which this has typically been meant is to debase God by putting Him on the same level as creatures. In the same way, the traditional, literal understandings of the Christian doctrines Incarnation and Atonement are both scientifically and religiously impossible. To understand the notions of God and the true import Christian doctrine requires that we place them in the context of our existential situation as understood by Heidegger. In this context, God and Christ answer and relieve our existential anxiety. God for us becomes the object of Ultimate Concern and the cash–value of the Jesus Myth (which is literally false as historical truth but which expresses an existential truth) that there is a New Life preached by Christ that is available to us, not merely in Heaven, but here and now in this life through faith and membership in the Church. Although Tillich's theology is couched in the portentous language typical of German philosophy and theology, it found popular expression in the English-speaking world in the writings of John Macquarie and especially in *Honest to God*,[1] written by then Bishop of Woolwich John A. T. Robinson, a theological best-seller in the 1960's.

It remains for Bultmann to draw the Feuerbachian implications of this way of thinking of things. For Bultmann, the twentieth-century man who understands the workings of the electric light can no more countenance the Christian *mythos* than he can the colourful myths of the Greek and Roman pantheon. Theology, then, must become a kind of existential anthropology, the central concern of which is to convert talk of God into talk about the human being and the human situation in order that it may retain some relevance to modern life. On this view, the deistic picture of Christ as a moral teacher whose "kingdom" is a this-worldly community of agapeistic peace and brotherhood animated by the ideal of Christian charity and tolerance emerges as the genuine core of Christian teaching, one which needs neither grounding in nor support from any supernatural force. With Bultmann, we are far along the way to a kind of Christianity that dispenses with God altogether.

---

1 Robinson (1966)

BRAITHWAITES'S PRESCRIPTIVISM AND CHRISTIAN ATHEISM

Whether intentional or not, Bultmann's existentialist interpretation of Christianity dovetails nicely with the logical positivist re–interpretation of religious language advocated by R. B. Braithwaite in his Eddington Lecture entitled "An Empiricist's View of the Nature of Religious Belief."[1] After rehearsing the standard verificationist arguments against the meaningfulness of religious statements when understood categorically, i.e. as substantive factual or descriptive statements, Braithwaite proposes to interpret religious assertions along the lines suggested by a sophisticated positivistic analysis of ethical assertions. According to this view, known as *prescriptivism*, ethical assertions, despite their apparently categorical form, are really disguised prescriptions expressing/revealing the speaker's intention to act in a particular way and thus committing himself to act in accordance with that intention expressed as a general policy. Such avowals are neither true nor false, but they can be either sincere or insincere, a judgment that can be justified by the observation of the individual's behaviour. Essentially, then, anyone who adopts the Christian faith commits him- or herself to an agapeistic life-style and the sincerity of that religious commitment can be tested in experience by observing his or her behaviour. Of course, religious people do, say and assert more than simply moral claims. Religious people pray, worship and repeat the stories that constitute the traditional lore of the community of believers to which they belong and many of these make factual, historical claims. Even so, the significance of these stories and practices for Braithwaite consists in the support they give to living in accordance with the moral values and moral code that constitutes the core of the religious mode of life and thus are capable of so functioning even if their literal truth is doubted or rejected on factual grounds. If the core of religion is a way of life, rather than a set of substantive factual claims about the nature of things, it can survive the rejection of the substantive historical or factual claims upon which it is founded. Even myth can be truth when it is properly understood as intended to illustrate and motivate the life of the believer.

Logical positivism also appears to have played a hand in the popularity of what is sometimes called Christian Atheism in the 1960's and '70's, known in the U.S. as "death of God" theology and associated in England with the writings of Don Cupitt (1934–). The most astute of the so-called "radical theologians", Paul Van Buren,[2] explicitly referred to the empiricist critique of religious language as one of the major

---
1 Braithwaite (1955) pages 1–32.
2 See Van Buren (1961).

reasons for abandoning traditional ideas about God. Yet, with the other members of this movement, he refused to see the death of God as the death of Christianity or of theology as an enterprise. Instead, the death of God became a challenge and an opportunity to produce a new, secular interpretation of Christianity capable of speaking to the modern person for whom traditional religious ideas are neither intellectually nor existentially meaningful. For the most part, however, the "death of God" movement failed to provide anything really new, ultimately simply retreading the deist conception of Christ as a supremely good moral teacher with an inspiring ideal for individual and communal existence in this world. Cupitt,[1] a former Anglican priest, preaches an "anti-realist" version of Christianity that firmly rejects the notion of salvation and any conception of the supernatural realm. Embracing a kind of nihilism inspired by Nietzsche, Cupitt maintains that there is no eternal or objective truth and that all ideas are created by human beings and justifiable only insofar as they prove useful in living one's life in this world. From this perspective, religious ideas need not be true in order to be credible; it is enough if they form part of a perspective on things that provides a way of getting through life and dealing effectively with its problems. If a secularized form of Christianity (or Christianity *cum* Buddhism) proves effective in so doing, it is as credible as any other system, given that none of them can claim a corner on the (objective) truth.

D. Z. Phillip's Wittgensteinian Analysis of Religious Language

Although Christian Atheism `a la* Cupitt would seem to be the *ne plus ultra* of non-cognitivism about religious language, it is in fact exceeded by a yet more radical perspective, that of the Welsh Wittgensteinian school associated with the University of Swansea and the group that formed around the American-born Welsh philosopher Rush Rhees, a favourite student of Wittgenstein, which included Peter Winch and D. Z. Phillips (1935–2006). Phillips[2] especially has devoted himself to the construction of a Wittgensteinian philosophy of religion that firmly rejects any notion that religious claims are to be understood as literally true while maintaining that they are of profound importance to religious believers. Since Phillips writes in a typically Wittgensteinian idiom, it is not altogether clear to an outsider like myself what his views actually amount to. However, I will at least attempt to give the flavour of his position. Let us begin with Wittgenstein himself.

After having abandoned the "picture theory" of language in the early 1930's,

---

1 See Cupitt (1981).
2 Among his many writings on this topic, see Phillips (1967) and (1976).

Wittgenstein returned to Cambridge where he propagated a new philosophy of language that became the basis for the "philosophy of the Later Wittgenstein."[1] According to this view, the mistake of previous philosophers was to suppose that the primary function of language was to *describe the world* or convey information about something pre- or non-linguistic in character. Working under this mistaken assumption, philosophers were able to generate all of the traditional philosophical problems and puzzles that have proven so frustrating and intractable. According to Wittgenstein, however, language cannot be properly understood by treating it instrumentally or as though it was beholden to something beyond or other than itself. Language in fact is a diffuse phenomenon and cannot be captured or understood from perspective outside of itself or in terms of some general theory about *the* nature and function of language. Language has no essential nature or primary function the understanding of which is the key to understanding the phenomenon of language-in-use. Instead, language can only be studied from a perspective within language itself, where specific expressions are placed and understood in specific contexts and the tendency to generalize or theorize stoutly resisted. This does not mean, however, that language is merely a set of conventions or somehow the product of human decision-making; language is the product of natural history and governs us with a kind of natural necessity from which there is no appeal. For this reason, any attempt to improve, reform or replace natural ('ordinary') language with something else, such as the empiricist language the Logical Positivists proposed, is completely wrong-headed.

In place of the picture theory of language, Wittgenstein proposes that language is more like a game governed by rules that determine what can and cannot sensibly be said in a particular context. Indeed, language is a network of such games each with its own set of rules or "logic." Since there is no perspective external to or beyond language, nor any "master game" that sets the rules to which all language-games must conform these varying games, each arising in natural language for a specific, limited purpose, do not necessarily form a coherent whole and the possibility of incommensurability cannot be ruled out. This is not a problem so long as we resist the notion that differences between various language-games need to be mediated or resolved; different areas of language, like different games, have different rules and this simply goes with the territory; in any event, we lack any kind of further point of view from which such languages can be compared and reconstructed in the first place.

---

1 For a summary account of this later philosophy Melchert (Fifth Edition, 2007, pages 620–641); for another interpretation of Wittgenstein's critique of philosophy, see Fogelin in Sluga and Stern (2004), pages 34–56.

The job of the philosopher, according to Wittgenstein and his followers, is to "lead the fly out of the fly-bottle" by exposing the errors and misunderstandings that traditional philosophers, guided by the picture theory, have brought to their understanding of ordinary language. Again, there is no general method or set of arguments capable of doing this; language does not provide us with those resources. Instead, the Wittgensteinian philosopher is like a psychotherapist, who has to deal with the specific confusions of each individual and provide a course of treatment tailor–made to relieve his or her philosophical delusions. This is done by taking the claims about the metaphysical or philosophical "commitments" or "implications" of ordinary language or the "common sense view of things" made by philosophers and showing that ordinary language has no such implications, largely through a close examination of what we do in fact say in accordance with the "logic" of ordinary speech in that context. This is a painstaking procedure in which various techniques in various combinations must be used, the purpose of which is not to win a philosophical argument but rather to dissipate confusion or, at any rate, to reduce the "patient" to silence by progressively shutting down each of his attempts to motivate a philosophical problem and thus leave him, like a Socratic interlocutor, not knowing what to say.

A recurrent theme of Wittgenstein's *Philosophical Investigations,* for example, is that the picture theory of language has created systematic confusion for philosophers in their understanding of "mental" talk. Assuming that words like "pain" are common nouns and that a statement such as "I am in pain" are simple categorical statements, philosophers quickly generate "problems" for themselves to discuss: What is the nature of this 'I'? What is 'pain'? Given that 'being in pain' is a subjective, private mental event, how can one ever know that anyone other than oneself is *really* in pain? And so on. While never denying that there is such a thing as pain or that we do in fact refer to subjective mental events when we use words like "pain", Wittgenstein does seem committed to the view that reference to subjective mental events or experiences is never *essential* to our understanding of pain-language as measured by our ability to use pain-language correctly according to its own proper "logic." First person pain-ascriptions such as "I am in pain" are more like saying "Ouch!" than asserting a categorical claim. Further, the criteria for both asserting and revising third-person ascriptions of pain (e.g., "He is in pain") are all publicly observable ones. Finally, it is not even possible for someone to learn "pain-talk" in the first place if this is not the case. Reference to 'pain' as a subjective private mental state simply drops out of the picture once we understand how "pain-talk" works and along with it the confusion that motivates "philosophical" questions about the self, mental states and other minds.

For Phillips, the philosophy of religion rests on a similar mistake. Since many religious claims have a categorical form and thus appear to be factual and descriptive, philosophical critics of religion demand proof, evidence or justification for claims like "God exists" sufficient to convince a neutral, non-religious person of its truth and theistic philosophers, taking the bait, attempt to supply these proofs. However, from the Wittgensteinian perspective religious language is a kind of *global* language game participation in which grounds a comprehensive "form of life" that is foundational for its participants. Religious language (or, more specifically, the Christian religion with its characteristic claims) is neither a theory about the world nor a description of it, let alone committed to any metaphysical position labelled "theism" by philosophers. It makes no substantive claims and rests in no way on any religiously-neutral facts or evidence; it is a completely self-contained set of practices for speaking and acting inaccessible and unintelligible to non-participants, entry into which is solely by a kind of conversion experience in which one's basic outlook on things is completely altered such that one now sees the world in a completely new fashion. As such, both defenders and attackers of "theism" simply fail to grasp what religion is all about and the complete irrelevance of their discussions to religion as actually experienced and practiced. Since religious claims are not substantive, they cannot be attacked by treating them as though they were and then declaring that when so treated they will not stand up to rational scrutiny. Nor can religion be dismissed as merely an irrational, gratuitous expression of "faith." For, in the first place, conversion is something that happens to one, not something one chooses for oneself. Secondly, the notion of "rationality" as some sort of neutral, context-independent standard for belief and behaviour is itself a philosopher's myth that has no standing within the general Wittgensteinian perspective; so the religious person cannot be faulted for failing to live up to it. There is, in fact, neither an external perspective of any sort on the religious form of life from which it can be understood by the outsider nor any way for the religious person to articulate what that perspective is like to those who do not share it. As such, the questions about religion that the philosopher would like to raise about religion cannot even be formulated, let alone discussed; in the end, there is only silence.

What *is* characteristic of the religious point of view, according to Phillips, is a kind of *unconditional commitment* that expresses itself in the Christian's subjective attitude toward life and events as expressed in his or her behaviour. The Christian responds in thanks to God regardless of what happens, because this is a necessary part of what it means to be a Christian: to love and trust God *no matter what*. The

Christian responds to the world in *agape* by loving God and neighbour not because of the hope of reward or out of gratitude for past favours but simply because that is what it means to be a Christian and live the Christian life. This *is* conversion and the only gift that God has to offer and confer upon us; indeed, only if God confers this gift on us is such a life possible for us at all. By experiencing this conversion and living this new life the Christian *knows subjectively* through his own experience that the truths of faith are "really true" even though they cannot be known to be objectively true from some neutral point of view. Nothing more can or need be said about what "really true" means in this context; all attempts to cash it out in other terms will fail since it is by its very nature a Kierkegaardian subjective truth.

If all one wants to do is insulate religious belief from philosophical critique, the Wittgensteinian approach is hard to beat. However, outside of the adherents of certain strains of evangelical Christianity notably popular in Wales, few are likely to find Phillips's views of either religion or Christianity an accurate depiction of the phenomenon. Most Christians, for example, do in fact believe that Christianity makes metaphysical claims both about this world and the world to come and that what happens in life can either help confirm or try one's faith, in some cases to the breaking point.[1] At any rate, the philosophical articulation and defence of theism in recent decades has taken another, more classical approach and it is that development that we will be following in the rest of this book.

THE "PARITY ARGUMENT": AN EPISTEMOLOGICAL COUNTERATTACK

By the mid-1960's, analytically-trained defenders of theism began to appear. These individuals were largely the product of small, Protestant colleges like Calvin College in Grand Rapids, Michigan and Wheaton College in Wheaton, Illinois who had earned doctorates at major American universities like Michigan and Yale. By the time they came on the scene, the Positivistic and Wittgensteinian preoccupation with the philosophy of language was beginning to weaken and the problem of "God-talk" was running out of steam,[2] thus creating the possibility for alternate approaches in the philosophy of religion. One such alternative grew out of an early theistic response to moderate Wittgensteinian C. B. Martin's book *Religious Belief*, a sophisticated compendium of the results of the language-dominated approach.[3] While the early chapters

---

1 For a critique of Phillips, see Helm (1997) pages 53–77.
2 Indeed, it is little discussed today. However, see Vesey (1972) for a collection of good papers on this topic.
3 See Martin (1959; second edition 1963); he is no relation to Michael Martin.

of the book were restatements of the by-then familiar critique of the meaningfulness of God-talk, in a chapter entitled "Seeing God" Martin considers whether claims to have directly experienced God – whether in mystical experience, in prayer, reading the Scriptures, or in visual and auditory experiences – can provide any evidence for God's existence.[1] If they can, then the theist can bypass the problems raised by the critique of the traditional arguments and even mitigate the problems of "God-talk" by appeal to experience. However, says Martin, such claims cannot accomplish their aim. Either we interpret these claims realistically, in which case the evidence will be insufficient to justify those claims, (being consistent with their falsity) or we must interpret them phenomenologically, in which case they no longer make any claim about the world. In neither case, then, does the evidence of experience suffice to justify those claims.

Martin goes on to argue that there is a crucial difference between the case of religious experience and my putative sense-experiences that makes the latter good evidence for claims about the world but not the former. In the case of ordinary sense-experience, there are established ways of *checking* our experiences in such a way as to confirm or corroborate them. For example, if it *seems* to be me that there is a blue piece of paper on the table before me, then that is generally regarded as good evidence that there *is in fact* a piece of blue paper on the table before me. True, that it seems to me to be the case does not entail that it is so, but if any doubts about the matter are raised, we all know how to go about checking whether what we say is so. We can look more closely, for example. We can photograph the piece of paper and consult the photograph to see whether an image of it is produced. We can ask other people and see if they report seeing the piece of paper, and so on. By contrast, however, religious experiences have the worst of both worlds, since they are uniformly personal experiences, not immediately shared by others (hence are *subjective* experiences) but purport to be experiences of an objectively existing reality that transcends the experience that reveals it. For this reason, there can be no publicly-applicable testing procedures that can either confirm or infirm such experiences. The believer is left with nothing but his putative experiences of God and no way to establish their veridicality. Even if he finds himself psychologically incapable of doubting the veracity of his experiences, the fact remains that his experiences provide no evidence whatsoever for his belief that God exists. This may not matter to the believer, of course, but it does to the philosopher – and, if that believer is a philosopher, it ought to matter to him as well.

Michigan's George Mavrodes (1926–), an evangelical Christian who is also an

---

1 Martin (1959, second edition 1963) pages 64–94.

analytic philosopher, takes up Martin's challenge in his book *Belief in God*,[1] first published in 1970 and at the time a lonely voice in defence of theism. Characteristically, however, Mavrodes does not argue that religious experiences are (contrary to Martin's claims) good evidence for God's existence. Instead, he argues that Martin's appeal to the presumably "public" tests that we rely on in sense-experience is *ultimately* no help in justifying or even corroborating the corresponding beliefs about the piece of paper. *All* experience is subjective in precisely the sense that Martin accuses religious experience of being and is thus in the same boat as religious experience. My only access to the world is through my personal subjective experience, whether it be direct visual experience of external objects, the contents of photographs or hearing the reports of others. If I cannot take at least some of these at face value, as providing evidence in and of themselves for the claims they are intended to support without further corroboration, then experience is useless as a foundation for our beliefs. If I can accept an experience as veridical only if I can corroborate it by some further experience, then the same will apply to that further experience as well, and we are off on an infinite regress. By the same token, if I fear that my original experience might be false or delusive, the same fear must infect the various experiences by means of which I attempt to verify or corroborate them as well. Suppose I have a vivid visual image of my dead grandfather sitting in the corner of my living room as though he were still alive, which is so clear and distinct that I find it indistinguishable from experiences that I would ordinarily regard as veridical. Realizing that I might be hallucinating, I consult my friends who assure me that, in fact, they do not see my dead grandfather. Now, it seems, I have conclusive "public" proof that my apparent experience of my grandfather is an hallucination. However, it suddenly occurs to me that, if I am hallucinating, my vivid visual experience of my friends all reporting that they fail to see my grandfather may itself be an hallucination, hence does not count as evidence that I am hallucinating after all. Seeking further "tests" along these lines will, of course, be quite useless. It does not follow from this, of course, that it is not rational for me to take my friend's testimony as grounds for believing that my putative experience of my grandfather is an hallucination; Mavrodes' only point is that the rationality of that taking is not justifiable by appeal to experience *as such*. The sceptic about religious experience, then, is faced with a dilemma: either experience in general is useless as a guide for belief or religious experience, despite its differences from other, more common forms of experience, is just as good a ground for belief in God as sense-experience is for belief in an external world. Mavrodes does not tell us which of these

---

1 Mavrodes (1970) pages 73–80.

two alternatives we ought to accept, but given the drastic consequences of the first alternative, the second seems obviously preferable.

Alvin Plantinga (1932–), then at Calvin College, takes a similar line in his first book, *God and Other Minds*, published in 1967.[1] Written firmly within the confines of the deductivist paradigm, Plantinga devotes the first two parts of the book to a discussion of the evidence for and against God's existence, looking first at natural theology and then at natural atheology, construing all of the evidence pro and con articulated as deductive proofs. He concludes, after an exhaustive discussion that displays considerable logical and analytical acumen, that neither the arguments for God's existence nor those against God's existence are ultimately satisfactory. In the third part of the book, however, Plantinga switches gears and begins to explore a different approach to assessing belief in God, one which, after a lapse of years, Plantinga will return to. Plantinga argues that our knowledge of other minds has no better justification than that supplied by Descartes' analogical argument in the *Meditations*; in particular, he rejects Logical Behaviourism and argues against Wittgensteinian analyses of mental ascriptions. At the same time, Plantinga argues that the analogical argument for other minds is flawed in a manner similar to that in which the teleological argument – also an analogical argument – fails as a proof for God's existence. Despite this, it is eminently rational for us to believe in other minds on the grounds provided by analogy; by the same token, it is just as rational for us to believe in God on the grounds provided by the teleological argument. So, either we must be sceptics about both of these things or accept them both at face value despite their lack of conclusive proof.

Plantinga's book was immediately recognized as an important contribution to the philosophy of religion. However, his conclusion was widely rejected as the position that since we have no good reason to believe in other minds, but we do anyway, we might as well believe in God as well. Plantinga would later reject the entire deductivist paradigm, contending that the rationality of our beliefs is a matter almost completely separate from considerations of proof or evidence; from this later position he would contend that, just as belief in other minds is eminently rational despite its lack of rational proof, so too is belief in God. For the present, however, what needs to be emphasized is the strategy represented by the so-called "parity argument," which has since been used by many philosophers to argue that religious experience is relevantly analogous to some other, generally accepted source of belief-formation, such that one is either forced to be sceptic both about religious belief and that other source of belief-formation, or to admit that both are acceptable sources of rational (i.e. probably true) belief.

---

1 Plantinga (1967)

A recent, sophisticated version of the "Parity Argument" strategy has been developed by William P. Alston (b. 1921–) of Syracuse University and is unfortunately too complex and detailed to be usefully summarized here. However, in various books published since 1989 (beginning with *Perceiving God*)[1] Alston argues that the claims to be made on behalf of *mystical perception*, i.e. putative experiences of God are as credible as those made on behalf of sense-perception. Alston denies that we have any non-circular justification for sense-perception as a source of knowledge about the external world. Nor is "sense-perception" the name of some sort of faculty of intuition. Instead, sense-perception consists in a set of doxastic (belief-forming) procedures that, beginning from some sort of non-doxastic input, arrives at occurrent beliefs about reality. The beliefs formed in accordance with these practices, while spontaneous and incapable of being controlled by the will, are nevertheless subject both to social control and change over time. Despite this, sense-perception in practice proves itself to be reliable when judged by its own standards, hence is "self-supported" by the facts that the doxastic practices involved in sense-perception result in many verified experiences and show themselves to be largely self-correcting. This is a form of circularity, since it presumes the reliability of sense-perception as a condition for evaluating sense-perception as a source of knowledge about the world; however, this is not a *trivial* form of circularity since there was no antecedent *guarantee* that sense-perception would prove reliable when judged by its own standards.

Alston then construes what he calls mystical perception as a distinct and independent set of doxastic practices arising from putative direct experiences of God. Although a bias in favour of "Eastern" mysticism among scholars of religion has led to an identification of mystical experience with what is often called monistic or unitative mystical experience, Alston argues that in the Western Christian tradition we have a much richer variety of putative perceptions of God, many of which have distinct phenomenological content and thus retain the subject/object distinction. Since these experiences form a distinct kind of experience of a unique object, mystical perception bids fair to be a mode of apprehension in its own right and thus not automatically subject to the evaluative criteria that apply to other, distinct sets of doxastic principles such as those governing sense-perception, memory, induction, deduction, and so on. Attempts to apply these standards to the case of mystical perception (usually with the intent of discrediting its claims) either fail to appreciate relevant differences between the putative objects of these experiences as revealed in practice or involve an unjustified intellectual imperialism. When judged in accordance with its

---

1 See Alston (1989a), (1989b), (1991) and (1993).

own standards, mystical perception proves to be both reliable and self-correcting, especially in relation to the realization of the ideal inherent in the practice of the religious life; this is *mutatis mutandis* the same sort of non-trivial circularity we find in the case of sense-perception. Further, *contra* the claims of C. B. Martin and others, it is simply false that there are no rules, standards or procedures for evaluating the veridicality of mystical experiences and while it is true that none of these tests are foolproof or "Cartesian-safe" this does not put mystical perception at any disadvantage in relation to, e.g., memory or sense-perception because none of the standards in play in these contexts can reach these standards either. Therefore, if sense-perception, memory and so on are rationally suitable grounds for belief formation, so too is mystical perception. Given the success of this "parity argument", it remains that one's only choices are either to reject the rationality of belief in sense-perception, etc. along with mystical perception or admit (however grudgingly) that it is just as rational to accept the "well-confirmed" deliverances of mystical perception as it is to accept those of sense-perception.

The "parity argument" strategy is something of a way-station on the road from Deductivism to Post-Deductivism and useful both to Inductivist and Post-Deductivist thinkers. Indeed, Alston has exhibited sympathies in both directions, endorsing in some contexts the inductivist "cumulative case" approach and in others the "Post-deductivist" rejection of evidentialism in favour of an account in terms of largely independent sets of doxastic practices that generate "basic beliefs" and whose deliverances we are either forced (at least sometimes) simply to accept at face value or otherwise forego entirely. We shall investigate the Post-Deductivist approach presently. For now, we will concern ourselves with the Inductivist paradigm which developed first.

Chapter Four

The Argument from Evil and the Origin of Inductivism

The year 1955 was to be a crucial one for the philosophy of religion, because it initiated one of the most significant disputes of late twentieth century philosophy, the dispute over the problem of evil. In that year the Australian philosopher J. L. Mackie published his paper "Evil and Omnipotence" in *Mind*, a paper whose argument was widely regarded as constituting a deductive *disproof* of God's existence by eliciting a contradiction from a set of non-negotiable commitments of traditional theism. Noting that analytic philosophers have largely accomplished the task of refuting the traditional arguments for God's existence, Mackie worries that theists may seek refuge in some form of fideism that discounts the need for rational argument to justify religious belief. As such, he regards it as incumbent upon the atheist to cut off this last route of escape by convicting the theist of *positive* irrationality inasmuch as the traditional theist inevitably contradicts him- or herself, forcing the theist to either abandon his or her position or to lapse into incoherence. Mackie's argument is not new: Plato, the Stoics, Epicurus and Cicero all discussed the problem of evil in Classical times; so did the Mediaevals, such as Augustine and Aquinas and modern philosophers such as Leibniz. However, Mackie's way of presenting the argument was new and, to many, so compelling that it made theism utterly untenable.

Mackie, of course, did not have the last word on this topic. However, the discussion of the problem his paper initiated was to produce a prodigious literature – it is estimated that more books and articles have been produced on this topic than any other philosophical issue in the last fifty years[1] – and a dialogue that has developed through a series of distinct stages. More than this, it has initiated paradigm change in the philosophy of religion. In this chapter, I will discuss the first stage of this change, the transition from the Deductivist to the Inductivist paradigm.

---

1 See the editor's introduction to Howard-Snyder (1996) page ix.

Mackie's Argument

As typically stated, Mackie's argument[1] takes the following form. The traditional theist maintains the following three propositions about the nature of God:

1. God is omnipotent.
2. God is omniscient.
3. God is wholly good.

Theists disagree about how to interpret these claims, but their natural tendency is to treat these claims as relatively unrestricted. Now, consider the proposition

4. Evil exists.

Unlike the other claims, which are conceptual, claim 4 is empirical and readily confirmed by ordinary sense-experience. However, if God is omnipotent, then He has the power to eliminate evil if he so chooses. If God is omniscient, then He is aware of all the evils in the world and knows how to prevent their occurrence. Finally, if God is wholly good, then presumably God would *want* to prevent all the evil in the world. Therefore, if the theistic God exists, evil will not exist. But evil exists. Therefore, God does not exist. To put it another way, we can deduce a *contradiction* from the set consisting of propositions 1–4 and any set of propositions from which we can deduce a contradiction is an *inconsistent* set of propositions, i.e. one whose members cannot all be true at the same time. If so, then in order to remove the inconsistency the theist must give up one of the claims forming the inconsistent set. According to Mackie, any adequate solution to the problem of evil must occur along this line. But which claim is to be given up?

Mackie cites what amounts to two main possibilities. One can either deny that evil exists or give up one or more of the claims constituting the traditional theist account of God. As far as Mackie is concerned, it does not matter which of these solutions one adopts, since adopting either alternative represents a major defeat for the theist. Mackie weighs in on the matter and is joined by others as well. If one takes the line that evil does not exist or that evil is only good improperly understood, one can escape the problem of evil but only at the cost of having to defend the highly implausible view that everything that happens, no matter how horrible and apparently gratuitous, is really good when viewed from the perspective of the "big picture" available from the God's-eye point of view or somehow necessary for some greater good to exist.

---

[1] See Mackie's essay in Pike (1964) pages 46–60.

Further, the thesis that evil is an illusion or a misapprehension is problematic in its own right, for after all is not the illusion or misapprehension of evil itself an evil, hence something that a good God would have ample reason to prevent? On examination, this way out does not seem very promising as a response to the problem of evil.

The only alternative, then, is to abandon at least one of the traditional divine attributes. This, however, is equally unsatisfactory, since it yields either an indifferent or malevolent God, a morally admirable but apparently impotent one or a God who is woefully ignorant of what is going on in the world. On any of these scenarios, the teachings of the traditional theistic religions have to be dismissed as false and many of their practices pointless. This may represent a victory for process panentheists, but very few theists are attracted to such a heterodox position. Furthermore, many theists who make these concessions do so only half–heartedly, giving only verbal assent to the required limitations while resisting the implications of these concessions.

Mackie realizes that theists will attempt to evade the dilemma by arguing that we can remove the appearance of a contradiction. Mackie regards all of these shopworn arguments as fallacious solutions to the problem of evil and critiques them on various grounds. For example, the claim that good cannot exist without evil or is a necessary counterpart to the good fails on two grounds. First, it implies that God is not omnipotent, because the truth of these claims would place limits on what a good God could do. Second, the defender of the position faces a dilemma: either good and evil are related in such a way that neither can exist without the other, in which case evil will be ineliminable in principle (even in Heaven) or they are not, in which case these claims are false. If there were only good and no evil then perhaps we would not have a concept of "good" for lack of contrast, but this does not mean that goodness would not exist. The suggestion that evil is necessary as a means to the good fails for the same reasons; not only would God not be omnipotent on such a scenario but evil would be ineliminable as well.

A third proposal, which suggests that the existence of evil makes goods possible that otherwise would not exist in the world, Mackie regards as much more challenging. On this view, first order physical evils, such as disease and disasters are necessary in order to make heroism and virtue possible. In a world in which these evils were absent, these great goods would not exist, so a world containing these evils is, on the whole, a better world than one in which they did not. Mackie offers a scattershot of objections to this solution. First, why suppose that worlds in which moral virtues are possible is better than one in which happiness is maximized? Second, if God permits natural evil in order than moral good might exist, can God be described as truly benevolent? Thirdly, what about the second–order moral evils (such as neglect, malevolence, indifference, cowardice, etc.) that the current setup allows? It is very unlikely that the amount of moral good outweighs the combined weight of natural and moral evil and thus that a good God would permit this. Nor does there seem to be any higher-order good for which moral evil is a necessary condition; so this solution proves inadequate as well.

A final solution investigated by Mackie fares no better in his view. This view suggests that perhaps free will is a higher-order good the existence of which is so valuable that it outweighs the moral evil that exists as a consequence of the abuse of that power. Mackie regards the notion of free will as incoherent but maintains that the appeal to free will cannot help the theist cause in any case because the theist inevitably lands in the same dilemma we have already seen. If God cannot control His free creatures, then He is not omnipotent. If He can control them, then He could bring it about that they always freely choose to do the good and moral evil will not exist. If we claim that God is omnipotent but permits his free creatures to do evil acts that He foresees and could prevent, then God is not good. Indeed, any talk of God having conditional obligations or binding Himself is nonsense; there is here a paradox of omnipotence that is strictly analogous to the paradox of sovereignty in British constitutional law.

Flew, McCloskey and Scriven

Mackie's deductive Argument from Evil received additional articulation and support from the contemporaneous writings of a great number of philosophers, most notable of whom were Antony Flew, H. J. McCloskey and Michael Scriven. In a second contribution to the *New Essays* volume,[1] Flew argues that it is not impossible for God to have created human beings who always do what is good hence that evil cannot be excused on the grounds that it is required for the existence of free action. Flew's argument presupposes the compatibilist account of free will, according to which one is free so long as one acts voluntarily in accordance with one's own desires and character rather than contrary to one's wishes through external threat or coercion. On this account of what it means to be free, there is no incompatibility in describing our actions as free even if they were causally determined by forces outside of our control. As such, God could have created human beings in such a way that they were pre-

---

1 Flew (1955), pages 144–69.

destined always to do the right and the good, to do so willingly and whole-heartedly and thus, in a compatibilist sense, freely. Indeed, many Christians believe that God is necessarily good and acts freely despite the logical impossibility of His performing any evil act. Many Christians also believe that one is truly free only when one acts in a morally good fashion and that the saints are preserved from all possibility of doing wrong. So there seems to be no reason to suppose that God could not have created His rational creatures in such a way that they were incapable of sin and presumably a good God would have done so. So the appeal to free will does not mitigate the problem of evil.

Just as Mackie had accused Hume of half–heartedness in his discussion of the problem of evil, H. J. McCloskey, writing in 1960, accuses Mackie of being soft on theism, a defect he intends to remedy in his essay "God and Evil."[1] Mackie makes things too easy for the theist by allowing him or her to assimilate all physical evil to moral evil. In fact, says McCloskey, there are numerous physical evils that cannot plausibly be thought to be necessary in order for free choice to be possible, so theists need a separate theodicy to account for these evils. Further, argues McCloskey, none of the usual reasons given to justify the existence of physical evil can justify all of the evils we in fact encounter in the world. It is simply false that pleasure cannot exist without pain, so it cannot be true that good cannot exist without evil. Nor is it plausible to suppose that physical evil is the just punishment for our sins, a warning to turn to God before it is too late or a goad to spur us to action. These will not explain the entirety of physical evil in any case; more importantly, however, a good God would have better ways of accomplishing these ends, such as making us less lazy or more naturally religious. The claim that physical evil is the by–product of the operation of the laws of nature that are on the whole beneficial does not absolve God from the duty to prevent those evils that result, something an omnipotent God could do simply by constantly intervening in nature to prevent those evils from occurring. Finally, while McCloskey concedes that there is some merit in the notion that physical evil might be justified as a necessary means to the production of good there are far too many gratuitous evils in the world for this claim to pass muster as a general explanation of physical evil.

Free will does no better as a solution for the problem of moral evil, according to McCloskey. Defenders of theism appeal either to the mere existence of free will as a justification for the existence of evil or to the goods made possible by the existence of free will, but neither of these appeals is sound. It is questionable on the face of it

---

1 Reprinted in Pike (1964), pages 61–84.

that free will is so valuable that a world containing moral evil is better than one in which free will does not exist. But if theists concede (as most of them do) that it was logically possible for God to have created a world in which free moral agents always do what is good and right, then a good God would have created such a world; on the other hand, if God was unable to actualize this logically possible state-of-affairs then He is not omnipotent. Free will, then, does not require the existence of evil in order to exist or to have a point. Further, McCloskey denies that the goods made possible by free will can be shown to outweigh the evils produced by moral agents or shown to be so valuable that a world containing them is plausibly thought to be better than one that would lack them. In a world of peace and happiness, many of the moral virtues we recognize and cultivate in this world would not exist or have little if any scope. If there were no hunger, there would be no need to mount campaigns to aid the starving. If there were no wars, there would be no need for military heroism or to defend the innocent against aggression. If there were no natural disasters, then great acts of caring, compassion and moral heroism would be unnecessary. Would this really be so bad? Besides, there is a paradox in this sort of reasoning. If moral evils are really so necessary for moral striving and the perfection of character – even though they often have the opposite effect – then do our attempts to eliminate these evils actually reduce the good in the world? And suppose we actually succeeded in overcoming them – what then? On this view we would have destroyed all possibility of developing these supposedly invaluable states of character through the very activity that was supposed to develop them!

In many ways, Michael Scriven's *Primary Philosophy*[1] is an atheist's scholastic manual. Although written as a textbook for introductory philosophy courses, it eschews any pretence of objectivity in favour of the advocacy of a specific set of philosophical positions. The thesis of chapter four of Scriven's book is that God does not exist and that this can be demonstrated by philosophical argument. Scriven proceeds by refuting all of the classical arguments for God's existence (construed as deductive proofs) and then arguing that the deductive argument from evil demonstrates the logical impossibility of God's existence. Scriven's version of the argument, however, takes a slightly different form. Scriven takes it for granted that a claim such as *it is wrong to permit the gratuitous torture of innocent children* to be a paradigm case of a self-evident moral truth and one that most religious people would agree to. Further, most of us would take this truth to imply that any suitably placed moral agent would have a moral obligation to prevent such acts: it would be wrong for me, for example,

---

1 See Scriven (1966).

to stand idly by while an innocent child was being tortured just for the fun of it and I would be morally blameworthy for failing to intervene on behalf of that child, especially if (like God) I could do so at no cost or danger to myself. Further, my failure to intervene in this way in these circumstances would certainly reflect against my claim to be a good person. However, religious people claim to believe in a God who is necessarily good, so that it is impossible for Him to do any evil act or refrain from doing any morally required one. Since God is omnipotent, omniscient and morally perfect, God is always suitably placed to prevent acts such as the gratuitous torture of innocent children and, if He existed, would recognize the moral requirement to intervene and thus inevitably act in such a way as to prevent such actions from occurring. But the gratuitous torture of innocent children does occur and does so with uncomfortable regularity. Since such acts could not occur if the theistic God existed, it follows that no such God exists. Q.E.D.

Pike and Plantinga: Refuting the Deductive Argument from Evil

In 1963, Nelson Pike (1926–), then of Cornell University, published his paper "Hume on Evil"[1] in which he attacked the consensus in favour of the argument from evil as a deductive disproof of God's existence. Essentially, Pike argues that the apparent contradiction involved in 1–4 above can be removed simply by adding a further proposition to the set:

> 5. God has a morally sufficient reason for permitting the evils we experience in this world.

If proposition 5 above is true, then there is no contradiction in supposing that an omnipotent, omniscient and wholly good God exists and that there is evil in the world. All that follows (says Pike) is that God must have a good reason or *reasons* for permitting those evils and not preventing them. The atheist errs, then, in thinking that the deductive argument from evil proves that theism is self-contradictory and thus his proposed disproof of God's existence fails.

Pike makes two further points in his paper that, when suitably expanded, are of relevance to our discussion here. First, Pike maintains that evil is evidence against God's existence only if we take theism to be some sort of *hypothesis* about the way the world is that is to be embraced or evaluated on the basis of neutral evidence. However, religious people do not treat belief in God as in any way hypothetical: belief

---

[1] Reprinted in Pike (1964), pages 85–102.

in God is posited by faith and faith is the ground for the religious view of the world, not the result of some sort of inference. The claims of faith, then, are not subject to evaluation by reference to neutral evidence; it is a sufficient defence of the faith to argue that it is internally coherent and logically consistent with everything else we know about the world. Secondly, proposition 5 above is a logical consequence of the theist's commitment to the joint truth of 1–4 above, not a claim for which the theist either has or needs confirmatory evidence. According to Pike, the theist is under no obligation to provide any proof or justification for proposition 5 above and is free to profess complete ignorance as to what that reason or reasons might be. Indeed, religious people have generally maintained that we have no access to the divine mind nor any detailed understanding of God's plans for the world other than what has been revealed to us and accepted in faith and trust by those who believe. The religious person's plea of ignorance in this context is not an attempt to evade the unpleasant facts of evil but merely a frank confession of the limits of our intellect. In these two points, made by Pike *en passant* and largely ignored at the time, we find the germs of the negative apologetics characteristic of what I will call the Post-Deductivist Paradigm in the philosophy of religion.

The influence of Pike's critique of the deductive disproof of God's existence from the fact of evil is evident in what transpired over the course of the next few years. Atheistic philosophers of religion quietly abandoned the deductive version of the argument from evil and no one defends it today. This does not mean, of course, that the problem of evil has gone away: Pike was completely mistaken when he claimed, at the end of "Hume on Evil", that "the traditional problem of evil reduces to a non-crucial perplexity of relatively minor importance."[1] Indeed, the next change of paradigm in the philosophy of religion emerged out of the atheistic response to Pike's refutation of the traditional problem of evil. I will return to this topic at the end of this chapter.

Alvin Plantinga takes a line very similar to Pike's in *God and Other Minds* and that he further refines in later works such as *The Nature of Necessity* and *God, Freedom and Evil*. Plantinga calls this the free will *defence*[2] in order to distinguish his appeal to free will from the classic Augustinian free will *theodicy*. A theodicy attempts to supply us with the actual reasons that justify God in permitting evil; a defence, however, simply attempts to supply a *logically possible* reason or set of reasons that would do this. A defence is sufficient to refute the deductive argument from evil and so is all

---

1 Pike (1964), page 102.
2 See Plantinga (1967), pages 131–55, (1974a) pages 164–96 and 1974b) pages 7–64.

that is required to exonerate theistic faith. However, even if the free will defence fails, this does not undermine the faith or re-establish the claims of the deductive argument from evil; not even a refutation of every reason that we can think of would do this. On the Pike/Plantinga line, it is sufficient to save the logical consistency of theism that it is logically possible that there be such a reason *whether or not we have any inkling of what it is*. The atheist who wants to prove that there is no God can only do so if he can prove that it is logically impossible that there is such a reason and it is difficult to imagine how one could even begin to go about doing this.

Nevertheless, Plantinga does think that his free will defence is sufficient to provide a plausible candidate for a reason that would, if true, justify God in permitting evil. Plantinga asks whether or not even an omnipotent God can create any universe He chooses. According to Leibniz, this does lie within God's power, but Plantinga denies this – if God is a necessary being, then given that God exists His non-existence is logically impossible. So, then, God could not create a universe in which He himself did not exist and thus cannot create any just any universe. There are limits on what even an omnipotent being can do.

Now suppose that human beings have *significant* free will, so that some of their choices are such that it lies within their power at that moment to effect more than one alternative at that time. It is nevertheless consistent with this that some free choices will be easily predictable given a standard description of the situation of choice. So, suppose situation S in which an agent who owns a Rembrandt is offered some trivial sum – say $5 and nothing else – for his Rembrandt in a situation in which that agent is fully cognizant of the value of the painting, clearly understands what he is being offered in exchange for it and has no other reason compelling him to sell such a valuable item for such a trivial sum. We can easily predict that the agent in question will freely turn down this offer. If so, then there is no universe God can create in which S obtains and the agent freely accepts $5 for his painting. (God could create a different universe in which some similar situation S' obtains in which the agent in question does accept $5 for his Rembrandt, but that is not the same thing.) It follows once again that there are universes, such as ones containing S but in which the agent accepts $5 for his Rembrandt, that even an omnipotent God cannot create.

Finally, let us suppose that there is a condition known as *transworld depravity* that essentially affects every moral agent. If an agent suffers from transworld depravity, then in every universe in which he or she might exist there will be at least one morally significant situation M in which the agent in question will freely choose to do wrong. If that is so, then it will be impossible for God to create a universe in which there are agents possessing significant free choice and yet no moral evil exists. Once again, it turns out that it is impossible for God to create a universe in which there is significant free choice and yet no moral evil. As such, God cannot be faulted for having failed to create such a universe. Now Plantinga does not propose that this is actually the case, only that it is possibly so, i.e. that the envisaged scenario is non-self-contradictory. Given that the foregoing is the case, it will be sufficient to refute the claim that it is inconsistent to affirm the existence of the theistic God while admitting the existence of evil. In the same way, Plantinga also removes the implicit contradiction represented by the existence of physical evil by proposing that disease, natural disasters and so on are really the result of the actions of Satan and his minions who delight in tormenting us and tempting us to our doom. Again, Plantinga does not assert the truth of this claim, only that it is possibly true and that its possible truth is sufficient to refute the deductive argument from physical evil to the non-existence of God.

John Hick's Irenaean Theodicy

Scriven's *Primary Philosophy* appeared in 1966. The same year, John Hick published his landmark study *Evil and the God of Love*[1] which was at one and the same time a history of theodicy and a proposal for a modern, liberal Christian solution to the problem of evil. Although it is something of an excursus, we cannot pass over this important innovation in theodicy without some mention.

Hick distinguishes two traditions in Christian theodicy. The first, known as the Augustinian tradition, is the mainstream tradition in Christian theodicy. According to the Augustinian tradition, God created both angels and human beings as fully perfect exemplars of their natural kinds and placed them in an optimal environment in which God's presence was palpable and in which all their needs were met. Nevertheless, both angels and men fell through disobedience and were deprived of the immediate presence of God. It is due to this fact that evil entered the world. Further, evil itself has no positive reality; instead, it is parasitic on the good and exists in the form of a privation of the good that is proper to something by nature, as the evil of blindness exists in the eye as the privation of sight. Evil exists in human nature due to the fact that proper ordering of the parts of the soul is absent; because of this all human beings are born sinful and will inevitably sin in consequence of their natural bent. At the same time, human beings retain their free will, such that on any occasion in which one actually sins, one could have refrained from that act in those circumstances; that

---

1 Hick (1966)

we are inherently sinners does not entail that we will commit any particular sin in any particular circumstances, only that we will inevitably sin on some occasion or other. Therefore, since both our sinful tendencies and our actual sins are the result of the abuse of human free will, it is human beings, not God, who are responsible for the existence of moral evil in the world and who are now helplessly enmeshed in the coils of sin. Although God could have abandoned us without any injustice to us, God loves us and through the Incarnation and Atonement of Christ has made our salvation possible solely through the grace. The Augustinian solution is rooted in Christian myth and offers primarily a religious answer to the problem of moral evil.

Although Augustine is the first to draw the distinction between moral and natural evil, he does not much concern himself with natural evil. Everything God has created is good and the universe overall is good as well. Further, it is part and parcel of the universe that it should be as rich and diverse as possible, reflecting in as many ways as possible its Creator and thus glorifying Him. The appearance that some things are evil results from our limited perspective on reality as a whole, from which we are unable to appreciate and/or understand either the necessity of those apparent evils for the overall perfection of the universe or their contribution to the beauty of the universe when appreciated as a whole. Even disease, predation and animal pain are part of the overall plan of the universe and contribute to its smooth operation as a fecund system of mutable forms and transitional types. More than this, God works to bring good out of evil so that even the evils that occur as a result of the operation of the processes of nature are in some way redeemed.

The problems with the Augustinian approach are well-known, despite its ongoing popularity with Christian apologists. However, says Hick, there is another, minority tradition in the history of Christian theodicy that takes its origins in the writings of Irenaeus of Lyon, one of the early church fathers. This version of theodicy de-emphasizes the mythical past and adopts a teleological perspective on evil, seeing it as a necessary – though merely instrumental and temporary – means to the primary end for which God created the universe, i.e. to confer eternal happiness on His rational creatures.

If one were designing a military training camp and did so with the comfort and ease of trainees uppermost in mind, one would have failed to create an optimally designed "boot camp." The reason is that the purpose of such a camp is to prepare potential soldiers both physically and psychologically for the hazards and rigors of the battlefield, to give them the skills and experience necessary to insure that they will be able to successfully accomplish military missions and, if possible, survive to fight another day. These tasks cannot be accomplished unless we use the means necessary to accomplish them and this means, in practice, that the trainees will have to be subjected to an arduous, rigorous and challenging regimen that will expose them to a great deal of physical and psychological stress as well as physical discomfort; unfortunately, some of the recruits will "crack" and have to be discharged. Yet, given that this is the necessary means to a morally legitimate end (such as the prosecution of a just war) the existence both of the camp and of its training methods are more than justified by reference to the ends they make it possible to achieve. The point, of course, is that whether or not this is the "best of all possible worlds" depends on the purpose for which the universe exists. Hume, Mackie, McCloskey and Scriven appear to think that the best universe could only be one in which the greatest logically possible balance of pleasure over pain would be guaranteed. But this is not the traditional Christian view of things.

The universe is not a "boot camp", of course, but according to Hick it is a "vale of soul-making", in which human beings are fitted out for their heavenly inheritance by being perfected in the image and likeness of God. This is the greatest good that the Creator can confer on His rational creatures, so we can expect that a good and loving God would provide it for them; however, without the proper training and experience they will be unable to fully enjoy and benefit from this gift. The world, then, was designed by God, not as a pleasure-dome for sentient beings who have no higher goal or call than to live lives of ease and sensual pleasure, but instead as the training–ground for rational creatures that need to be perfected in order to fully appreciate and participate in the joys of the next life. The solution to the problem of evil, then, is prospective rather than retrospective; it is not original sin that explains moral evil, but God's offer of salvation in the life to come. For while God could have made us morally perfect from the very beginning, our personal, loving response to God cannot be compelled: it has to be a free and willing act of self-surrender to God's will. In the 1932 film *Svengali*, the title character hypnotizes Trilby, the artists' model and makes her an opera star. Each night before he puts her to bed, he makes the hypnotized girl repeat "I love you, Svengali" just to hear her say the words, all the while knowing that the free, conscious Trilby would never return his love for her. In a like manner, in Kierkegaard's[1] story of the King and the maiden, the young king falls in love with a milkmaid but fears that if he were to appear before her *in propria persona* she would be so dazzled that she would fall in love with him *qua* king rather than with him *qua* the person he is; thus, he adopts the expedient of disguising himself as a humble shep-

---

1 See Kierkegaard in Oden (1978) 40–45; originally from the *Philosophical Fragments*.

herd in order to win her love on his own account, only then to reveal himself as what he truly is. God is in a similar position, says Hick, with regard to His finite rational creatures; He needs to woo them but only indirectly so that their free response to Him will not be impaired. Then He needs to hone and perfect them so that they will be capable of entering into a full, complete and mature relationship with Him in a future life.

According to Hick, we find the general outline of such a theodicy in St. Irenaeus' "soul-making" theodicy, dating from the fourth century CE. For Irenaeus, the fall of man is not the story of man's loss of grace and expulsion from a perfect world but a "fall upward", the loss of innocence that occurred when human beings first became self-conscious, free moral agents. Men were created "fallen", i.e. imperfect and the world created to provide an optimal environment for perfecting them by contending both against recalcitrant nature and against their own "lower natures", neither of which will be completely mastered and overcome in this life. While we work to eliminate evil, we will never entirely succeed and it is right and proper that this should be so, since evil plays an ineliminable role in the salvation of every generation of human beings. For Hick, the process of soul-making continues into the next life and the ultimate goal, eternal life in the company of God, more than makes up for the rigors and sufferings encountered along the way. In heaven, the need for struggle and further perfection no longer exists so the blessed will live in a realm that is free of evil, pain and suffering and the good they will enjoy will so far outweigh any earthly sufferings they have endured as to make them trivial by comparison.

In the course of developing his theodicy, Hick becomes increasingly heterodox from the point of view of traditional Christianity. Although the view as sketched so far is unconventional, it is not contradictory to any central dogmas of Christianity. However, Hick feels naturally led – not logically compelled – by the Irenaean approach to adopt further positions that most Christians are likely to find unpalatable. First among these is the doctrine of *universalism*, according to which all rational creatures, even Satan and Hitler, will eventually be converted, saved and inherit the Kingdom of God. The harrowing of hell is not a one-time event, but the long-term goal of our Creator and one that will be accomplished in a finite amount of time. Hick denies the existence of an everlasting Hell in which those who have been reprobated will endure endless suffering. Although a few Christians have held this view, the overwhelming consensus of Christian tradition is that this is heresy. Hick compounds his error in their eyes by endorsing a further form of universalism known as *religious pluralism*, usually contrasted with the doctrine of *particularism*, according to which only those who make an explicit faith-commitment to Jesus Christ will be saved – a view that is central, for example, to most forms of evangelical Christianity. Hick's universalism maintains that, at least as far as the world's great religions are concerned, each is as good as any other as a path to salvation. None of those religions is the whole truth about the Transcendent and all of them are false in their distinctive teachings and claims to exclusivity or pre-eminence. At the same time, there is a broad agreement among the great religions on the need for salvation and with regard to their moral teachings, at least if taken at a suitably abstract level, so that each can plausibly be regarded as "different paths up the same mountain" and equally effective for their followers. Although the Catholic Church, especially since Vatican II, has come around to the view that some people have "implicit faith" and thus belong the Church even without making formal profession to it,[1] Hick's view goes far beyond anything that traditional Christianity has been willing to countenance. This position has led Hick into further controversy due to his rejection of some central Christian teachings as Tillichian "myths". For example, in his contributions to *The Myth of God Incarnate*[2] and his critique of T. V. Morris's model for the incarnation presented in *The Logic of God Incarnate*,[3] Hick has in effect denied the historicity of the Incarnation and the divinity of Christ, something that no orthodox Christian can possibly endorse. Since the Christians that were to come to the defence of theism in the 1970's were of a decidedly more conservative cast, this has limited the influence of Hick's ideas in the philosophy of religion, a field that he subsequently left in order to become a scholar of world religions.

THE ATHEISTIC RESPONSE TO PIKE AND THE TRANSITION TO INDUCTIVISM

The general response of atheistic philosophers of religion to Pike and Plantinga was to reformulate the problem of evil as a *probabilistic* or *inductive* argument against theism. Granted that the truth of theism is barely *logically* consistent with the existence of evil, mere logical consistency by itself is not enough to make theism *rationally credible*. Instead, unless theists are able to provide a plausible explanation for the existence of evil given the hypothesis of an omnipotent, omniscient and omnibenevolent God, they can still be convicted of wilful, culpable irrationality. The problem of evil, then, is retooled as a challenge to the rationality of theism rather than as

---

1 See (2001) sections 854–857, which officially condemns the view that only those who have made an explicit submission to the Catholic Church can be saved.
2 In Hick (1977), pages 242–61.
3 See Morris (1986); for Hick's critique see Hick (1993) pages 47–60.

a rational disproof of the existence of God and thus remains a formidable objection to religious belief. So natural and automatic was this response that it seems to have occurred to everyone at once; it cannot be tied to any one article that first formulated it or figure who first "discovered" it. However, by the mid–1970's this version of the argument had quietly replaced the earlier, deductive version of the argument.[1]

In responding to this argument, theistic philosophers have divided into two basic camps. The first, consisting of philosophers like Hick and Swinburne, actually propose a theodicy intended to provide plausible reasons for supposing that the evils that we see about us are compatible with the actual existence of an omnipotent, omniscient and omnibenevolent God. In Swinburne's case, theodicy is part of a full-blown inductivist defence of theism; this will be our topic in the next chapter. The second alternative – which I call the "hard-nosed" approach – is characteristic of Plantinga and his many followers and constitutes an entrenched development and defence of Pike's position in "Hume on Evil." According to this view, the rationality of theism does not depend in any way on the theist's being able to meet the atheist's demand for a theodicy. To the contrary, the theist maintains that we have no reason to suppose that we would be privy to the reasons that justify God in permitting the evils we see around us. In time, Plantinga develops Pike's "agnosticism" about our cognitive powers to comprehend such reasons into an entire ethics of belief that becomes known as Reformed Epistemology. We will consider this development, which I will call "Post-Deductivism" in the penultimate chapter of this book.

To conclude this chapter, let me note some of the important changes initiated by this "paradigm shift" in the philosophy of religion. In the emerging inductivist paradigm, shared by most analytic atheists as well as theists like Mitchell and Swinburne, the question of whether or not belief in God is rational is no longer one to be settled solely by means of deductive proofs but rather by reference to the reasonableness of belief in God given the total evidence for and against the existence of God. On such a view, belief in God is treated as a kind of hypothesis that posits a theoretical entity, God, as the best or only explanation for certain features of the world and claims that an examination of the relevant evidence justifies belief in God or makes it rational/reasonable to believe in God according to some appropriate standard for what counts as rational or reasonable in this context. No assumption is made that the evidence will be completely unambiguous; what it is rational or reasonable to believe on the basis of the evidence will involve a judgment about what the preponderance of the

---

1 For a classic statement of the probabilistic argument from evil, see Peter H. Hare and E. H. Madden, *Evil and the Concept of God* (Springfield, IL: C. C. Thomas, 1968).

evidence will support.

Furthermore, though this went largely unnoticed at the time, the inductivist paradigm loosens the connection between theism, considered as a philosophical or metaphysical position, and religious belief. On the deductivist approach, monotheism cannot be true unless theism is true, since the former entails the latter, so that a successful refutation of theism likewise entails the falsity of theism by *modus tollens*. On the inductivist approach, however, this logically tight connection is broken. A more complex hypothesis, such as Christian theism, may contain resources that make it more plausible, given the evidence, that the relatively more simple hypothesis of unadulterated theism. So, even if the latter performs poorly relative to the whole body of relevant evidence, it does not follow that the former will do so as well. So the philosophical defence of theism *per se* is no longer life and death for religious belief. By the same token, since it is really e.g., Christianity that is actually the "hypothesis" at issue, it therefore becomes legitimate for Christian theists to appeal to distinctively Christian beliefs, accepted on the basis of Scripture and tradition as parts of the hypothesis to be tested against the evidence, a device that Christian philosophers have employed in various ways and in varying degrees under the aegis of this new paradigm.

Although I have proposed that the discussion of the problem of evil was instrumental in the emergence of the inductivist paradigm, there is good independent reason to suppose that the deductivist paradigm was largely played out by the beginning of the 1970's. Evidence for this can be seen in the remarkable convergence of deductivist philosophers, such as Plantinga, Keith Yandell and Richard Gale all of whom were at one time explicitly committed to the deductivist approach to the question of God's existence. Yandell,[1] agreeing with the earlier conclusions of Plantinga, argues that all the arguments for God's existence fail and that all of the arguments against God's existence likewise fail. For Gale,[2] all the attempts to demonstrate that the concept of God is somehow self-contradictory are merely opportunities for the theist to clarify and modify the concept of God in order to avoid these problems, and that this can be done without sacrificing much of importance to the theist. On the other hand, even the best versions of the ontological, cosmological and teleological arguments are flawed, so that no proof of God's existence is extant or likely to be forthcoming. Yandell proceeds to sketch out a limited version of Inductivism, while Gale endorses

---

1 Yandell (1984) *passim*, see especially pages 272–85.
2 Gale (1991) *passim*, see especially page 387. I may err in thinking that Gale is being serious rather than ironic; in his case, as in Hume's, it is not always easy to tell.

a Kierkegaardian leap of faith as the best option for believers!

It is indeed notoriously difficult to provide deductive proofs for any substantive philosophical thesis outside the realm of formal logic. It is hardly to be expected that the philosophy of religion will be any different.[1] If this is the appropriate standard for permissible philosophical belief, then an almost universal scepticism will be the outcome, not just with regard to the question of God but with regard to every philosophical issue. But just what is the appropriate standard for philosophical rationality and thus for the permissibility of philosophical belief? This is the question that gives rise to discussion of the ethics of belief and of the proper methods of philosophical inquiry. We shall that such issues inform the development of the philosophy of religion down to the present time.

---

[1] It by no means follows that interest in the traditional arguments as proofs for God's existence has disappeared. See, for example, Davis (1983) and (1997) and Sobel (2003).

Chapter Five

The Inductivist Paradigm

Although the inductivist approach to the question of God's existence had already been employed by F. R. Tennant to good effect in the 1920's, it was not until the 1970's that the inductivist paradigm emerged as a self-consciously distinct alternative to the earlier deductivist approach to the main questions of the philosophy of religion. Two figures, Basil Mitchell and Richard Swinburne, both of whom would serve as Nolloth Professors at Oxford, were especially significant in the development of this paradigm. In this chapter we shall examine the approach of both men and then consider some of the potential for the further development of this tradition.

BASIL MITCHELL: THE JUSTIFICATION OF RELIGIOUS BELIEF

In 1968, Ian Ramsey was appointed Bishop of Durham and resigned the Nolloth chair. He was replaced by long–time Oxford figure Basil Mitchell, who had been associated with C. S. Lewis's Socratic Club and was later a prominent member of the Metaphysicals as well as an Anglican priest. In 1973, Mitchell published a surprisingly contemporary essay entitled *The Justification of Religious Belief*[1] in which he initiated the contemporary discussion of what I am here calling Inductivism. In the first two chapters, Mitchell argues a thesis that by now was becoming a commonplace among theistic philosophers: that theism could neither be proved nor disproved by any sort of formal argument, whether deductive or inductive in structure. The deductivist approach had failed of its promise, and the alternatives seem either to deny that rational evaluation has any role whatsoever to play in religious belief or to find some other way to approach the question. In this short book, Mitchell proposes to provide such an alternative, what he calls a *cumulative case* for theism, suggesting that while none of the classical arguments for God's existence will work as proofs for God's

---

1 Mitchell (1973)

existence, the sort of evidence they present for God's existence can provide a kind of circumstantial case for theism, much like the sort of circumstantial case that a detective or a lawyer tries to construct in order to identify or convict a killer in the absence of eyewitnesses or other direct evidence. While none of the bits of evidence by itself is sufficient to gain a conviction, their combination all point to the accused as the most likely perpetrator of the crime and, if sufficiently numerous and of high enough quality, make it rational for the jury to convict.

Suggestions to this effect in the past have always been dismissed in the abstract as reliance on the "ten leaky buckets" strategy. According to Flew,[1] for example, if none of the arguments for God's existence is sound, the defect cannot be made up by combining them, any more than ten leaky buckets can be put together in some fashion so that they hold water. Mitchell challenges the metaphor, however. What we are talking about, says Mitchell, is a comprehensive metaphysical worldview, Christian theism, and asking how well on the whole this worldview fits the facts. Any particular fact pointed to by the theist – the contingency of the universe, the appearance of teleology and design in nature, the experience of moral obligation, religious experience, etc – can be explained by the atheist in such a way as to be accommodated to a metaphysical naturalist worldview. The atheist therefore wants to deal with each of them in a piecemeal fashion, in isolation from the others, explain away each in turn and then declare victory. However, this procedure is unfair to the theist, who sees these features of the universe and human experience as complementary to one another and mutually reinforcing and thus properly to be considered as a group, not just individually. Just as in the circumstantial case in court, the preponderance of evidence all points in the same direction or supports the same hypothesis, thus making it rational to convict on the whole body of evidence even though no one piece of evidence is conclusive by itself and there are no strict standards for determining what the threshold for proper evidence consists in. The question, says Mitchell, is what the proper standards are for evaluating belief-commitments formed in this way.

Mitchell compares the evaluation of religious commitment to our evaluation of different historical, literary or philosophical hypotheses. In these cases, rival interpretations deal with the same data – a poem, an historical event, a philosophical text – and there is no prospect in most cases of discovering any new relevant evidence to break ties between rival interpretations, let alone the possibility of doing experiments or making novel observations that will confirm one interpretation and refute another. Yet the consideration of various interpretations of literary texts or reconstructions

---

1 Flew (1966) pages 62–3.

of bygone events is hardly irrational or merely a matter of taste. Anyone who is acquainted with a body of scholarly literature has a set of rough and ready criteria for selecting between rival interpretations. After all, the purpose of interpretation is to *understand* something, such as the meaning of a text or the proper order of a set of events occurring within a particular historical situation, and in the context understanding has a large intuitive component. We prefer and endorse those interpretations that do the best job of providing that understanding. Quoting Passmore,[1] Mitchell notes that an interpretation of a philosophical text that "unlocks" that text, that (e.g.) illuminates formerly obscure passages, provides overall unity and coherence to the reading of the text and/or explains the inevitable presence of the errors and contradictions that undoubtedly are there – in short, one that makes the best overall sense of the text in question – is the best interpretation of that text. The same holds for the interpretation of a poem or an historical reconstruction despite our inability to justify our judgment by formal deductive or inductive procedures.

The great strength of natural science, according to those critics who want to dismiss the foregoing as too loose to count as a rational decision procedure, is that scientific theories are testable in experience, i.e. capable of direct empirical confirmation or falsification. However, Mitchell notes, the researches of modern historians and philosophers of science have shown that things are much less straightforward than logical positivists, working in the abstract, have depicted them. Scientific theories are never *deductively* confirmed by observation and experiment or conclusively falsified using *modus tollens*. Opponents and defenders of such theories always have the option of offering an alternate explanation or of altering their theories so that they "predict" the supposedly incompatible results, thus saving the theory in the face of the evidence or blunting its confirmatory force. This holds even in the case of so-called "crucial" experiments. That these experiments are accepted as confirming one theory and refuting another is not a matter of deductive proof or falsification. Other factors are at work deciding the issue.

The course of "normal" science, which takes place within a reigning scientific paradigm with an agreed framework for what counts as an observation, a fact, proof and evidence, etc., disguises this from us. However, as Kuhn and Lakatos have persuasively argued, it becomes all too obvious in times of scientific revolution, when competing, comprehensive paradigms, each of which is compatible with and capable of accommodating all the data at least as well as its rivals become the objects of choice. Here there is a certain degree of incommensurability between rival concep-

---

1 Mitchell (1973) pages 54–5.

tions resulting from their differing understanding of the basic terms involved affecting how they describe the phenomena to be explained and thus what counts as a proper explanation and proper evidence for confirming an hypothesis. To the extent that each account is plausible, it tends to manufacture the evidence that confirms it and it becomes difficult to find any neutral point of view from which to compare rival conceptions. Indeed, the transition from one paradigm (in Kuhn's technical sense of that term) to another is often likened to a religious conversion by those who undergo it; they use language reminiscent of Ian Ramsey: "the ice breaks, the penny drops, the scales fall from one's eyes," one finally "gets it." This results not from the neutral examination of evidence or by being convinced by an argument but rather by a kind of perceptual act: it is as though one had always seen only the duck and not the rabbit aspect of the duck–rabbit drawing, but now suddenly does grasp or apprehend the rabbit aspect for the first time.

Although many historians and philosophers of science, including Kuhn in some of his moods, deny that paradigm-shift is a rational procedure and suppose that the explanation for this phenomenon is purely sociological, Mitchell stops short of this point of view. Instead, he claims, the transition from one paradigm to another is a rational procedure despite the fact that it cannot be modelled by formal argument either of the deductive or inductive variety. We are out for truth and understanding and we naturally gravitate toward the account that appears to provide them, toward the view that possesses both "empirical fit" and explanatory power. Exponents of Christian theism tend to find in that worldview just such a combination; their adoption and persistence in it, then, is fully rational in the foregoing sense.

At the same time, this does not mean that Christians regard the Christian faith as a kind of hypothesis to be held tentatively on the basis of publicly available evidence; the religious believer does *not* apportion belief to available evidence or change his or her mind with every alteration of its force. This is partly because the nature of faith is not just propositional but, as Mitchell argued many years earlier in his contribution to the theology and falsification debate, trusting faith in a personal God. But Mitchell also notes that there are many other analogues to the case of the religious believer. The modern Briton's belief in liberal democracy far outruns the evidence for its value as a political system. The scientist's faith in induction and the scientific method remains largely intact despite the attacks of anti-realists and "sociologists of knowledge." The common man's belief in the external world and the reliability of memory largely withstand sceptical doubts produced by a consideration of the paucity of evidence for these claims. A man's belief in his spouse's faithfulness is expected to persist and (generally does so) in the face of evidence that would be sufficient to produce doubt in a neutral observer, and so on. Nor would liberal democracy, science, common life or romantic love be possible unless people were prepared to have this kind of total commitment and to be shaped by it in thought and deed. Religious belief is no less rational than commitments of this sort.

While Mitchell talks about the project of constructing a cumulative case for Christian theism, he in fact makes little effort to do this in *The Justification of Religious Belief*. He merely hints at what the elements of such a case might be and discusses the possibility of such a case from the abstract point of view. For the actual construction of such a case, we need to turn to Mitchell's successor in the Nolloth chair, Richard Swinburne who, in a dozen books, constructs the sort of case that Mitchell envisages for Christian theism while using formal probability theory as a framework for the presentation of that case. To Swinburne, then, we now turn.

SWINBURNE'S INDUCTIVIST THEISM: THE GENERAL STRATEGY

When Mitchell retired from the Nolloth Professorship in 1981 (he was still a presence at Oxford a quarter of a century later) Richard Swinburne, an Anglican layman who had previously taught at Hull and then at Keele, was appointed to replace him. A life-long Christian and himself an Oxford product, Swinburne had already published the trilogy of books – *The Coherence of Theism*, *The Existence of God* and *Faith and Reason* – that would serve as the core of his inductivist theism. But there was much more to come. Surprisingly, there has to date been no full-length treatment of Swinburne's system.[1] What follows is an attempt to give a useful summary and overview of Swinburne's defence of theism spread over several books and several decades, making only occasional references to the development of his views during that time.

HYPOTHESIS AND EXPLANATION

Like Mitchell, Swinburne takes theism to be a global metaphysical hypothesis or worldview competing with other such hypotheses such as physicalist naturalism and absolute idealism. Swinburne recognizes, of course, that Christian theists do not take Christianity to be a hypothesis to be held tentatively on the basis of an objective assessment of evidence; however, in the philosophy of religion our concern is

---

1 For an account of Mitchell's and Swinburne's early views, see Prevost (1990).

the degree to which the metaphysical core of Christian commitment is amenable to rational justification. As such, we are here operating outside the context of faith and making an appeal to all rational inquirers by taking a neutral stance with regard to the evidence. An hypothesis is an *explanation* intended to account for data by providing a causal account of its origin and occurrence. From first to last, Swinburne supposes that causation is a productive relation between discrete substances by means of which one thing acts so as to bring about another, typically by affecting something else in some way through the exercise of its innate causal powers so as to realize the capacities of whatever it affects. Both causal relations between events and the operation of causal laws can ultimately be reduced to productive relations between substances characterized in terms of capacities and powers. He thus rejects explanations in terms of laws and initial conditions, although he uses this language because of its greater ease and familiarity. Even so, laws have no ontological status in Swinburne's philosophy of explanation. Rather, to explain something is to explain its occurrence or existence in terms of the operation of its cause. At the same time, nothing hangs on whether or not this account is correct, according to Swinburne.[1]

Swinburne distinguishes two different and, he argues, irreducible forms of substantive explanation: *scientific* explanation and *personal* explanation.[2] Scientific explanation (more typically called impersonal or inanimate explanation in Swinburne's writings) explains states-of-affairs in the universe by reference to the causal powers and capacities inherent in material bodies and their interaction with one another. In this case, the cause precedes the effect and operates automatically within the context to produce its effect either with causal necessity or with statistical probability just in case the context is not fully determinate with respect to the outcome of the cause's influence. This is the sort of explanation we associate with the scientific explanation of events occurring in the non-human, physical universe composed of material things. In this case, the cause is a material substance exercising its causal powers on another substance or material medium with the capacity to be changed or altered by that exercise. In personal explanation, the cause is a person and the effect is an observable action, which may be either a basic action or a mediated one, either sort of which may give rise to some further effect, such as a physical change in the world. Whereas we may conveniently characterize scientific explanation in terms of laws and conditions giving rise to effects, in personal explanation the production of action is made intelligible by reference to the acting person's (or *agent's*) beliefs, desires,

---

1 Swinburne (2004) pages 26–35.
2 Swinburne (1996) pages 20–25 and (2004) pages 35–45.

intentions and reasons. Swinburne argues in several places that personal explanation cannot be reduced to scientific explanation and that the exercise of personal agency is free at least in the sense that it is not produced by the operation of physical causes operating beyond our control.[1]

Theism regards God as the ultimate reality and thus God's primary agency as the final explanation of everything that exists. However, to understand exactly how God explains the observable physical universe requires that one distinguish a number of kinds of explanations: full, complete, ultimate and absolute.[2] A *full* explanation is one that cites a cause and a reason that necessitates the observed effect. An explanation can be a full one without, however, without mentioning all of the factors involved in producing that effect. The operation of a roulette wheel explains why Jones lost his fortune without our having any further explanation for why the wheel operated in just the way it did to secure that result. A *complete* explanation is a full explanation that includes reference to all the relevant background conditions necessary in order to produce the effect, which may include reference to higher-order theories or laws describing very general conditions obtaining at the time the effect was produced. An *ultimate* explanation is a complete explanation that terminates in conditions for which there is no further explanation but whose existence or operation simply has to be accepted as a surd, brute fact. An *absolute* explanation would be an ultimate explanation the terminus of which was in some manner self-explanatory or logically necessary, a claim typically made for the theistic God. Swinburne, however, maintains that there cannot be an absolute explanation for any contingent fact or state-of-affairs. He therefore rejects the notion that the theistic hypothesis proposes an absolute explanation for the observable universe. Instead, God is the ultimate explanation for all things in Swinburne's technical sense but in Himself lacks any further explanation; God's existence and nature, then, are surd or brute facts about the universe.[3]

The theist's claim, then, is that the postulation of God's existence and nature is the best ultimate explanation for the existence (etc.) of all things other than God and, in particular, superior to physicalist naturalism (what Swinburne in one place calls *materialism*) which postulates matter and the laws of physics as the ultimate explanation of all things. Theism, then, proposes that personal explanation in terms of the action of God, a supreme personal agent, is the ultimate explanation for everything we see around us, whereas physicalist naturalism supposes that scientific explana-

---

1 Swinburne (1986)
2 Swinburne (2004) pages 75–80.
3 Swinburne (2004) pages 148–9.

tion is ultimate and that we need seek nothing beyond the laws of nature in order to ground all phenomena. Both theories are very general and both are compatible with everything we observe about the world. How, then, can we choose between them, if at all? To answer this question requires that we consider, in general, what the grounds are for choice between hypotheses.

SIMPLICITY AND THE CHOICE OF THEORIES

Swinburne notes that there have been a number of criteria offered as grounds for choice between potential theories; however, all of these reduce to or are aspects of one central criterion, that of *simplicity*. In his 1997 Aquinas lecture, *Simplicity as Evidence of Truth*,[1] Swinburne identifies four criteria for selecting between hypotheses, two of them *a priori* and two of them *a posteriori*. The *a priori* criteria are *content* (how extensive the claims made by the theory) and *simplicity*, the a posteriori criteria are those of *yielding the data* and *conformity to background knowledge*. He then goes on to argue that all of the other three are either aspects of or crucially governed by considerations of simplicity. Theories with lesser content, for example, are more likely to be true than those with greater content because they are simpler. Further, since there are an infinite number of theories that possess empirical fit (both yield the data and conform to background knowledge) considerations of simplicity play the decisive role in which competing hypotheses to seriously consider and which one to ultimately accept. Swinburne recognizes that hypotheses can diverge with regard to the application of these criteria and that sometimes (e.g.) an hypothesis that has greater content is preferable to a one with less content – General Relativity is an example of this. However, even in such cases, the palm goes to the theory with the greatest *overall* simplicity, as judged along a number of dimensions: number of entities postulated, types of entities postulated, complexity of predicates (e.g. grue vs. green) attributed to entities, number of laws postulated by a theory, number of variables contained in those laws, their length and the number and complexity of terms employed in the equations expressing those laws.[2]

Swinburne vehemently rejects *predictive power* as a central criterion for evaluating theories.[3] Exponents of verifiability and falsifiability insist that no hypothesis is worth its salt unless it is testable in experience and that this requires the hypothesis in question make predictions about future experiences testable by observation or

---

1 Swinburne (1997)
2 Swinburne (1996) pages 25–31, (2004) pages 52–61 and (2003) pages 74–102.
3 Swinburne (2003) pages 221–32; see also Swinburne (2004) 69–70.

experiment. According to Swinburne, however, all theories of this sort unjustifiably privilege *novelty* evidence, i.e. evidence acquired after an hypothesis is formulated, over evidence known prior to its formulation, committing them to the view he calls *predictivism*. However, this means that one and the same theory, judged on the same evidence, will be of differing degrees of credibility depending on *when* that theory was formulated, which seems absurd. If an hypothesis h is probable on the whole relative to evidence e, then e makes h likely to be true regardless of whether or not it was known or discovered prior to the formulation of that theory. As such, it is irrelevant whether or not a theory can be confirmed or falsified by reference to novelty evidence. Overall simplicity, therefore, remains the ultimate determinant of selection between hypotheses; indeed, Swinburne goes so far as to claim that it is an *a priori* synthetic truth that the simplest hypothesis is the most likely to be true.

Applying this to the case under discussion, Swinburne argues that the theistic hypothesis is simpler than its rivals, in particular, physicalist naturalism.[1] Theism postulates the existence of a personal, providential creator God, a single entity of great internal simplicity as the ultimate explanation for the universe, whereas physicalist naturalism postulates the whole physical universe, a complex system consisting of a very large number of basic things possessing many basic powers and capacities and governed by a set of contingent physical laws as a brute fact incapable of any further explanation. Theism, thus described, outperforms physicalist naturalism along a number of dimensions by means of which we measure simplicity. First of all, personal explanation is, in itself, a simpler form of explanation than scientific explanation and so any hypothesis that "bottoms out" in a personal explanation for things is already more likely to be true than one that "bottoms out" in some sort inanimate explanation.[2] Secondly, it is much easier to account for the existence of the physical universe in terms of the action of a person than to explain the emergence of persons from a purely impersonal, material substrate. Thirdly, theism postulates a single substance as the ultimate cause of everything else, which is simpler than postulating the entire world-system, with all its elements, as surd facts. Fourthly, the kind of person postulated by theism is Himself simple due to his being infinite, i.e. possessing all His essential properties to their maximum degree (omniscience, omnipotence, eternity, etc.) so that the question – "Why so much and not more?" cannot arise in the case of God as it can in the case of the physical universe.[3] Given the foregoing, theism is sim-

---

[1] Swinburne (1996) pages 38–47 and (2004) pages 93–109.
[2] Swinburne (1979) page 102.
[3] Swinburne (1979) pages 102–106 and (2004) page 97.

pler than naturalist physicalism and thus, on *a priori* synthetic grounds, more likely to be true than its competitors.

THE PROBABILITY OF THEISM

However, the foregoing considerations are not enough by themselves to justify theistic belief. The relative probability of theism does not by itself establish that theism is reasonable to believe. In order to claim this, we must be prepared to go on to argue that theism is more likely to be true than not. Expressed in the language of formal probability theory, this requires that we argue that the probability of theism is greater than .5, at any rate to the extent that it is possible to judge that this is the case. In order to argue that this is the case, Swinburne turns to confirmation theory, an application of formal probability theory to the evaluation of hypotheses, both in the sciences and by extension to metaphysical theories as well. Swinburne's commitment to confirmation theory, not just in the philosophy of religion but in the philosophy of science and epistemology as well, make him a leading exponent of this approach in philosophy generally.[1] Central to the confirmation theory approach is Bayes's Theorem, an extension of elementary probability theory to cases involving conditional probabilities. Bayes's Theorem is not an easy formula to understand and Swinburne formulates it in a number of different ways in various works. However, the basic strategy involved in its use appears to be something like the following:

> First, determine the *prior probability* of the hypothesis (h), which is the sum of its *a priori* or *intrinsic* probability (probability on no evidence) *and* its probability on background evidence (k)
>
> Then, *given* the foregoing, use Bayes's theorem to calculate the *posterior* probability of the hypothesis by considering, in addition
> > the likelihood that h is *true* on the basis of additional evidence (e)
> > the likelihood that h is *false* given that evidence and
> > the likelihood that e would have obtained in the absence of h.
>
> We do this by adding the first two quantities, multiplying the result by the prior probability of theism and then dividing that result by the third.
>
> The result will be the probability of h given the *total body* of relevant evidence.

Since Bayes's Theorem is a mathematical formula, it works best when actual numbers can be used to take the place of the variables in the formula. There is no prospect

---

1 See Swinburne (1973), (2003) pages 102–7 and (2004) pages 66–72.

of this happening in most cases and certainly no likelihood of this in the case of the evidence for theism; nevertheless, Swinburne maintains that the Bayesian approach is viable and useful despite that fact.[1]

Applying this to the present case, we have already seen that Swinburne regards the intrinsic probability of theism as higher than its competitors. Further, in those cases in which the relevant background evidence is tautological, the prior probability of h will be equivalent to its intrinsic probability. Swinburne apparently takes this to be the case in this instance since theism is a global hypothesis. Swinburne then proceeds by marshalling the positive evidence for theism consisting in considerations upon which the traditional arguments for God's existence were based, such as the contingency of the world, its order, the existence of self-conscious rational beings, the fact of moral obligation, religious experience and miracles; this is the positive evidence for theism. The positive evidence against theism is represented by the fact of evil in the world which, like Mitchell, Swinburne admits counts against the existence of the theistic God but not decisively so. Finally, in considering each of the positive arguments for theism, Swinburne also considers how likely the evidence in question would have obtained in the absence of the existence of God and concludes that this is not likely at all. In later discussions, he contents himself with simply arguing that, since the likelihood of all of the positive evidences for theism occurring together in the absence of God's existence is significantly less than their joint occurrence in a world containing God, that the theistic hypothesis is well-enough supported to be reasonably thought to be above .5. Of course, one is free to dissent from that conclusion; still, it does not follow that one who assents to it is necessarily irrational.

SWINBURNE'S POSITIVE ARGUMENT FOR THEISM

Swinburne distinguishes two kinds of inductive arguments for God's existence.[2] An argument is a good *c-inductive* argument if the truth of its premises makes its conclusion more probable than it would be otherwise. An argument of this sort need not claim to raise the probability of its conclusion to greater than .5 in order to be successful. An argument is a good *p-inductive* argument if the truth of its premises raises the probability of the conclusion to more than .5, thus making it rational to believe. In

---

1 For criticism of Swinburne's Bayesianism, see Prevost (1990) pages 14–55 and 70–77; Plantinga has also criticized Swinburne's general approach: see (e.g.) his discussion in Sennett (1998) pages 174–80. Swinburne, however, remains firmly committed to Bayesianism, not just in the philosophy of religion: see his (2003) for a stout defense of Bayesian epistemology.

2 Swinburne (2004) pages 13–14.

presenting the evidence for theism, Swinburne echoes Mitchell's "cumulative case" idea by proposing that a series of successful c-inductive arguments for God's existence could amount to a good p-inductive argument for God's existence. Thus, on this view the theist does not have to put all his or her stock in a single argument for God's existence and can admit that none of the arguments by themselves are sufficient to justify belief in theism while still maintaining that their concatenation can and does do so. To the extent that the various arguments are found to be mutually reinforcing, this is further evidence for the theistic hypothesis. Swinburne hopes to build a significant case that the atheist will not be able to rebut and that uncommitted individuals will find persuasive. We must now look at his positive case to see how he attempts to manage this.

Swinburne rejects the traditional arguments as demonstrations or proofs of God's existence. As we have already seen, Swinburne holds that there can be no deductive proof for any contingent fact. However, there is another way to use the traditional arguments, i.e. to argue that postulating God as the ultimate brute fact about reality is superior to postulating the universe itself as the ultimate brute fact and this is what Swinburne proposes to do. We will now illustrate this strategy with regard to the major traditional arguments for God's existence.

The Cosmological Argument

Take, for example, the cosmological argument. Swinburne rejects the five ways of St. Thomas as fallacious, at least as presented by the neo-Thomists, and turns instead to the versions of the cosmological argument formulated by Leibniz and Clarke in the eighteenth century.[1] According to this version of the argument, it is the physical universe as a whole (rather than a particular contingent thing) that is the focus of the argument and it is assumed both that the universe may have existed for an infinite amount of time in the past and that each member of this infinite series has a full explanation in terms of the causal activity of a previous member of the series. Swinburne then asks whether this is sufficient to provide a full explanation for the existence of the physical universe as a whole. Many philosophers, such as Hume and Edwards, have thought so, but Swinburne disagrees. On the supposition that each member of the series has a full explanation in terms of the operation of a previous member of the series, then the earliest member of any segment of that series will be the cause of all

---

1 See Rowe (1975) and references; for Swinburne's presentation of the argument, see Swinburne (2004) pages 133–52; compare Swinburne (1979 and 1991a).

the rest, so if a is caused by b, b by c and c by d, then d will be the cause of a+b+c. The cause of any such segment will always be some cause that is not itself a member of the series explained by it; this will hold as well for every series, no matter how long it is. However, in an infinite series, there is no first member, hence no member that accounts for all the others in the series. It follows, then, that either the cause of the whole series is something external to that series as a whole or that the series has no cause and that its existence must be postulated as a brute fact. The theistic God suggests itself as the natural candidate for such a cause and this naturally motivates the atheist to adopt the second alternative. However, given that the prior probability of theism is higher than that of the hypothesis that postulates the existence of the complex, contingent physical universe as a brute fact, theism is clearly more probable, hence more likely to be true, than the alternative. The cosmological argument, then, provides a good c-inductive argument for theism though, being too weak by itself to establish that God's existence is probable, not a p-inductive argument for God's existence.

Teleological Arguments

Swinburne then moves on to teleological arguments. There are two kinds of order that evoke our wonder and admiration: *temporal order*, constituted by the recurrent regularities of succession we see about us in nature and *spatial order*, the regularities of co–presence and mutual interdependence we observe in the world around us.[1] Both of these are a consequence of the initial conditions and the most basic laws that govern the universe and, for all we have reason to expect, they might have been vastly different in many ways. What we do know, however, is that these laws and conditions have produced a very complex, highly ordered and beautiful cosmos when no such world need have existed. Even if the world we see around us is the inevitable operation of those laws given those conditions, from the scientific point of view there can be no explanation why just these laws and conditions obtain rather than any of the countless other possibilities that would have produced much less complex, orderly and beautiful universes than the one that actually exists. If physicalist naturalism is true, this was just the luck of the draw. More than this, however, it is actually contrary to what we would expect to be the case if physicalist naturalism is true, just because there are so many other, simpler (hence more likely) universes that could have existed in preference to this one. No rational inquirer, then, is likely to be satisfied with the

---

1 See Rowe (1996) pages 48–68 and (2004) pages 153–91.

assurance that "that's just the way it is."

If theism is true, however, there is ample reason to predict that the world would not only be complex, orderly and beautiful but also governed by a system of universal, simple laws of the sort that science is progressively discovering, because God is both rational and good and thus will prefer to create an orderly over a chaotic world. After all, a rational being acts purposively, with an end or ends in mind and will use effective means to attain those ends; in turn, those ends will be reflected in the products of that action, giving the impression of having been designed for a purpose even if through the mediation of processes (like evolution) occurring within nature. Further, God is good and will want to share existence with as many different kinds of things as is compatible with the overall good order of the whole. We can thus expect any universe created by God to be constituted by a few simple laws governing a set of basic constituents possessing a few basic powers and capacities, the operation of which produces an incredibly diverse and fecund number of types of things. Further, we would expect that, viewed from the perspective of the whole, the overall universe would possess great beauty. In fact, we find all of these to be the case, so that to the extent that the universe is as we would expect it to be if the theistic God had created it and not as we would reasonably expect to find it if its basic laws, constituents and initial conditions had been the product of pure chance, the overall evidence of apparent design and order in the universe favours theism over its main opponent, physicalist naturalism. We thus have another c-inductive argument for theism, one which not only raises the probability of theism versus physicalist naturalism but also does so in absolute terms as well.

The argument is greatly strengthened, of course, by reflection on the fact that the physical universe contains human beings, who are themselves self-conscious rational agents.[1] It is highly probable that if God created a physical universe that it would contain such creatures, since only such creatures would be capable of knowing and loving God, a state-of-affairs that a good and loving Being would have ample reason to bring about. Whereas physicalist naturalism gives us no reason to expect any sort of world-order and must accept the world-order we observe as mere brute fact, theism predicts that the basic laws and conditions governing the universe would be such as to inevitably give rise to beings such as ourselves. It thus makes a strikingly specific claim about what sort of universe we ought to expect to exist. Of course, God has other ends and goals in creation besides bringing it about that human beings should exist; nevertheless, that such beings as ourselves should exist is obviously one such goal and the attribution

---

1 See Swinburne (1996) pages 69–94.

of such a goal to God goes a long way in explaining why the universe is as it is.

In the first place, only a relatively few sets of laws, constituents and initial conditions will be such as to produce beings like ourselves, even in an infinite amount of time. Even if those conditions are met, however, it is still far from inevitable that evolution would produce us – or, even if it is, this in itself is somewhat surprising. It nevertheless remains that it happened, something that we had antecedently very little reason to expect. More than this, the idea that the production of human beings is an overriding goal of divine creation both reinforces the earlier arguments for theism and also helps explain some of the otherwise anomalous features of reality. For example, it reinforces the notion that God would have created an orderly universe, since only an orderly, reliable universe would be one in which the human intellect and will (and, to a lesser extent, those of other animals as well) would have scope to learn and to act effectively. It also explains many other features of the world as well as we shall see when we turn to Swinburne's theodicy.

THE ARGUMENT FROM CONSCIOUSNESS

Given our knowledge of the physical laws and initial conditions that obtain in the actual world, we have no antecedent reason for supposing that there would be any such thing as consciousness as we experience it in ourselves in the form of sensations, feelings, mental states and acts, etc.[1] Indeed, consciousness seems anomalous on the assumptions of physicalist naturalism inasmuch as the existence of consciousness would not be predicted by such a theory. Even if evolution can explain the persistence of consciousness and even some of its features, it cannot explain the coming into existence of consciousness in the first place. Yet we are more certain that we are conscious beings than we can possibly be about the truth of any scientific theory.

Exponents of materialism in the philosophy of mind are embarrassed by consciousness and have devised numerous means of coping with it.[2] One program, reductive materialism, hopes to reduce mental properties and states to states of the brain, much as heat was reduced to mean kinetic energy or light to electromagnetism. However, Swinburne points out that in each of these cases the reduction was effected by distinguishing the phenomenal and noumenal aspects of these realities and evacuating the phenomenal aspects (sensations of heat and light) to the mind. When it comes to mind itself, however, this same device will not work; in this case there is nowhere else to which we can evacuate the contents of consciousness. Other, so-called identity theo-

---

1 See Swinburne (2004) pages 192–212.
2 See Swinburne (2004) 201–9 and Swinburne (1986).

rists, maintain that the mind is the brain, thus denying that "mind", whatever it is, is ontologically distinct from the brain. Swinburne uses thought experiments to critique this position. Suppose, for example, that my brain is divided in half and transplanted into two different bodies. Which, if either of those persons, would be me? They can't both be me, on logical grounds: if they were both me, they would have to be identical with each other, which clearly they are not. But the possibilities that neither of them is me, or that one or other but not both is me cannot be excluded by anything we know about "my" brain. Nor is it a merely trivial matter that can be settled by convention. If I were told that one of the halves of my brain would exist in a person who would live a life of bliss and the other in a person who would live a life of unrelieved misery, it would be a matter of some concern to me that I not end up being the latter. Further, it seems perfectly conceivable, hence logically possible, that I, who exist now, might still exist in a year's time even if my entire body (including my brain) were utterly destroyed tomorrow. If that is possible, however, then it cannot be the case that I am identical with (let alone nothing but) my brain or even my body as a whole. If I am not identical with my body, however, then even now I exist as a substance distinct from my body.[1]

The data, then, strongly suggest the truth of substance dualism of the sort defended by Descartes, a position incompatible with physicalist naturalism since it requires the existence of something in addition to the physical universe governed by the laws of nature. This fact no doubt explains the unpopularity of dualism among contemporary philosophers of mind, but that is no argument against it in and of itself. Dualism not only conforms to everyday experience, which informs us that some of our mental states (e.g. sensations of pain) are caused by bodily states and that some bodily states (e.g. my raising my arm) are caused by mental acts of choice but, according to Swinburne also offers the only plausible metaphysical analysis of personal identity over time.[2] The main argument against dualism is the famous interaction problem, but Swinburne dismisses this as overrated; one can be perfectly persuaded that a causal connection exists even in those cases in which we are unable to grasp the mechanism by means of which cause and effect are related.

If immaterial substances, minds or (Swinburne's preference) *souls* actually exist and there is no prospect for explaining the existence of such souls through any sort of (non-question-begging) natural mechanism, then clearly the existence of souls requires a special, non-physical cause. The theistic God, Himself an immaterial, spir-

---
1 Swinburne (2004) pages 197–198.
2 See Swinburne and Shoemaker (1984) pages 3–66.

itual substance, naturally suggests Himself as the obvious candidate. Further, since consciousness and self-consciousness are necessary conditions for the full-blown rationality and capacity for free choice necessary for beings capable of knowing and loving God to exist, God would have good reason to create such substances and to "fit" them to individual physical bodies in order to create finite persons such as human beings. Further, God could decree that certain brain-events should be correlated to certain mental states, something that science has no prospect of explaining, thus establishing the fundamental mind–brain correspondences that evolution modifies over time. Once again, theism "predicts" substance dualism whereas physicalist naturalism does not and, indeed, appears to "predict" the opposite. Once again, theism both outperforms physicalist naturalism and finds additional confirmation in the data of consciousness. Thus, this "argument from consciousness" provides a further c-inductive argument for the existence of God.

THE MORAL ARGUMENT

Swinburne rejects the traditional moral argument for God's existence that attempts to explain the existence of the objective moral law or moral values by reference to God's nature or will as its *fons et origo*.[1] Since the fundamental principles of morality are very likely necessary truths, they are in need of no ontological grounding. However, Swinburne does argue for God's existence from the fact that we possess distinctively moral beliefs. If God creates human beings with a significant capacity for free choice, God would have good reason to make sure that human beings possessed the capacity to form moral beliefs and be inclined to allow their behaviour to be directed by those principles, since unless this were so no significant moral choices would be possible. By contrast, we have no reason to believe that the natural order as understood according to the principles of physicalist naturalism would produce such beliefs. Provided that such beliefs antecedently existed, the mechanism of evolution can explain the persistence of such beliefs by reference to the survival-value they confer upon the communities governed by them. Further, we can perhaps explain the evolution of "altruistic" behaviour on the basis of self-interested motives *a la* `Hume as the Sociobiologists of the 1970's proposed. However, that is not the same thing as full-blown moral consciousness that sees moral obligation as something categorically obligatory, not merely fortuitous or as merely advantageous in the long run. Only the former can be the basis for significant moral choice in which competing motives

---

1 Swinburne (2004), pages 215–19.

are not merely alternatives but temptations to deviate from the good. The existence of moral knowledge of this sort, then, is once again something that theism would "predict" about the world but that physicalist naturalism would not. So, once again, theism outperforms naturalism and, to the extent that the existence of moral knowledge of this sort confirms the theistic hypothesis, we have an additional c-inductive argument for God's existence.

SWINBURNE ON EVIL AND THE HIDDENNESS OF GOD

We have seen that, according to Swinburne, we have good reason to believe that God would have created a complex, orderly and beautiful world containing finite rational beings such as ourselves capable of knowing and loving Him. That, of course, is precisely the sort of world we live in; so far forth, things are precisely as we would expect them to be if the theistic hypothesis were true. However, it will not do just to consider the positive evidence in favour of God; we must also consider the evidence against God's existence and assess its strength as well. Without a doubt, the major evidence weighing against God's existence is that provided by the existence of evil in the world. Of course, from the inductivist point of view the existence of evil is hardly make or break for theism – even if it is *prima facie* evidence against God's existence, it is probably not decisive by itself given the weight of the positive evidence in favour of God's existence. Nevertheless, it remains very puzzling why a good and loving God of the sort postulated by theism would permit any evil at all, let alone all the evil that we see around us and few rational inquirers are going to be inclined to accept the explanation that God must have a good reason but that it lies beyond our ability to know. It is evident that evil is at least *prima facie* evidence against the existence of God and it is disingenuous to suppose otherwise.[1] Further, we know that an omnipotent, perfectly good God would prevent every gratuitous evil from occurring if He existed. So, if there are gratuitous evils, i.e. evils that serve no greater purpose, then this greatly diminishes the probability of theism. So, then, theodicy is not a luxury for theists but something they are required to provide in defence of the claim that God exists. Swinburne therefore attempts to allay our worries about evil by constructing a theodicy, a justification of God's ways to man. Swinburne originally hoped to provide a theodicy that did not rely on any specifically Christian ideas and presents such a theodicy in *The Existence of God*. However, he later changed his mind about this

---

[1] See Swinburne's essay in Howard–Snyder (1996), pages 30–48; also Swinburne (1996), pages 95–113 and (1998), pages 14–29, especially page 29.

and constructed a full-blown Christian theodicy in a later book, *Providence and the Problem of Evil*. Since the approach taken in both places is roughly the same, however, I will deal with them as a single, unified view.

Swinburne's Theodicy

If sensations of pleasure are the only intrinsic good and sensations of physical pain the only intrinsic evil, then the universe we live in is clearly not the universe that we would expect a perfectly good God to create. Theism, however, plausibly denies that this is the case; most of us would not choose a life of childish pleasures over the adult state even if it were only moderately happy, and most of us would be willing to undergo pain, suffering and even loss of life if some great good could be secured as a result. Even in our sybaritic culture, most of us think that at least a large part of the good life is one in which we are able to develop and use our capacities in significant ways. If these ideas are correct, then the world in which we live looks as though optimally designed to make this possible. Swinburne even goes so far as to suggest that this is a further c-inductive argument for God's existence, the so-called argument from providence.[1]

We have already seen that God would have good reason to create rational beings with intellect, free will and the capacity to form and be motivated by moral beliefs. If so, God would also have good reason to create bodies for such beings, since they need these bodies in order to interact with and learn about the external world and that these bodies are vulnerable both to natural forces and to the actions of others, i.e. liable either to being harmed or helped by them. Only in this way will be we able to be of use to one another, providing opportunities for others to aid and support us just as others provide such opportunities for ourselves, both of which are good things. However, without natural evils and the possibilities of harm and damage inherent in our environment, our responsibility for ourselves and others would be greatly diminished. Further, if God were to constantly intervene in nature and human life in order to insure that nothing bad – or at any rate *very* bad – could ever happen, especially to the morally good or the innocent, our lives would once again be robbed of a great deal of their poignancy and significance. However, if God has given us our intelligence and free will in order to love and serve each other and to be loved and served by others in their turn, then the world as we see it looks well-designed to achieve this end.

---

1 See Swinburne (2004), pages 219–35.

Of course, given that we have the free will necessary in order for us to possess genuine moral agency, the possibility of the abuse and neglect of ourselves and others cannot be excluded. We can fail to do our duties to others, to help them when they need it and even to ignore what is best for ourselves through selfishness, laziness or the pursuit of pleasure. Even worse, however, we can use our knowledge and power to bring positive harm to others out of hatred, contempt or to serve our own self-interest. This, of course, is the moral evil that men commit against each other. God could intervene to prevent such evils from occurring, either by cancelling the effects of such actions or by immediately punishing those who committed them, but once again for God to do this would undermine the moral seriousness of our free choices both to do the good and avoid evil by eliminating any genuine choice between them. By the same token, however, God has taken steps to place natural limits on our ability to abuse and cause harm to others. Human life and the human tolerance for pain is limited just as is our capacity to do good for others and to repent of the evil we have done. The fact of death itself reinforces the significance of our moral choices. Further, according to Christian theism, God promises eternal life to all and this holds out the possibility that God will be able to compensate those who have suffered and to punish those who have caused suffering in the next life, something that we would expect a just God to do.

In sum then, the world appears as we would expect it to appear if we had been created by a good God who has left us largely in charge of ourselves in order that our free choices, especially those that involve moral matters, should form and express our characters either in acts of loving concern for ourselves and others or in contempt and indifference to our moral obligations; nor is it altogether implausible that the theistic God should have chosen to do so, especially given the possibility that the scales of cosmic justice will be balanced in the life to come. But there is more. On the Christian theist picture, our evil actions are more than merely immoral: they are also *sinful*, evincing an arrogant contempt for God as well as our neighbour. Although God has every right to utterly destroy us for our sins, God exercises forbearance during this life while the possibility of repentance remains, thus making Him vulnerable to our actions insofar as He allows His will for us to be frustrated. By the same token, love of neighbour can also evince love of God when we do for others in God's name and for God's sake. If certain other Christian doctrines are true, such as the Incarnation, Atonement and Resurrection of Christ, then we have good reason to think that God has taken human form, suffered with us and for us and thereby secured the possibility of salvation for all human beings through the grace of Christ offered freely to all, accepted and at work in all who believe.[1]

THE PROBLEM OF DIVINE HIDDENNESS

At the same time one may well ask, if this is so, why God doesn't make his existence more evident to human beings? After all, there are many honest non-theists who decline belief in God on the basis of insufficient evidence despite having studied the theist's case for God. To these queries Swinburne responds that, while there must be enough evidence to make God's existence reasonable to believe (and, for Swinburne, this means enough to make it more reasonable than not to believe) there cannot be *overwhelming* evidence for God's existence, since once again the free choice to believe in God and live a godly life would be critically undermined. Nor could God have endowed us with a stronger sense of His presence, since this too would undermine our freedom. Our good desires both to be liked by good persons and to secure our own long–term self-interest would combine to make a free choice for God virtually impossible; paradoxically, too strong of a conviction of God's existence would make it too easy to be good! Although Swinburne remains committed to the idea that there is, *in fact*, sufficient evidence to justify belief in God, the delicate balance between the need for God to be "hidden" enough to be an object of a free response and the evidence justifying that choice must make honest non-theism a genuine possibility; so, that there are honest non-theists is predictable on the assumptions of Christian theism and so cannot be construed as evidence against it.[2] Thus, that honest agnostics should exist is a good thing and even a good thing for the agnostic, since he or she retains the free will to decide whether or not to become a morally good person. That honest agnostics should exist is likewise a good for the believer, since it provides an opportunity to witness, both in word and deed, to the agnostic and perhaps be an agent of conversion.

THE SUFFERING OF ANIMALS

Animal pain and suffering is probably the greatest challenge to the contemporary theodicist, given our tendency nowadays to regard animals as strong candidates for membership in the moral community. Animals do not have free will or, it is generally thought, immortal souls. They have not sinned and yet they feel pain. Why?

---

1 See Swinburne (1989)
2 Although his argument is flawed in execution, Brams (1981) suggests the utility of applying Game Theory to the divine hiddenness problem.

Swinburne's primary response to the problem of animal suffering[1] is that animals possess, to a lower degree, the same capacities for learning and caring behaviour as we do and that it is good that they should be able to develop these capacities and display these traits, which they cannot do unless they are subject to real threats that sometimes result in serious pain and suffering to individual animals. Animals cannot learn to protect themselves from danger unless dangers exist and they witness what happens to other animals that fall prey to those dangers. By the same token, animals can only care for their mates, their young and take risks to protect or rescue them if there are dangerous circumstances that call forth such behaviours. It is a good thing that animals should have an opportunity to do such things. Further, Swinburne suggests that the primary function of pain, both in humans and animals, to signify bodily damage and its causes and thus set up an aversion to those things, is largely good. It is also questionable whether or not animals suffer, as opposed to merely feeling sensations of pain that evoke an automatic response and how far down the scale of living things awareness of pain extends. At any event, witnessing the sufferings of animals is also instructive for humans, a source of beneficial information derived from animal experimentation and, at the same time, capable of evoking compassion from humans and thus providing an additional outlet for our love and caring.

Despite having said all this, Swinburne still apparently regards evil as weighing against the truth of theism and thus as lowering the overall probability that God exists, though to an extent that is difficult to quantify. This is largely because the ways in which the various goods and evils we experience in this life are intertwined with one another are difficult to untangle and our judgments about alternatives taken in conditions of extreme ignorance. Evil does count against the existence of God, according to Swinburne, but we cannot judge that it does so decisively, given that there is a strong positive case to be made for God's existence on other grounds. The foregoing exercise in theodicy is intended to mitigate the force of the evidence for evil and suggest that it is, despite appearances, compatible with the existence of a perfectly good God after all, but it certainly stops short of proving this or resolving every hypothetical puzzle-case that we can imagine. In the end, it perhaps amounts more to a theodical defence rather than a full-fledged justification of the ways of God to man.

---

1 Swinburne (1998), pages 171–5 and Swinburne (2004), pages 243–5.

Swinburne on Religious Experience and Miracles

In his defence of theism from the problem of evil, Swinburne ultimately feels it necessary to make appeal to some of the distinctive teachings of Christianity in order to make his case, apparently believing that, at least where the problem of evil is concerned, Christian theism is more plausible than mere unadorned theism taken by itself. However, to make this move raises the question of the propriety of the evidential grounds for those beliefs. In the case of Christianity, these grounds are two: first, the religious experiences of Christians, both as individuals and corporately, taken as a group and second, the historical witness to the founder of Christianity given in the Scriptures, in which Christ's miracles, especially his the Resurrection from the dead, are prominently featured. Not surprisingly, Swinburne wants to argue that both of these are reliable, credible sources of information about God and thus provide additional evidence for the existence of a theistic God.

Miracles

Swinburne examines the credentials for the biblical revelation and the canons for its interpretation in his book *Revelation*[1] and defends the propriety of accepting it as (largely) historically accurate with regard to its supernatural content. However, this will only be the case if the very notion of supernatural intervention is coherent. Not all supernatural interventions in the natural order are miraculous, of course, and in his early monograph *The Concept of Miracle*[2] Swinburne examines the Humean argument against miracles with an eye to characterizing what a miracle would be. He concludes that the Humean analysis is essentially correct: a miracle is a unique and unrepeatable supernatural intervention in the natural order that involves the violation of a law of nature. Hume, of course, notoriously maintains both on *a priori* and *a posteriori* grounds that no credible miracle claims are likely to be found and, more than this, that they are so intrinsically unlikely as to be beneath rational investigation, so that they may be safely dismissed out of hand without any examination whatever. At the end of *The Concept of Miracle* Swinburne claims that whether this is true or not depends on what whether or not we think it likely that a theistic God exists; Hume's arguments will only carry the sort of weight that they are intended to if it is highly unlikely, on balance, that such a God exists. Different people, then, will make different judgments about the likelihood of miracles given their different estimates regarding God's existence.

---

1 Swinburne (1992)
2 Swinburne (1970)

Swinburne takes up the topic of miracles again in *The Existence of God*.[1] If the only evidence relevant to evaluating miracle-claims is that provided by natural science, then Swinburne is inclined to agree with Hume that the evidence for miracles provided by testimony, etc. is insufficient to outweigh the empirical evidence in favour of the laws of nature. The intrinsic probability that the theistic God exists is apparently not enough to make such reports credible, so it is doubtful that Swinburne would agree with those Christian apologists who want to make a direct appeal to miracle-claims, such as the bodily resurrection of Jesus, as proof for the Christian religion. However, says Swinburne, the scientific evidence on behalf of the laws of nature is not the only evidence that is relevant to the assessment of miracle-reports. The previous c-inductive arguments for God's existence have greatly augmented the intrinsic probability that God exists residing in the inherent simplicity of that hypothesis. The evidence of evil, though ultimately weighing against the existence of God, has been blunted by theodical considerations so as not to count decisively against it. Furthermore, if a theistic God existed, He would have good reason to communicate with us and reveal His presence to us in a manner provided adequate but non-compulsive evidence both for God's existence and His providential care for us. Given that this is the case, the *prior probability* that miracles would occur if a theistic God existed would be fairly high and, Swinburne thinks, high enough to be credible on the basis of well-attested reports.

Of course, not every putative miracle-report is intrinsically credible even if the foregoing is true; many of them are too trivial and fantastic to take seriously and may be reasonably disregarded. However, there are classes of miracle events that God would have good reason to perform, such as to testify to some important truth that God wants us to believe (e.g. that Jesus is the Messiah), to advance the divine plan when its course is blocked by human intransigence (e.g. the ten plagues visited on the Egyptians that secured the freedom of the Israelites) or as the free response to heartfelt faith (as in the case of a miraculous cure worked in response to petitionary prayer.) Miracle-reports of these types, being the sort of acts that we would reasonably expect a theistic God to perform do merit investigation and rational acceptance provided that they are well-attested by credible witnesses. In his book *The Resurrection of God Incarnate* Swinburne argues at length that this is the case for the central miracle of Christianity, the bodily resurrection of Jesus Christ.[2]

---

1 Swinburne (2004), pages 273–92.
2 See Swinburne (2003).

RELIGIOUS EXPERIENCE

In a certain sense, to discuss the topic of miracles is already to broach that of religious experience, since most miracle-reports (e.g. Moses and the Burning Bush) involve an element of religious experience as well. Whereas Swinburne's defence of theism has been largely the effort of one man – he has not established a school or a movement as Plantinga has – one area in which his work has had some influence on others is in the investigation and defence of religious experience; several writers on this topic have acknowledged Swinburne's influence.[1] Swinburne's defence of religious experience as a source of rational belief about God is part of his overall examination of the credibility of testamentary evidence in general. Although Swinburne's position on this topic develops over time, I will attempt to present it from the point of view of the completed doctrine, which is roughly the opposite from the way it developed in Swinburne's work.

Swinburne takes it to be the case that on any non-sceptical account of empirical knowledge the process of rational belief-formation based on sense-experience will involve the reliance on what he call the *Principle of Credulity*,[2] which may be stated as follows:

> PC: The prima facie best explanation for X's appearing to be F is that X is F.

Thus, it is rational for us to presume that our first-person perceptual experiences are veridical *unless and until* we have good reason to doubt them. This does not mean, of course, that every experiential judgment will be reasonable to believe *ultima facie*; there are numerous conditions that can override the initial presumption in favour of first-person experience most of which involve special conditions affecting perception or subsequent disconfirmation of one's apparent experience. Even so, it is impossible for us to proceed on any other supposition than that our everyday experiences are largely veridical.

In turn, however, the Principle of Credulity licenses and supports a further principle, the *Principle of Testimony* which we can formulate as follows:

> PT: The prima facie best explanation for A's reporting that he or she experienced P is that A experienced P.

If we were not willing to credit the testimony of others without further corroboration,

---

1 See Franks Davis (1997) and Gellman (1998); the latter presents a nice blend of both the Inductivist approach and the Post-Deductivist perspective of Alvin Plantinga.
2 Swinburne (2004), pages 303–325.

at least on a preliminary basis, our empirical knowledge would be limited solely to what we could directly confirm for ourselves and this is far too small a foundation for most of our beliefs about the world. The alternative is to accept the claims of others at face value unless there are good reasons to do otherwise. At the same time, the number of overriding conditions, while including all those that apply to first-person experiential claims, is greater in the case of third-person reports and include questions about the intrinsic improbability of what is reported, the reliability of the witnesses, their honesty and so on. Nevertheless, in most cases it is eminently rational to accept the testimony of others at face value.

There is no reason, according to Swinburne, to exempt claims about religious experience from the foregoing. If someone claims to have experienced God under certain circumstances and appears to be an otherwise sane and reliable witness, it is eminently rational to accept their reports as veridical unless and until some subsequent condition defeats their claim. Of course, if claims of this kind were routinely overturned by subsequent investigation or experience, we would not credit them. However, Swinburne argues that an examination of the varieties of religious experience by scholars of religion shows that this is not the case and that, despite problems of interpretation and so on there is a significant number of undefeated claims to religious experience and a relatively neglible amount of "anti-religious" experience. He therefore concludes that religious experience constitutes a strong c-inductive argument for God's existence.

J. L. Mackie's Critique of Swinburne

Swinburne concludes by reckoning up the positive evidence for God's existence and concluding that all of the positive evidence for God's existence taken together, even when the residual evidence against God's existence represented by evil is factored in, constitutes a successful p-inductive argument for God's existence, i.e. an argument that makes it more probable than not that God exists. Since it is not possible to quantify the amount of evidence that each of these independent lines of argument contributes to the case for theism or the amount of residual force residing in the evidence from evil, Swinburne's claim to this effect must inevitably constitute a "judgment call" for each individual reader. Nevertheless, Swinburne would certainly want to claim that enough evidence has been presented to make it reasonable for the reader to conclude as he has, even if not every reader has been convinced.

J. L. Mackie's *The Miracle of Theism*[1] appeared posthumously in 1982 and was essentially a broadside response to the burgeoning revival of theism occurring in the mid-to late-1970's. Although it was not written specifically to critique Swinburne's *The Existence of God*, Mackie shows himself to clearly understand the basic structure of Swinburne's approach and that he has acquaintance with Swinburne's specific arguments. Indeed, Mackie largely agrees with Swinburne in taking the Bayesian approach to the question of God's existence. However, after a thorough review of the evidence, Mackie not surprisingly comes to a completely different assessment of the probability of theism, maintaining that the evidence provided by miracles, religious experience, the existence of the world, its order, consciousness and morality is negligible, making it neither more probable than physicalist naturalism nor more probable than not taken on its own. According to Mackie, the Bayesian approach just illustrates the paucity of evidence for theism and the only miracle that genuinely needs explaining is that some intelligent, educated people still believe in God. Mackie found it quite easy to adjust to the new, inductivist paradigm and, had he lived, undoubtedly would have continued to be a major contributor to the debate over God's existence.

In the appendix to the 1991 revised edition of *The Existence of God*,[2] Swinburne responds to three of the specific criticisms made by Mackie of his argument for theism. Mackie argues that Swinburne's attribution to God of the power to cause the universe directly, without any intervening mechanism or pre-existing material to affect, is unintelligible because "completely unfamiliar" to us. Swinburne responds that it is neither. We each of us experience something akin to such a power in the initiation of in intentional action. While it is true that our direct actions are realized through neuromuscular mechanisms occurring in the body, it nevertheless remains that we do not need to consciously direct those processes; they happen automatically in response to our act of willing. God's direct power to cause is simply a further extension of this familiar idea. At any rate, the simplicity of an explanation is not determined by its familiarity and the attribution to God of such a power recommends itself on grounds of simplicity in abeyance of any reason to suppose otherwise.

Mackie also questions whether or not explanation in terms of God's willing or choosing that such-and-such be the case really amounts to any kind of explanation at all. Does "God willed it so" provide any illumination when offered as an explanation of the fact that a sense–datum of redness is experienced when the eyes are affected by a particular wave–length of light? Swinburne responds that his use of personal

---
1 Mackie (1982)
2 Swinburne (1991), Appendix A, pages 293–99.

explanation is not merely a "God-of-the-gaps" appeal. The theistic hypothesis has definite content such that not just any, let alone every universe could plausibly be thought to be the product of divine creative activity; indeed, there are many universes that would give us no reason whatsoever to believe that it was created by a god and others that would definitely be ruled out on that hypothesis. The great surprise is that, if Swinburne's arguments are sound, the universe that actually exists is such a world and this must be accounted strong evidence for God's existence.

Or would, if the features we observe the universe to have were in fact as unique and unusual as theists tend to take them. This brings us to Mackie's third criticism. Why suppose that a complex, orderly and beautiful universe like this one is so unlikely unless a god existed to bring it into existence? Isn't Swinburne just assuming without argument that a random, featureless universe is more likely than one that is orderly and thus apparently "designed"? To this Swinburne responds that he is not just assuming this without good reason. The prior probability of a random, featureless universe is much higher than that of a complex, orderly one just because there are so many more ways for a universe of the former sort to come about than one of the latter, so that a universe such as ours would actually exist is a surprising fact, one that finds a natural explanation in terms of the intentions of the theistic God. Swinburne has had other critics, of course.[1] However, we will have to leave this topic for now and to recount further developments in the philosophy of religion.

Inference to the Best Explanation and the Future of Inductivism

While Swinburne articulates his version of Inductivism by relying on Bayesian Confirmation Theory, other exponents of Inductivism have adopted a less formal approach that can be traced to Peirce, often called *Inference to the Best Explanation* (IBE).[2] According to exponents of this version of Inductivism, theism is the best explanation for certain familiar and very general facts about the universe and thus preferable to alternatives such as physicalist naturalism. It is thus rational to believe in preference to those alternatives. Exponents of this version of Inductivism do not generally suppose that it is necessary to argue that the probability of theism on the whole is greater than .5 and are content with a much more fluid account of the grounds of rational belief.

---

1 In addition to Prevost (1990) already cited, see also Gutting (1982) who attacks both Swinburne's and Mitchell's positions.
2 See Herrick (1999).

Peirce[1] advocated the use of a generalized scientific method as part of his pragmatic realism, which he reduced to three basic steps each characterized by its own peculiar form of reasoning. First, there is abduction, or hypothesis formation: in the face of a surprising phenomenon, we ought to ask ourselves what would have to be the case in order for this phenomenon not to be surprising, but to be expected. If we can successfully answer this question, we will be able to arrive at a plausible hypothesis to explain those facts. Second, there is deduction, in which we deduce observable consequences from our hypothesis in an attempt to provide conditions for the confirmation or falsification of that hypothesis. Finally, there is induction, the process by means of which confirmation or falsification of that hypothesis is actually undertaken. Peirce recommends this general pattern of reasoning not just for natural science, but for philosophy in general, including metaphysics. In an essay entitled "A Neglected Argument for God's Existence"[2] Peirce suggests that it is applicable in the philosophy of religion as well.

Of course, the application of the generalized scientific method (nowadays IBE) to the evaluation of worldviews such as theism and physicalist naturalism is a good deal more limited. After all, since (as Mitchell emphasizes) worldviews or "world hypotheses" are both abstract and very general, it is difficult to specify any sort of novelty evidence that would decide between them – there are no "crucial experiments" in metaphysics as there are in physics. Further, the scope and vagueness of such theories makes it difficult in many cases to evaluate them with regard to the very general sort of "evidence" available to us for making such evaluations. Still, exponents of IBE have suggested that something like Peirce's scheme might be workable if we are able to develop a set of quasi-scientific canons for the for evaluation of metaphysical constructs similar to those used to evaluate scientific theories of great scope and regularity.

One such list of canons or criteria is the following:[3]

1. *Internal coherence*, which may range from mere lack of internal contradiction to the mutual deducibility of each part of the hypothesis from other parts of that hypothesis.
2. *External coherence* with other well-established theories, which again may range from mere lack of contradiction to deducibility from those other well-

---

1 See Anderson (1995), especially 155–62.
2 In Anderson (1995), pages 118–35.
3 This list is my own, based on my reading of a number of presentations of the canons of IBE in various authors, especially Herrick (1999), pages 791–2.

established theories.
3. *Explanatory Power*, which includes: *scope*, the degree to which the hypothesis is applicable and unifies and systematically connects otherwise disparate data, and *fecundity*, the capacity of the hypothesis to suggest further useful ideas and potential explanations over time.
4. *Empirical Fit*, which can be construed either
    positively, as the measure of the performance of the hypothesis in relation to new evidence, or
    negatively, as the degree of its *ad hocness* in response to anomalous or "recalcitrant" data.
5. *Simplicity*, which as we have seen can be characterized in several different and potentially conflicting ways.

Further, given that we are dealing with worldviews that have implications for how one lives ones life, we can add to this list the following:

6. *Illumination*, the capacity of the worldview to make sense of life and to provide the prospect of a meaningful existence.
7. *Practical Efficacy*, the capacity of the worldview to found a coherent, practical and fulfilling way of life.

Given agreement to this (or some other, similar) standard list of criteria for evaluating "world hypotheses", one could then set about comparing competing worldviews, such as theism and physicalist naturalism. For example, a theist could marshal the sort of evidence for God's existence as presented by Swinburne and then argue that theism is the best overall explanation for the existence of the physical universe, its order and complexity, the existence of conscience and morality, and reports of miracles and religious experience, the sorts of evils that we regularly become aware of in the course of human history and experience, as well as many other features of the universe, when judged according to the foregoing criteria, ultimately reaching the conclusion that the world, though initially a puzzling and surprising phenomenon, is as we would expect it to be if it were created by the theistic God. By contrast, the theist would continue, the world is not as we would expect it to be if physicalist naturalism is true, so that e.g., even if the naturalist can "explain away" the data of theism, this will be at the cost of both explanatory power and of increased *ad hocness*. The defender of physicalist naturalism, of course, would presumably attempt to argue the opposite.

IBE shows some promise as a further medium in which the evidence for and against theism might be considered from a rational point of view. However, as yet the canons or criteria for evaluating hypotheses are still too vague and underanalyzed to cut much ice in the evaluation of worldviews; it is currently too easy to justify competing, mutually exclusive worldviews simply by weighting some of the criteria more decisively than others. Even if we cannot hope to achieve the sort of rigor and decisiveness that is the ideal of mathematical physics, we still need more than what we currently possess. IBE still awaits its John Stuart Mill who will accomplish for it what Mill did for causal inference using his famous "Methods". In the meantime, exponents of IBE in the philosophy of religion need to continue to refine this approach in the course of applying it.

Chapter Six

The Ontological Argument Redivivus

In the next three chapters, I propose to interrupt the main course of my historical narrative and instead examine the discussion of the major arguments for God's existence during the years since 1970. Although it is often said that nothing ever changes in philosophy and that each generation simply trots out the same shop-worn positions and arguments as its predecessors, this cannot be said about the philosophy of religion in the last three decades of the twentieth century. In fact, two major intellectual developments – the discovery of possible world semantics and "Big Bang" cosmology – had a tremendous impact on the fortunes of the traditional arguments for God's existence, resuscitating them when they seemed on the point of expiring and making them more formidable than they had seemed to be in many centuries. In this chapter we will look at the ontological argument. The next two chapters will deal with the cosmological and teleological arguments respectively.

The ontological argument is not one argument, but rather a family of arguments for God's existence that share in common the intention to prove God's existence *a priori* solely from the conceptual analysis of the notion of God. In every case, a particular analysis of the concept of God is given, according to which God is the in-principle most perfect possible being, unsurpassable even by Himself. Given this account of the concept of God, proponents of the argument go on to argue that existence or (perhaps) necessary existence is deducible from that analysis by a *reductio ad absurdum* on the claim that God does not exist and that consequently, God (necessarily) exists. Neo-Thomists reject this argument as unsound, usually by quoting Thomas's one-line refutation of the proof summarized in the slogan "what holds of the conceptual order need not hold of the actual one." The suggestion here is that even if the argument is a sound one and yields the conclusion "God exists", it does not follow that God actually exists, only that if God exists, then He exists necessarily. This, as even atheistic critics of the argument have noted, is simply question-begging; one might as well argue that square circles might exist even though the concept of a square circle contains a contradiction on the same ground. If the ontological argument is a sound argument, its conclusion will be true and as credible as the conclusion of any other deductive argument.

THE CLASSICAL ONTOLOGICAL ARGUMENT(S)

Although the ontological argument was first formulated by Anselm of Canterbury around 1080, the most familiar form of the argument was that formulated by Descartes in his *Meditations*,[1] which may be summarized as follows:

1. I have a clear and distinct concept of God as a perfect being.
2. Whatever I clearly and distinctly perceive to belong to any being according to my concept of it really belongs to that thing.
3. I clearly and distinctly perceive that existence belongs to the concept of God in the same way that "having three sides" belongs to the concept of a triangle.
4. Hence, just as I cannot conceive of a triangle with less than three sides, neither can I conceive of God as non-existent.
5. Therefore, existence belongs to God according to my concept of God.
6. Therefore, it really belongs to God to exist.
7. Therefore, God exists. Q.E.D.

Although this argument attracted numerous criticisms from Descartes' contemporaries, the standard objections to Descartes' argument, generally repeated by opponents of the ontological argument, are those derived from Kant's analysis of the argument in the *Critique of Pure Reason*.[2] According to Kant, the argument fails because it regards existence to be a perfection, which in turn requires that existence be a property that something can either have or lack. However, says Kant, "existence" is not a predicate, hence existence not a property of things and thus not a perfection that they can possess. Therefore, says Kant, existence cannot be an essential property of any thing and thus cannot belong to the concept of anything. Thus, Descartes is wrong when he claims that existence is part of the concept of God. Kant goes on to offer a different analysis of existential statements in terms of judgment, i.e. mental acts of *positing* or *refusing to posit* something in actuality. According to Kant, to say that X exists is to say no more than that X is real or actual and to say that X does not exist is

---

1 See *Meditation* V in Cottingham, Stoothoff and Murdoch (1984), Volume II pages 45–7.
2 See Kant (1998) pages 563–71.

simply to say that it is not real or actual.

Kant's rather sketchy analysis appears to draw significant confirmation from modern symbolic logic. According to Russell,[1] for example, the logical form of a statement such as "A red thing exists" is (roughly) "Some thing is a red thing", expressed in the propositional calculus as (Ex)Rx – "There is an x (i.e. a concrete, existing individual thing) such that x is Red." In this scheme, existence is expressed by the existential quantifier translating the phrase "There is an x" so that existence never appears in predicate position in an existential statement and thus never functions as a property–name. The statement as a whole, then, simply expresses what Kant would call a judgment of existence, such that when I deny existence to something I reject it along with all its properties. Russell offers the same analysis of statements that contain general terms, such as the names of natural kinds. Thus, if I say that Giraffes exist, the symbolic logic translation reads (Ex)Gx, "There is an x such that x is a Giraffe" and if I deny that unicorns exist, the symbolic translation will be ~(Ex)Ux, "It is not the case that there is an x such that x is a unicorn." In this context, it is common to talk about natural kinds, essences or properties as being *exemplified* or as *failing to be exemplified* by individuals. This becomes even clearer when we express negative existentials using the formally equivalent translation (Vx) ~Ux, "For all x, it is not the case that x is a unicorn." Using this device obviates the need to refer to non-existent things by insuring that reference is always to actually existing things; it thus offers a way of understanding existential statements that treats "existence" as an unanalyzed primitive concerning which any philosophical speculation is idling. On this view, the nature of "being" or "existence" is a philosophical pseudo–problem in no way evoked by reflection on statements of existence as used in ordinary language. As such, traditional Greek and Medieval metaphysics is shown to rest on a mistake.[2]

Anselm's argument in *Proslogion*,[3] chapter II, often regarded as the precursor of Descartes' argument and thus also called the ontological argument, was not entirely eclipsed by the more intuitive Cartesian version of the *a priori* proof of God's existence. Anselm's classic proof can be stated as follows:

    1. God=df 'a being greater than which none other can be conceived.'

---

[1] See Russell (1950) pages 41–56; the formal exposition as given here uses symbolization from a later time.

[2] Of course, not all philosophers agree; according to Moreland and Craig, for example, existence is a kind of second–order property, namely, the property of having properties; see Moreland and Craig (2001) pages 187–93.

[3] Anselm in Deane (1962), page 7.

2. No one can deny the existence of God, so defined, without conceiving Him as defined above.
3. If anyone conceives of God as so defined, God exists in his understanding.
4. If one denies God's existence, then one is claiming that God exists solely in the understanding.
5. In that case, God could have existed in actuality as well as in the understanding.
6. It is greater to exist both in the understanding and in actuality than it is to exist in the understanding alone.
7. Thus, if God exists solely in the understanding, then God could have been greater than He is.
8. By definition, God could not be greater than He is.
9. Thus, God cannot exist solely in the understanding.
10. Thus, God must exist both in the understanding and in actuality.
11. Thus, God exists in actuality, which is to say:
12. God actually exists.

This argument has evoked numerous criticisms. The most important of these, however, was formulated in Anselm's own lifetime by a fellow monk, Guanilo of Marmoutier[1] and standardly known as the Perfect Island objection, attempts to show that the foregoing argument must be invalid. Guanilo imagines an island he calls Lost Island, an island a greater than which none other can be conceived. He then creates a parody argument by replacing each occurrence of "God" in the above argument with "Lost Island", thus yielding the conclusion that Lost Island exists. However, since we know that there is no Lost Island, something must be wrong with the original argument. The natural suggestion is that argument is either invalid or commits some sort of informal fallacy; different critics have differing accounts of what the error consists in.

Defenders of the argument contend that there is another way in which the parody argument can fail,[2] i.e. the concept of a perfect island may simply fail to be coherent. For example, it is claimed that there is no intrinsic maximum for the natural kind "island" and that therefore the notion of an unsurpassable island has no content. It is also claimed that islands are by their very nature contingent beings, hence that the notion of a necessarily existent island is incoherent. Since this is largely an histori-

---
1 See Gaunilo's 'In Defense of the Fool' in Plantinga (1964); the argument is repeated by many others, including Scriven (1966) pages and Martin (1990) pages 75–99.
2 See the article by Stephen Davis in Copan and Moser (2003), pages 93–110; see especially pages 108–109.

cal survey, we will not linger here over the ongoing dispute about these responses. Instead, let us turn to the contemporary discussion of the ontological argument.

HARTSHORNE, FINDLAY AND MALCOLM: THE MODAL ONTOLOGICAL ARGUMENT

In a series of books and articles[1] beginning in the early 1940's, Charles Hartshorne, an American process philosopher who taught at Chicago and later at the University of Texas at Austin, began defending a modal version of the ontological argument that he claimed to have discovered in *Proslogion*, chapter III, an argument distinct from and independent of the famous Anselmian argument. Despite believing in a "dipolar" God that asymptotically approaches but never actually realizes his nature as a perfect being, Hartshorne is quite comfortable in supposing that this God is identical with the one of Anselmian conception and thus necessarily existent. According to Hartshorne, Anselm's second *a priori* proof of God's existence argues from the mere logical possibility of God's existence to His actual existence. The form of the argument is quite general and does not favour process conceptions of God over the classical "Anselmian" one, so it has been discussed by many philosophers of religion. We can perhaps best approach the argument by considering first of all J. N. Findlay's ontological disproof of God's existence, first published in *Mind* in 1948.

In "Can God's Existence be Disproved?"[2] Findlay, Professor of Philosophy at the University of London and a thinker with deep idealist roots, argues that it is a necessary condition for God to be supremely worshipable that His great-making features belong to Him essentially, in such a manner that it is impossible for God to have lacked them; otherwise, God lacks the kind of unsurpassable supremacy that evokes our standard religious feelings. Findlay is at one with Anselm and Descartes in asserting that it is a conceptual truth that God is a perfect being, one a greater than which cannot be conceived, even in principle. However, says Findlay, notice what follows from this. If the theistic account of God is correct, then God is not the sort of being who could *just happen* to exist; God's existence, like His other qualities, must be one of his essential qualities and it ought to be impossible for us to conceive of God as non-existent. However, most theists admit that it is at least possible that there is no God hence that God's non-existence is conceivable. In that case, it follows straightaway that God does not exist and, indeed, that God's existence is impossible. If God

---
[1] See Hartshorne (1941), (1961), (1962) and (1965).
[2] See Findlay's article in Plantinga (1964); Findlay later repudiated the argument; see Findlay (1963) and (1970). Findlay's paper was reprinted in Martin and Monnier (2005) without this being noted.

did exist, then His non-existence would have to be inconceivable, just as Anselm and Descartes maintain, because to conceive of God as non-existent would be like conceiving of a triangle with only two sides or a mountain without a valley. Since this is clearly not the case, God's existence is not logically necessary; the only alternative, then, is that God's existence is logically impossible, from which it follows that there is no God.

Fifteen years later, however, Findlay admitted that his ontological disproof of God's existence, though still important, had failed to prove God's non-existence. According to Findlay, Hartshorne had convinced him that the theist could "reverse the argument" using Anselm's Proslogion III modal proof for God's existence, arguing that if God's existence is even so much as logically possible, something that most atheists are willing to concede, then God's existence is logically necessary. Although Hartshorne first presented the argument in his book *Man's Vision of God* published in 1941, the explicitly modal version of the argument did not appear until 1962, by which time Norman Malcolm, an American student of Wittgenstein and professor of philosophy at Cornell, had published his article "Anselm's Ontological Arguments" in *Philosophical Review*.[1] Since Malcolm was a *bona fide* analytic philosopher, his interest in and endorsement of the proof gave it sudden prominence and plausibility, generating new philosophical interest in the argument. Like Hartshorne, Malcolm claims to have discovered a second, distinct modal ontological argument in the text of *Proslogion* III. The new version of the ontological argument became known as the Hartshorne/Malcolm proof for God's existence. Since Malcolm's version is easier to follow, I will consider it here:

1. If God does not exist, then His existence is logically impossible.
2. If God exists, then His existence is logically necessary.
3. God's existence is either logically impossible or it is logically necessary.
4. If God's existence is logically impossible, then the concept of God is self-contradictory.
5. The concept of God is not self-contradictory.
6. Therefore, God's existence is logically necessary.
7. Therefore, God exists.

Of course, this straightforward and apparently compelling argument was too simple to pass muster with philosophers and a number of criticisms quickly appeared. The major virtue of this new version of the ontological argument was that it avoided the

---

1 Reprinted in Plantinga (1965), pages 136–59.

major Kantian criticisms of Descartes' version of the argument, since it is not existence *per se* but instead necessary existence that is treated as a perfection attributable to God. Still, in the minds of most philosophers, more than this was needed to vindicate the argument. Some philosophers argued that premise five was false and that, on one ground or another, the concept of God could be shown to be self-contradictory.[1] Ultimately, however, none of these arguments has proven to be persuasive; the refutation of the deductive version of the argument from evil was especially telling in this regard. Other critics suggested that perhaps Guanilo-style "parody" arguments could be constructed against this version of the argument, just as they can against the *Proslogion* II argument.[2]

By far the most serious criticisms of the argument revolved around the obscurity of the notion of "logically necessary existence." Malcolm follows Findlay in assuming that only a God whose non-existence would be logically impossible would be a fit object of the sort of unreserved worship that theism demands of its adherents. According to Plantinga, for example, the traditional notion of "necessary existence" refers to supposed divine attributes such as eternity, aseity and infinity, none of which are plausibly connected to the notion of *logically* necessary existence but which have usually been regarded as sufficiently exalted properties to command human worship and abjection.[3] John Hick reinforces this sort of claim by arguing that not even these properties are plausibly required for the God of biblical religion, who is considerably more anthropomorphic than the "God of the philosophers" but no less demanding of full-blown and exclusive *latria* despite that fact.[4] So it is not clear that God must be conceived of as necessarily existent.

Further, the notion of "logically necessary existence" is itself obscure and problematic. Necessity is usually thought to be a property of propositions rather than of things, and the relation between necessity *de dicto* (concerning propositions) and necessity *de re* (concerning things) was at this time seen to be quite obscure, so much so that many philosophers of the day rejected the notion of *de re* necessity altogether. Retreading one of the classic criticisms of Descartes' version of the argument, Hick maintains that the conclusion of the argument expresses a merely conceptual truth, one that holds of our concept of God as understood according to one possible definition of "God", but denies that this conception must be instantiated in reality; in effect,

---

1 See the papers in Urban and Walton (1994)
2 See Martin (1990)
3 Originally published in *Journal of Philosophy* in 1961; reprinted in Plantinga (1965) pages 172–80.
4 See Hick in McGill (1966) pages

Hick denies that 7 above follows from 6 above. Plantinga also argues in *God and Other Minds* that all that follows from the premises of the argument is that "necessarily, God exists" (*de dicto*), which is not equivalent to and does not demonstrably entail "God necessarily exists" (i.e. *de re*).[1]

The difficulties here, as it turns out, arose from an inadequate analysis of modal concepts. While Aristotle, the Megarians and the late Mediaevals all investigated modal arguments, the beginnings of a plausible modal logic had to wait until the early twentieth century, when C. I. Lewis and C. K. Langford,[2] both of Harvard University, created the first axiomatic formal system of modal logic. Although modal logic was further developed in the English-speaking world by such figures as Arthur Prior[3] at Cambridge and Ruth Barcan Marcus[4] at Princeton, modal logic remained an uninterpreted formal system of uncertain application. The mainstream of American logicians remained sceptical about the soundness of the modal systems developed by Lewis and Langford, especially the provocative S5 modal system, the one relied upon by Hartshorne in his reconstruction of the *Proslogion* III proof. No less a figure than Harvard's W. V. Quine published a powerful critique of the S5 modal logic and the very idea of *de re* modality in his important article "Reference and Modality."[5] The "new" ontological argument, though tantalizing, remained under a cloud as a consequence of these obscurities. However, this was all about to change as the result of a revolution in the logic of modality.

POSSIBLE WORLDS

Beginning in 1959, a Nebraska high school student named Saul Kripke began to publish a series of papers that culminated in his "Semantical Considerations on Modal Logic" in 1963.[6] This work became the basis for what became known as possible world semantics, a break–through in modal logic that would become the focus of a number of important late–twentieth century analytic philosophers including David Lewis, David Kaplan and Robert Stalnaker. However, by far the most important figure in the popularization of modal logic and its metaphysical applications was Alvin Plantinga. In his paper "*De Dicto* and *De Re*",[7] Plantinga not only answers Quine's critique of

---

1 Plantinga (1967) page 341–56.
2 See Lewis and Langford (1932).
3 See Prior (1957)
4 See Marcus (1993), especially pages 3–35 and 215–32.
5 Reprinted in Sleigh (1972), pages 131–51.
6 See Kripke (1963)
7 Reprinted in Sleigh (1972), pages 153–72.

S5 but shows how we can relate/intertranslate *de dicto* and *de re* modalities. More importantly, his 1974 book *The Nature of Necessity*[1] presented an accessible account of possible worlds semantics and scouted its numerous applications to the formulation and solution of problems in the philosophy of language and metaphysics. While we cannot go into all of this here, we will summarize the results of these developments – currently available in many elementary logic texts – and their application to the ontological argument.

A possible world is, to put it most simply, a way that the world could be. More technically, Plantinga defines a possible world as a maximal state-of-affairs, such that, given any possible world W and any proposition P, either P or its negation (~P) is true in that world. Since the actual world (called K) is a way that world could be, it is also a possible world; Plantinga, along with most exponents of possible worlds semantics, maintains that K is the only possible world that actually exists. Truth in K, then, is straightforwardly truth in the correspondence sense; "truth-in-a-world" for any world W other than K is parasitic on truth and falsity in that sense and means, roughly, that P is true in W just in case, had W been the actual world, P would have been actually true. Since there are an infinite number of ways in which the world might have been different than it is, there are an infinite number of possible worlds corresponding to each of those differences conceived of as elements of some maximal state-of-affairs or other. Although philosophers disagree about the ontological status of non-actual possible worlds, for our purposes we may consider them as merely imaginary, heuristic devices. However, just as we can talk of propositions being true-in-a-world, we can also talk about things existing-in-a-world, such that X exists in W just in case, supposing W to have been the actual world, X would have actually existed.

This means that both propositions and things have *modal properties*, properties they possess across possible worlds. The basic *de dicto* modalities can be defined as follows:

> A proposition is *possibly true* if it is true in at least one possible world.
> A proposition is *possibly false* if it is false in at least one possible world.
> A proposition is *necessarily true* if it is true in all possible worlds.
> A proposition is *necessarily false* if it is false in all possible worlds.
> A proposition is *contingent* if it is true in at least one possible world and false in at least one possible world.

It is to be noted that while necessary truth and necessary falsehood are contraries,

---

1 Plantinga (1974a), pages 44–65.

possible truth and possible falsehood are not; as such, every contingent proposition will be both possibly true and possibly false in every world regardless of its truth in that world, though of course there will be no world in which that proposition will be both true and false. Further, a proposition's contingency as defined above needs to be distinguished from its *contingent truth*. A proposition is contingently true just in case it is both contingent *and* true in the actual world; consequently, contingent truth is not a modal property but rather a property that a proposition possesses only in the actual world.

We are now in a position to characterize the corresponding *de re* modalities, where X is any thing we might care to mention:

> X is *possibly existent* if it exists in at least one possible world.
> X is *possibly non-existent* if it fails to exist in at least one possible world.
> X is *necessarily existent* if it exists in all possible worlds.
> X is *necessarily non-existent* or *impossible* if it fails to exist in all possible worlds.
> X is *contingent* if it exists in at least one possible world and fails to exist in at least one possible world.

Here the same caveats apply. Possible existence and non-existence attach to every contingent thing in every world, regardless of whether or not X exists in that world (as defined above). Contingency is a modal property of contingent things; *contingent being*, however, is not since it refers only to those things that are both contingent (as defined above) and *that actually exist* (i.e. exist in the actual world). This is a status that an X can only have in the actual world and that many contingent things will lack.

There are standard examples for each of the *de dicto* modalities:

> The Earth is round.
> The Earth is flat.
> The Earth is either round or not–round.
> The Earth is both round and not–round.
> The Earth is round, The Earth is flat.

Of these examples, the Earth is round will be both contingent and contingently true, whereas the Earth is flat will be a contingent falsehood.

There is a bit more controversy about modality *de re*. George W. Bush, who exists in the actual world but (many people will say thankfully) does not exist in all possible worlds, illustrates the first two and the fifth of the *de re* modalities as defined above, and square circles illustrate the class of impossible beings. However, are there any examples of necessary beings? One might suppose that, since 2+2=4 is a necessary truth, that the number 2, for example, must exist in all possible worlds; however, not all philosophers are realists about numbers. Nevertheless, Plantinga claims that there is at least one necessary being, i.e. God and that given the foregoing, we can use the ontological argument to make this claim credible.

PLANTINGA'S ONTOLOGICAL ARGUMENT

In *The Nature of Necessity*, Plantinga applied the possible worlds scheme to questions in philosophical theology, later revising and excerpting those chapters for independent publication under the title *God, Freedom and Evil*.[1] Having already defended the traditional ontological argument from the standard criticisms in *God and Other Minds*,[2] Plantinga now undertakes to reformulate the Hartshorne/Malcolm argument using the new "possible worlds" approach to modal logic. The result, he claims, is a valid and apparently sound ontological argument. We can formulate his argument as follows:

1. God=df a maximally great being, i.e. one that exemplifies maximal excellence in every possible world.
2. Maximal greatness is possibly exemplified.
3. If so, then God exists in some possible world.
4. God cannot exist in some possible world without existing in every possible world.
5. So, if God exists in any possible world, then God exists in every possible world.
6. So, God exists in every world.
7. The actual world is a possible world.
8. Therefore, God exists in the actual world, which is to say
9. God exists.

According to Plantinga, *maximal excellence* is the property of being omniscient, omnipotent and omnibenevolent in some world. Since we can imagine a being possessing maximal excellence in some worlds but not others, mere maximal excellence (or even maximal excellence in every world in which that being exists) falls short of divine perfection, since such a being would be exceeded by a being that possessed

---

1 Plantinga (1974a) pages 197–221 and (1974b) pages 85–112.
2 Plantinga (1967) pages 26–94.

those properties in every world. Thus, to capture the idea of divine perfection, we need to stipulate that God is not merely maximally excellent, but *maximally great* as well, meaning that God possesses these properties essentially and in an inseparable manner, such that God is conceived of as maximally excellent in every world. This, of course, entails that God exists in every possible world if He exists in any world in accordance with the foregoing argument.

At the same time, it does seem to be the case that the property of maximal greatness is possibly exemplified; for there is no obvious impossibility or incoherence in the notion of maximal greatness. Indeed, most atheists are willing to admit that God's existence is at least possible. If so, God exists in at least one possible world. However, since God cannot exist in any possible world without existing in every world, since maximal greatness entails maximal excellence in every world, if maximal greatness is exemplified in any world, it will be exemplified in every world. This is to say, of course, that God is a logically necessary being, one that exists in every possible world. Therefore, since the actual world is a possible world, maximal greatness is exemplified in the actual world, which is to say that God actually exists.

Having clarified the notions of necessary truth and necessary being, Plantinga is able to reconstruct the argument without the ambiguities apparently fatal to earlier versions of the modal ontological argument. While not everyone was persuaded, most philosophers of religion are willing to admit that the new ontological argument is at least valid. Even so, Plantinga wants to emphasize that his version of the ontological argument is not a *proof* for God's existence, if for no other reason than that we cannot prove that maximal greatness is possibly exemplified. Nevertheless, given the lack of any plausible argument that it is impossible for maximal greatness to be exemplified in some possible world, there seems little rational basis for resisting the argument. Indeed, the atheist who does so appears to be assuming a daunting burden of proof; his inability to prove that God's existence is impossible (using, e.g. the deductive argument from evil) seems to leave his or her position without rational support.

Before we leave this topic, we may note in passing that there may be an argument for premise 2 above, suggested to me by some remarks made by Kurt Gödel in an unpublished manuscript on the ontological argument.[1] Let us define a *positive property* as any property with a.) coherently conceivable positive conceptual content that b.) adds to the reality of whatever it qualifies. (This definition excludes any merely negative or privative properties, as well as relational, conjunctive and disjunc-

---

1 See Sobell's essay in Thomson (1987), pages 241–61 and Sobell (2003) pages 115–167. Sobell rejects Godel's argument as based on questionable axioms.

tive properties reducible without remainder to positive properties as defined above.) Necessarily, no positive property can be conceived of *as such* (i.e. *qua* property) unless we conceive of it *as possibly exemplified*, i.e. as present in a possible subject that it qualifies. But, then, it is likewise necessary that every positive property (as characterised above) has the property of being *possibly* exemplified since properties are inconceivable *as such* apart from this. Now, if every positive property is possibly exemplified, then there is something in at least one possible world in which that property is exemplified. But maximal greatness is a positive property, so it too possesses the property of being possibly exemplified, which is to say that something in some possible world exemplifies maximal greatness. From this it follows straightaway by the ontological argument that God exists.

I leave this argument for the reader to consider!

Chapter Seven

The Cosmological Argument *Redivivus*

The withering criticisms levelled against the Five Ways in the 1950's and '60's of the last century were standardly repeated in every discussion of the cosmological argument and largely regarded as unanswerable, so that the cosmological argument itself seemed as good as buried. However, in 1975 William L. Rowe (1932–) of Purdue University, then known primarily as a scholar of early modern philosophy drew the philosophical world's attention to another, later version of the cosmological argument, the one developed by Leibniz and Samuel Clarke. According to Rowe, this version of the cosmological argument was much more sophisticated and plausible than any of those produced by Thomas, and free from many of the defects of those arguments. Once separated from its nearly complete identification with the Five Ways and its variants, the cosmological argument began to receive new attention. As we have already seen, Swinburne rejects the five ways – specifically noting Kenny's treatment in a footnote – and adopts the Leibniz/Clarke argument – citing once again Rowe's treatment. This "new" cosmological argument, then, becomes the focus of discussion in the philosophy of religion.

The Leibniz/Clarke Argument

Leibniz and Clarke both intended that the argument should pass muster as a deductive proof for God's existence – witness the title of Clarke's book: *A Demonstration of the Being and Attributes of God*.[1] Rowe takes this seriously in his exposition and analysis of the argument, which we may reconstruct as follows:

1. For everything that exists there is a sufficient cause or reason for its existence.
2. This cause or reason is either intrinsic to it by nature or extrinsic to it by nature.

---
1 Clarke (1994)

3. Any being the cause or reason for the existence of which is extrinsic to its nature is a *contingent* (i.e. dependent) being.
4. Not every being could be a contingent being.
5. Therefore, at least one being is a non-contingent or *necessary* being, whose cause or reason for existing is intrinsic to its nature.
6. This being possesses by nature all of the traditional divine attributes.
7. Therefore, that necessary being is God.

The crucial premise of the argument as reconstructed here is premise four, the claim that not every being could be a contingent being. Suppose that there exists some being, A, that is a dependent being. By definition, this being depends for its existence on the operation of some other being B. If B is in turn a dependent being, then it depends for its existence on the operation of some further cause C, and so on. No matter how far back we go in this series, so long as it always terminates in some further dependent being, we never find a complete explanation of A's existence; to extend the series to infinity only compounds the problem infinitely. Even if it did not, the whole series, consisting as it does of nothing but dependent beings, might have failed to exist; so, postulating an infinite past series of such beings, each of which is dependent in exactly the same way as the being it was invoked to explain, does not explain why any of them exists rather than not.

Rowe considers a number of objections to the argument for this premise.[1] One common argument is that the theist is committing a fallacy of composition, assuming that since each member of the infinite series is a dependent being that the series itself is a dependent being. Another is that the theist is supposing that, since each of the members of the series has a cause, that therefore the series as a whole needs a cause, which obviously does not follow. A third objection asserts that, given that each of the members of the infinite series has an explanation, this suffices to explain the series as a whole, thus blocking the demand for any further explanation for its existence. Rowe takes these objections seriously, but in the end he rejects them all as successful criticisms of the argument.

The first two objections can be considered together. Rowe denies that the proponent of the cosmological argument need make either of these errors in legitimately pressing his question concerning the existence of the whole. The collection of all human beings is not a human being, but this does not make the question as to why any humans exist at all otiose, at least on the supposition that there need not have been any human beings. By the same token, unless we have some reason for supposing that

---
1 See his summary of the argument of Rowe (1975), pages 115–67.

the infinite series of dependent beings is itself independent, the question concerning its existence remains open and legitimate. Furthermore, given the premise one above – a version of the *Principle of Sufficient Reason* or *PSR* – every positive fact needs an explanation, so the fact that the series exists at all, being a positive fact, will also need an explanation.

In the end, then, the atheist's critique of the argument hinges on the third objection, which claims that the series does have a sufficient reason for its existence, namely, the fact that each of the members of the series has a sufficient reason for its existence in the operation of the earlier members of the series upon which it depends. However, consider the following two questions:

1. Why does each member of the infinite series of dependent beings exist?
2. Why does an infinite series of dependent beings exist?[1]

It is intuitively obvious that an answer to the first question, even for each member of the series, is not an answer to the second question. For, given that none of the members of the series is a non-dependent or necessary being, it remains conceivable that none of them need have existed at all; in such case, neither would the series have existed. As such, the infinite series need not have existed at all and the fact that it exists has not been accounted for, despite the fact that, *on the supposition that such a series exists*, the explanation of each of the members can be explained by reference to the operation of other members of the series.

At this point, the atheist will most likely throw in the towel and reject the first premise of the argument, the PSR, and assert that the existence of the whole series is simply a surd fact without any further explanation. There is no positive proof, after all, that the PSR is true, nor could there be, since according to Leibniz and Clarke, it is a self-evident first principle. If the atheist declines the PSR, insisting on reflection that it is not self-evident or rationally necessary to him, the Leibniz/Clarke argument will fail as a proof for God's existence. This, of course, is what Rowe concludes; since the argument will only persuade those who accept the PSR as a rationally self-evident principle, it fails as a *demonstration* of God's existence; therefore, it does not provide the rational proof for God's existence that it promises. At the same time, it does not follow that those who accept the conclusion of the argument on the minimal assumption of the PSR are somehow irrational or dogmatic.

Discussion of the Leibniz/Clarke argument is ongoing. In 2004, for example,

---

1 Rowe (Fourth edition, 2007) pages 26–30.

Richard Gale who, like Rowe, is an atheist proposed a further clarification of the argument that succeeds in weakening premise one while strengthening the argument's conclusion. He argues, among other things, that the principle of sufficient reason can be derived from a weaker principle, that such an explanation is merely possible.[1] In addition, Garrigou-LaGrange offered a derivation of the PSR from the principle of non-contradiction.[2] If either of these lines of argument produces any results, then the atheist will have to argue not merely that it is possible that there is no explanation for the origin of the universe, but that no such explanation is even possible. This appears to be a formidable burden of proof for the atheist to carry.

THE NEW PHYSICO–THEOLOGY I: THE "BIG BANG" COSMOLOGICAL ARGUMENT

Since the beginning of Western science, the decided preference of cosmologists has been to suppose that the universe has always existed. Aristotle defended the thesis of the eternity of the world and his authority among scientists made it the mainstream view down to the twentieth century. However, in one of the most remarkable reversals in the history of science, the thesis that the universe had a beginning in time – or rather that time and space themselves had a beginning – seemed well established by the turn of the 21st century.[3]

Beginning in the 1920's, data gathered from the huge reflecting telescopes at Mt. Wilson and Mt. Palomar in California began to cast doubt on the eternity of the world. In 1922, Edwin Hubble was able to confirm the Island Universe hypothesis put forward by Kant and LaPlace in the eighteenth century. Instead of the universe consisting of a uniformly distributed pattern of individual stars, Hubble observed that the Milky Way was just one among a vast number of galaxies separated by vast distances and that some regions of space were rather more densely packed with galaxies than others. If the universe were eternal, one would have expected the former sort of universe; the data, however, suggested the latter.

Even more surprising, however, was the data derived from the "red shift" in the light from distant galaxies. Light approaching an observer tends to increase in frequency, which is detected by scientific instruments as belonging to the "blue" range of the colour spectrum; light moving away from an observer tends to "stretch out" and get shifted into the "red" end of the spectrum. The "red shift" suggested that the

---

1 See Gale in Peterson and Vanarragon pages 114–130 and 132–34
2 Garrigou–LaGrange (1934) pages 176–181; the argument was apparently originally devised by Wolff.
3 In what follows I am largely following Herrick (1999), pages 202–18.

distant galaxies were moving away from the Milky Way, the galaxy containing the Solar System, at a high rate of speed. This suggested that the universe was expanding like a beach ball attached to a bicycle pump. This discovery was also troublesome for defenders of the eternity of the universe. If the universe was infinitely old and had been governed by the same system of laws for all time, then the galaxies ought to be both uniformly distributed and infinitely far apart; once again, however, the data suggested otherwise.

In 1927, the Belgian physicist Georges LeMaitre came to the idea that the present distribution of matter in the universe might be explained in terms of an explosion of some kind. Using Hubble's data, LeMaitre "ran the film backwards" and proposed that at one time all the matter in the universe had been packed into an infinitely small concentration known as a "singularity" and that this singularity had subsequently exploded with a "great noise" about 10 billion years ago. This hypothesis, if true, would mean that the universe had a discrete beginning: not only matter, but space and time itself came into existence at a calculable moment in the past. This, of course, was incompatible with the thesis that the universe had existed forever.

Although the "Big Bang" hypothesis (as its opponents called it) attracted some early support, most notably from Einstein, the great majority of physicists resisted the notion that the universe had come into existence in this way. In 1948, the "Steady State" hypothesis, championed by the English astronomer Fred Hoyle, proposed that the universe had been expanding forever and was infinitely big, but that new matter "popped" into existence *ex nihilo* in accordance with some unknown physical law to fill the gaps left behind as galaxies drifted apart, thus creating the impression of a "young" universe. The "Steady State" theory had the look of an *ad hoc* construction about it from the very beginning, but the inherent (and probably quite rational) conservatism inherent in rational inquiry made it seem an attractive alternative to the more straightforward "Big Bang" hypothesis. At this point, after all, no decisive empirical proof for the "Big Bang" was forthcoming.

All of this changed, however, in 1965. In the late 1940's two physicists, Alpher and Herman had predicted that if the "Big Bang" had actually occurred that there would be residual radiation in the form of extremely "cool" microwave radiation perhaps a few degrees above absolute zero. At the time, there was no way to detect this radiation if it existed and no will or finances to build a device that would do so. In 1965, two engineers working at Bell Labs in New Jersey, Arno Penzias and Robert Wilson, built a radio telescope to aid them in their research into the satellite transmission of radio waves. They detected an unexpected static and, after many attempts to eliminate it, eventually discovered that the source was extremely cool microwave radiation (approximately 3.5 degrees above absolute zero) bombarding the Earth from all directions at once. They published their results in a scientific journal, but it was not until a chance meeting between Wilson and an astronomer that the true significance of the discovery was understood. The "Big Bang" appeared to be confirmed at last by "novelty evidence" and Penzias and Wilson were awarded a Nobel Prize in Physics for what was undoubtedly one of the major discoveries of the twentieth century.

Today the "Big Bang" seems to be as well-established as any empirical thesis about the natural history of the universe can expect to be. The Galileo and Hubble space probes have seen to the "end of the universe" and our current best guess is that the universe is not only finite but also a "one-shot" phenomenon; it does not appear that there is enough matter in the universe for gravity to "reverse" the process of expansion and produce a "great crunch" to counteract the "Big Bang." If so, the universe will continue to expand indefinitely into the future until all the matter in the universe is spread so far apart that gravitational attraction will cease; at this point, the "heat death of the universe" will occur, and all physical processes in the universe will cease as well. The universe is not only finite in size and in the amount of matter it contains, it also has a calculable beginning moment and (apparently) a calculable final one as well. The universe, then, turns out to be the opposite in every respect of what it was supposed to be for so many centuries and our conception of the universe radically altered by the course of less than a century of important scientific discoveries.

Theists showed significant caution in embracing the apparent implications of "Big Bang" cosmology. In 1951, in an address to the Papal Academy of Sciences, Pope Pius XII acknowledged the "Big Bang" as "unexpected confirmation" of the Christian faith but emphasized that religious belief could not be based on the results, however suggestive, of the science of the day and that the only sure foundation for rational belief in God resides in the Five Ways of St. Thomas. However, as confidence in the "Big Bang" continues to mount, the question of the origin of the singularity naturally obtrudes. Since the singularity apparently could not have existed eternally prior to the "Big Bang" – since there existed nothing external to the singularity hence nothing that could induce it to explode out of a quiescent state – it seems to be the case that the occurrence of the "Big Bang" is simultaneous with the coming into existence of the singularity itself. This resonates quite nicely with the *fiat lux* of Genesis and suggests a further version of the Cosmological Argument:

1. The universe came into existence at a finite time in the past.
2. Nothing physical existed prior to the existence of the universe.

3. The physical universe did not come into existence out of nothing.
4. No chance mechanism could have produced the universe.
5. Therefore, the initial state of the universe must have had a non-physical cause.
6. The theistic creator God is a natural candidate for such a cause.
7. Therefore, God exists.

This, of course, is not a deductive proof of God's existence, but it has the cast of a scientific argument about it, one as well confirmed as any empirical claim about the universe can be expected to be.

Not surprisingly, most physicists and many philosophers have been no less resistant to this version of the cosmological argument as they were to the "Big Bang" itself and the search for a non-supernaturalistic explanation of the initial state of the universe has been a growth industry since even before the "Big Bang" was as firmly established as it appears to be today. In the 1950's, Brandon Carter proposed a "Many Worlds" interpretation of quantum theory, according to which every time a quantum-indeterministic event occurs, two separate universes come into existence; on this view, the "multiverse" is bound on chance alone to contain a universe like this one. In the 1960's, John Archibald Wheeler proposed a "Bang-Crunch" model according to which there have been an infinite number of cycles of expansion and contraction of the universe, at least one of which on chance principles is bound to be a universe like this one. Either of these views, if true, would provide an alternative to divine *creation ex nihilo*.

In the 1970's and '80's, many other speculative models for the origin of the universe have been suggested, far too many to be summarized here. Each of these challenges one or more of the above premises, by suggesting that there is something that existed prior to the existence of the universe (such as George Guth's "inflationary mechanism" that randomly generates universes) or some law ("the wave function of the universe") that somehow dictates that universe "pop" into existence out of nothing at a random moment. It has even been suggested that the whole question of the origin of the singularity can be avoided (or at least indefinitely postponed) by denying that there was a first moment of time, only a limit that scientific investigation can asymptotically approach but never actually reach.

To this point, none of these speculations has achieved general acceptance among cosmologists. Most of them are not testable even in principle and those that are, to the extent that they are, appear to be conclusively refuted by the relevant evidence. There are also obvious conceptual difficulties in many of these theories. A current lull in such speculations suggests that, for the moment at least, we have hit a dead end in this line of investigation.[1] Still, it is always premature to close the book on the future course of scientific research. Nothing in the natural sciences, especially in the volatile field of cosmology, is in principle unrevisable; indeed, nothing goes out of date faster than "the latest science" and philosopher who builds his system on it is likely to find that he or she has built on a foundation of sand. The only conclusion that we can draw from the foregoing is that the trend in scientific cosmology for the last century or so is strongly convergent with the claims of theism. This is both a surprising and a tantalizing result; how ultimately solid it proves to be remains to be seen.

THE *KALAM* COSMOLOGICAL ARGUMENT

Another new wrinkle in the ongoing history of the ontological argument is the revival of a neglected argument for God's existence popular among mediaeval Islamic and Jewish philosophers as well as a few Christian Platonists of the high Middle Ages. This argument, known as the *Kalam* cosmological argument, was first formulated by a Greek-speaking Syriac Christian neo-Platonist, John Philoponus, the premier Aristotelian scholar of his generation. In his commentary on the *Physics* and in independent treatises on Aristotle and Proclus, Philoponus claims to find a contradiction between the Greek pagan insistence on the eternity of the world and the Aristotelian rejection of the existence of any actual infinite. Since Philoponus accepts the soundness of Aristotle's arguments against the actual infinite, he rejects the thesis of the eternity of the world in favour of the Genesis account of creation by God *ex nihilo*. In 1979, an American philosopher and evangelical Christian apologist, William Lane Craig, revived this argument and has defended it against all comers within the context of modern physical science.[2]

Although Philoponus may have originated this argument, it received its fullest articulation at the hands of Muslim and Jewish exponents of *Kalam*, a word that literally means "speech" but which, like the Greek *logos*, can also mean "argument" or "rational discourse." *Kalam* is thus a kind of rational theology or apologetics, the use of reason by believers to justify the basic metaphysical presuppositions of the faith and to answer philosophical objections to it. Since all monotheists accept the *Genesis* account of creation in some form or other, it is not surprising that exponents of *Kalam*

---

[1] See Copan and Craig (2004) pages 219–266.
[2] See Craig (1979), especially pages 69–102; he has further developed and defended the argument in Craig and Smith (1993) as well as in many other places.

would use any available philosophical resources to defend the truth of this doctrine. In this way, the *Kalam* cosmological argument came to occupy a central position in Muslim and Jewish apologetics. Craig gives these thinkers the lion's share of credit for the formulation and defence of this argument, which he formulates as follows:

1. Whatever begins to exist has a cause.
2. The universe began to exist.
3. The universe has a cause.

The crucial premise, of course, is premise 2 above. Craig proposes the following argument for this premise:

1. An actual infinite cannot exist.
2. An infinite temporal regress of physical events is an actual infinite.
3. Therefore, an infinite temporal regress of physical events cannot exist.

Craig contrasts an *actual* infinite with a merely *potential* infinite. An actual infinite is a group or class consisting of an infinite number of members all of whom actually exist or have existed. A potential infinite is a class or group generable by an operation that has no terminus, such as additive succession or division; thus, a line is infinitely divisible since we can continue dividing it forever, at least in principle. Aristotle is willing to countenance the potentially infinite, but not an actual infinity. The modern account of infinity due to Cantor has not altered the situation, according to Craig; Cantor's theory of transfinite numbers is nothing more than an abstract, heuristic construct derived from conventionally adopted axiom system. It does not nor could it correspond to anything real.

The reason for this is that the notion of the actual infinite is incoherent. Craig argues for this by reference to a number of consequences of the notion of an actual infinite. For example, he mentions the paradox of Hilbert's Hotel, a hotel containing an infinite number of rooms each of which is occupied. Despite this, on the scenario just outlined, the hotel can accommodate any additional number of guests. Suppose an additional guest shows up. We can simply instruct the person in Room One of the hotel move to Room Two, telling the person in Room Two to move to Room Three, and so on *ad infinitum*. A similar expedient will allow us to accommodate any additional number of guests, even an infinite number of new arrivals! Russell's Tristam Shandy paradox illustrates another absurdity involved in the idea of the infinite. According to Sterne, Tristam Shandy writes his autobiography so slowly that it takes him a year to record the events of a single day; it appears from this that he must fall farther and farther behind the longer he lives. In fact, however, supposing that

Tristam Shandy lives for an infinite amount of time, there is no difficulty in principle in his having completed his autobiography, since he has lived as many years as he has days. By the same token, suppose that there exists a library consisting of an infinite number of books and that someone takes out a book. Common sense tells us that there is one less book in the collection than there was before; in fact, however, since there are an infinite number of books in the library, an infinite number remain, so that in fact there are no fewer books now than there were before. This will be so even if we double the number of books in the library, or halve it.

Nor could the past consist of an actually infinite series of previous events, since the past was formed by additive succession, and additive succession can never yield an actually infinite set of events. This is illustrated by the old saw "you can't count to infinity." If I begin counting now, no matter how long I continue to count – indeed, *even if I count forever*, I will only ever have counted to a finite number; nor will there ever be a point at which, by adding one more number, I will have gone from an infinite to an infinite set of counted numbers. So, given that the past is formed by additive succession, one event at a time, neither can the past constitute an actually infinite series of events. But if it is impossible for the past to constitute an actually infinite series of events, then it must consist of a finite series of such events. As such, there must have been a first event in the series and this requires an external cause. Once again, the theistic God naturally suggests itself as the likely candidate for such a cause.

The concept of infinity is tricky and few people understand it. Undoubtedly, this accounts for some of the diffidence that Craig's argument evokes. Defenders of the idea of the actual infinite maintain that the supposed paradoxes and incoherencies that Craig identifies in the Cantorian conception of the infinite are only *apparent* and not real; the impression that they are arises from confusing the infinite with a very large finite set. But the expectations and conditions that apply to finite sets are inappropriately applied in the case of infinite ones so to claim that the notion of the actually infinite is incoherent is really a kind of category mistake. So, while many people have been intrigued by Craig's argument and he has defended the argument against numerous critics – including mathematician and atheist philosopher Adolf Grunbaum – he remains its only significant exponent.

In addition, his stout defence of the argument has forced Craig to adopt a number of counterintuitive positions. For one thing, he has to reject the reigning 4-D conception of space-time in favour of genuine temporal succession in order to avoid the possibility that time constitutes a McTaggartean "B series" given all at once rather than one event at a time.¹ Secondly, he seems prepared to deny that there are an infinite number of truths, propositions and integers as well, since these would constitute actual infinities, albeit of abstract rather than concrete objects. Thirdly, Craig is forced to maintain that God existed timelessly but became a temporal being once He created the universe.² Craig argues with great skill for each of these claims and offers independent reasons for supposing them to be true wherever possible, but the overall impression that one comes away with is of someone in the grips of a theory.

Perhaps the main contribution of the *Kalam* cosmological argument is the suggestion that the past could not both be infinite and yet formed by additive succession. Exponents of the "infinite regress" objection to the cosmological argument usually assume the possibility that the past is infinite, while assuming that each of those past events is to be explained by previous events in the series. Both of these claims are necessary if the exponent of the infinite universe is to maintain both that a) there was no first moment of the universe and b) that the series of the whole is self-explanatory insofar as the occurrence/obtaining each of the events in the series can be explained by earlier moments in that series. However, if Craig is right, these two theses cannot be maintained together and the "infinite regress" objection to the cosmological argument is thus greatly weakened. At any rate, we can well agree with Rowe that the Cosmological Argument is certainly healthier now than it was fifty years ago and will undoubtedly continue to be discussed for the foreseeable future.

---

1 See Craig (2000a) and (2000b); in the first book he criticizes and rejects the tenseless or B theory of time; in the second, he argues for a reinterpretation of general relativity that makes it consistent with the objectivity of temporal passage (the A theory of time) and the Newtonian conception of absolute time.

2 Moreland and Craig (2001) pages 511–15. See also the works by Craig referenced there.

Chapter Eight

The Teleological Argument *Redivivus*

The teleological argument was the premier argument for God's existence in the eighteenth and nineteenth centuries, eclipsing both the ontological and the cosmological arguments. The reason for this was largely because it was regarded as a scientific argument, one implied by and justified by the New Science. All of the major figures of the scientific revolution in England – John Ray (the father of Natural History), Robert Boyle (the father of modern chemistry) and Sir Isaac Newton (father of modern physics) – were all extremely interested in religious questions and believed that in studying natural science they were discovering the divine plan for the universe. Ray initiated the modern design argument in his *The Wisdom of God Manifested in the Works of Creation* (1691)[1] and Boyle established a lecture series at Cambridge specifically intended to demonstrate that modern science reinforces the Christian faith. Newton wrote more on the interpretation of Scripture than he did on natural scientific questions. Although Boyle, Newton and Clarke were hardly orthodox Christians, they were nevertheless all theists and convinced of the religious value of scientific inquiry. Einstein once said that all he desired to do was to understand God's thoughts; British scientists of the late seventeenth century believed that they were actually achieving this. The marriage of science with religion is reflected by the large number of clergyman–scientists (which included Erasmus Darwin, grandfather of Charles Darwin) that populated the eighteenth and nineteenth centuries.

The key to this union of science with religion was the notion of *design*. The world as we see it around us is an extremely complex, orderly and beautiful arrangement of mutually adjusted elements, a *cosmos* or "beautiful order" that operates in such a manner as to achieve certain ends. The notion that such an order could have come

---

1 This book is no longer in print. However, there is a contemporary book that incorporates a good deal of Ray's text, as well as that of Robert Boyle's *The Christian Virtuoso*: see Cotton Mather's *The Christian Philosopher* (1994); the text was edited by Winton Solberg.

about by mere chance was too incredible to countenance and even Hume's arguments against "natural religion" had very little impact on either academic or popular commitment to the classic argument from design.

The happy marriage of science and philosophy was not to last, however. According to one popular reconstruction of the progress of human knowledge, as our knowledge of the natural world increased in the eighteenth century, nature became increasingly desupernaturalized, so that by the turn of the nineteenth century, the "clockwork universe" of Newtonian mechanism could now be seen as an eternal, self-contained and self-sustaining system governed by a set of immanent laws built right into the fabric of matter itself. Thus, when LaPlace replied to Napoleon that he had no need for the hypothesis of God in his cosmology, he was simply reporting the fact that scientific progress had eliminated any need for God either as the first cause or the designer of the physical universe. However, one area in which the spectre of design remained untouched was in the realm of biology, where the obviously teleological character of the bodily organs and the amazing adaptations of organisms to their environments seemed impossible to account for on any hypothesis other than that of divine design.

Darwin, of course, changed all that. His *Origin of Species*,[1] published in 1859 showed how a combination of chance and necessity, i.e. of random variation and natural selection, could explain both the diversity of species and their apparent adaptation without recourse to an overall plan or design for the universe, and thus without reference to a Designer. The implications of this discovery for the teachings of natural religion were immediate and obvious: the classical design argument seemed fatally undermined. In the U.S., for example, a liberal Unitarian like Harvard philosopher Francis Bowen and a conservative Reformational Protestant like Charles Hodge of Princeton Theological seminary could share a common resistance to Darwin, since despite their sectarian differences, both were adherents of the Scottish philosophy and regarded the argument from design as the primary rational basis for belief in God. Not surprisingly, both wrote in opposition to Darwin's *Origin of Species*.[2] Nonetheless, Darwin's natural history proved so compelling that it very quickly became ensconced at the heart of modern science.

Not only was the argument from design apparently fatally undermined, but the cause of irreligion gained a tremendous boost from Darwinism. Darwin and Huxley

---

1 See Darwin (1995).
2 See Kuklick (1988); not all exponents of Christianity and Scottish Common Sense philosophy opposed evolution; see Benz (1967).

proclaimed themselves to be agnostic about God's existence. Marx and Engels hailed Darwin's discovery as the final blow against the Christian view of the world. Richard Dawkins claims that Darwinism made it possible for one to be an intellectually satisfied atheist. As a consequence of fundamentalist opposition to evolution, many people, including intellectuals, have been tempted to convert Darwin's theory from a well-confirmed hypothesis in natural history into a kind of speculative cosmic philosophy entailing the atheistic worldview and capable of explaining, among other things, both the origin and persistence of religious belief. On both sides we find the dogmatic insistence that belief in God and acceptance of the evolutionary hypothesis in natural history is impossible. More generally, we find many scientists and philosophers who believe, and even some who argue, that science refutes religious belief. Things have come full circle.

However, the circle may be turning again. Just as the ontological and cosmological arguments have received new life as the result of innovations in formal logic and astronomy, so too has the teleological argument received new attention from philosophers and scientists as the result of recent discoveries in cosmology and astrophysics. To this remarkable reversal of fortune we now turn.

F. R. TENNANT'S TELEOLOGICAL ARGUMENT

The flickering flame of the teleological argument was kept alive throughout most of the twentieth century by F. R. Tennant, a Cambridge theologian whose two–volume work *Philosophical Theology*,[1] first published in 1930, remained influential for the next fifty years. Tennant, who pioneered the inductivist approach in the philosophy of religion, presents his version of the teleological argument in the first four chapters of volume two of this book. It represents a new kind of teleological argument, one that the contemporary "Fine Tuning" argument resembles in important ways. Although Tennant was not an analytic philosopher and wrote before the period concerning us here, he is clearly a precursor of the contemporary teleological argument. So it is with his version of the argument we will begin. However, given the complexity and scientific sophistication of Tennant's treatment, what follows will be a reconstruction (or perhaps more accurately an *impression*) of the basic structure of the argument rather than its detailed exposition.

Tennant explicitly adopts an "empiricist" approach to natural theology, reminis-

---

1 Tennant (1930), Volume II, pages 1–120.

cent of that adopted by Cleanthes in Hume's *Dialogues*.[1] We must first marshal the evidence from experience in favour of theism and then use that data to construct a theoretical model of the theistic God. In this, Tennant takes himself to be adopting the same strategy used by the natural scientist in investigating nature within a broadly "realist" conception of the scientific enterprise. We do not apprehend the external world *as such*, according to Tennant; it remains a Kantian *noumenon* so far as we are concerned. Rather, we immediately apprehend only states of our own minds which we take to be *phenomena*, i.e. subjective appearances of external objects in experience existing there as the effects of the influence of those objects on our minds. Our only clues to the nature of these objects are these phenomena, and scientific theory is the "interface" between the phenomenal and the noumenal realms for us. Our careful observation of the phenomena suggests hypotheses to us which we formulate and test in experience; on the basis of such testing, we form a theoretical conception of the noumenal world that transcends our consciousness. However, this procedure in no way rules out the possibility that phenomenal experience might suggest to us the existence of a noumenal reality other than and additional to what we are able to capture in the net of science, in which case we will have no less (though no more) reason to suppose that the phenomena that present themselves as the effects of the activity of that additional reality are just as veridical as those that lead us to postulate the world described by our physical models. In such case, theology will be no less "scientific" than is science itself conceived along realist lines. Since such a possibility cannot be ruled out *a priori*, it remains that we must inquire as to whether this possibility is realized. Tennant, of course, believes that it is.

We can characterize Tennant's version of the teleological argument as follows:

1. The phenomenal universe gives every appearance of being a teleological system.
2. This is not the consequence of any inbuilt teleological principles or processes inherent in nature itself.
3. Nor is it merely the expression of human cognitive psychology.
4. Nor is it merely the consequence of human imagination or convention.
5. Either this appearance of being a teleological system is a mere illusion or it has its source in some explanation that lies beyond either nature or the finite human mind.
6. Given the pervasiveness of teleology in nature, it is not credible that the appearance that the universe is a teleological system is mere illusion.

---

1 See Hume (1980), especially pages 15–22.

7. The only principle of teleological order with which we are acquainted is personal agency, which uses intellect and will to form purposes, to make plans and execute them in intentional action.
8. The theistic God is only the only credible candidate for such an agent.
9. Therefore, God exists.

Or rather, God *probably* exists, since the evidential basis for the conclusion is inductive rather than deductive. This does not mean, of course, that there is anything defective about the conclusion of the argument on that score; for Tennant, there is no reason to believe that the conclusion of the argument might not be as credible as the results of any scientific inquiry and thus recommend itself with the same degree of confidence as we routinely invest in those results. Scientists do not generally qualify the results of their inquiries with the adjective "probably" despite the fact that they are proven by inductive procedures. Neither is it required that theologians do so if the procedures they use and the evidence they acquire are roughly of the same order as those of the scientist.

The Phenomenon of Law-Like Regularity in Nature

Tennant begins with a long examination of the concept of a law in science. In modern mathematical physics, physical theories are mathematical models the central elements of which are *laws* taking the form universal generalizations that assert that, given certain conditions are met, certain results will follow. Tennant compares these laws to the standard patterns of inference in logic; they themselves entail no substantive conclusions but any scientific argument instantiating any of them will be valid as a consequence. This seems clear enough but in fact, says Tennant, the concept of a law in science is highly problematic. Despite what many philosophers have said, scientific laws are not merely empirical generalizations based on observed regularities in experience. Laws are expected (e.g.) to support counterfactuals; if it is a law of nature that copper expands when heated, it will also be the case that *this* piece of copper *would have* expanded *if* it had been heated, despite the fact that it never was. Laws claim a kind of necessity that makes them applicable beyond the range of both actual and possible experience. At the same time, it is not easy to explain what this necessity consists in. It is not logical necessity, for example; if it were, we would be able to know the laws of nature *a priori* and only one set of such laws would ultimately be possible. However, the laws of physics are clearly contingent and knowable only *a posteriori*. Nor can this necessity be explained *a la`* Kant, as merely reflecting the constitutive powers of the human mind and the necessary conditions for anything to be possible as an object of experience for us, since in any case these "laws of constitution" are no less contingent and fortuitous than the scientific laws that they ground. If Kant claims that space, time and the categories are necessary conditions for anything to be an object of experience *simpliciter*, then he goes far beyond what he can prove; if he makes the more modest claim that this is what is required in order for anything to be an object *for us*, this leaves open the possibility that there might be other categorical schemes that other beings might have instantiated in preference to our own. Conventionalist or relativist accounts of scientific law are equally suspect, says Tennant. It is simply an historical fact that the pressure of inquiry constrains what theories we ultimately adopt and forces sincere inquirers toward at least a rough consensus with regard to what the laws of nature are; this gives the lie to the notion that they are merely the product of imagination, convention or some purely political mechanism. We do not legislate for nature; we can only discover what laws actually obtain there by empirical scientific inquiry.

Further, so far as laws are merely mathematical constructs, they are abstract or ideal objects seemingly incapable of any causal influence; so much so, that in actual practice these laws always have to be adjusted or "fitted" to the empirical context in order to be useful for making specific "real world" predictions. Yet neither can laws be characterized as expressing relations of causal necessity between noumenal objects given their inherent and dispositional properties and thus in that way reducible to them. For we have no access to noumenal objects and their properties; these remain theoretical entities for us, so that we attribute the properties to them (especially the *mikra*, the supposed ultimate constituents of external bodies) that are required in order to make the laws work, rather than the other way round. Such a procedure, then, is bound to be circular. But even if we could justly cash out the operation of laws in terms of processes and mechanisms connecting cause and effect, at some point we will have to admit some immediate causal connections, on pain of infinite regress; when we do this, we will have bottomed out in something both contingent and inexplicable. It remains, say Tennant, that we have no plausible explanation from within nature itself either for the existence of the laws of nature or of their objectivity and apparent necessity. At the same time, the entire weight of scientific inquiry appears to presuppose and to reinforce both of these claims. Laws are absolutely essential to our understanding of nature but do not seem to be deeply embedded either in our psychological make–up or in the noumenal realm our scientific theories are designed to make intelligible to us.

The presence of law-like regularity in nature, then, is a pervasive phenomenon that fairly cries out for an explanation and for which no immanent explanation is forthcoming. If the universe were self-explanatory, we would feel no compulsion to go beyond it and postulate the existence of anything beyond the world described by physics. That, however, is not what the data of experience suggests. Instead, the presence of law-like regularity in nature, a presupposition of the very possibility of scientific inquiry and research, naturally leads us (as we have seen even Hume admits) to seek its cause in something other than the physical universe as revealed to us by science. Experience itself, then, broadly construed, testifies to something existing beyond the world revealed to us by mere sense-experience; to deny this is to arbitrarily ignore the data in favour of a preference that the physical world be the only world, which Tennant would say is hardly the objective attitude embodied in science. Perhaps, but why then suppose that this cause is anything like the theistic God?

An Anthropic World

Law-like regularity strongly suggests the hand of intelligence in the structure of the world, since mind is a principle of order. This, however, is a far cry from anything like the theistic God. Tennant therefore supplements his evidence from law-like regularity with additional observations that suggest that the world has an overall plan or purpose, one in which the production of human beings plays a prominent (if not exclusive or overriding) part. We live, Tennant says, in an *anthropic world*, a world as though designed to bring about the existence of persons such as ourselves. We find the basic structure of the world, with all of its laws and processes, such as to favour the production of beings such as ourselves, something that we would have neither right nor reason to expect if the physical universe were merely the product of chance. As such, the universe presents itself to us in experience as not merely law-governed but *purposive*, and this strongly argues for an intelligent, purposive designer of the sort that the theistic God is taken to be. But what is the evidence?

Tennant presents five putative facts about the world that he maintains are best explained by postulating that the physical world is a teleological system that was designed and instituted by the theistic God. We may summarize them as follows:

> 1. *The Universe is intelligible to us* The first "cosmic coincidence" noted by Tennant is the connaturality of mind and world that makes science and knowledge possible in the first place. Having argued at length in the firstvolume of *Philosophical Theology* that mind and soul as revealed to us in con-

sciousness are governed by principles very different from those that dictate the behaviour of inanimate nature, there appears to be no immanent explanation for the mutual adjustment of mind to world. Yet such adjustment there evidently is and it is totally unexpected on naturalism.

2. *The Course of Natural History* Tennant accepts the notion that human beings are the product of evolution. However, even given the mechanism of evolutionary development, there is no reason whatsoever to suppose that beings like us should have ever existed, nor indeed that any complex organisms should exist at all. Yet human beings do exist despite the long odds against it given natural selection and, contrary to all expectations were produced by that process in a surprisingly short period of time. It is as though the evolutionary process were being guided by some force to realize a particular end.

3. *The Hospitability of the Universe to Life* A third unexpected aspect of our world is that it is hospitable to the very process of evolution to begin with. Again, there is no law that dictates that this should be the case and presumably, not just any world is a world in which the evolutionary process will even be possible, let alone actually occur. The possibility of evolution presupposes a surprisingly large number of physical conditions that it can neither produce nor explain. When placed in this wider context, evolution is just as mysterious as any other law-governed process operating in the physical world.

4. *The Beauty of the Universe* Human beings in all times and places have marvelled at and been ravished by the order, complexity, integration and balance to be observed in nature; this includes not only children and common folk but also great artists and scientists as well. While some will naturally tend to dismiss the aesthetic qualities of nature as mere bathos, taking the facts at face value the gratuitous beauty of nature is as surprising as it is unexpected.

5. *The Phenomenon of Morality* Man is a natural product, but also a moral agent. Since nature itself is amoral, it has no potentiality in and of itself to produce either moral agency or an awareness of moral obligation. Yet, unless we are willing to put aside morality itself as a sham, the fact that moral agents have emerged from the evolutionary process requires an explanation. This is not, Tennant would say, simply a matter of using Evolution to explain how moral *behaviour* emerges – as Socio-biology would claim to do forty years later – because this simply explains it away as the cunning of the selfish gene. If genuine moral obligation exists and emerges from nature, we have a serious puzzle on our hands.

Tennant's explanation for these facts is to propose that appearance reflects reality: the universe is an anthropic system, a teleological process purposely designed to produce beings such as ourselves – self-conscious, rational moral agents. This hypothesis unifies all the data we have reviewed, data which is wholly unexpected on purely naturalistic grounds and thus constitutes "recalcitrant data" for that hypothesis. The naturalist can both shrug his or her shoulders and say "Well, that's just the way it is", refusing to offer an explanation for these facts or adopt the *ad hoc* procedure of either attempting to explain each of these separately or try to discount them altogether. Further, attempts to avoid theism and replace the telic motor of the universe with *élan vital* or some other, impersonal, sub–rational force makes it just as mysterious how the universe developed its apparently purposive cast. Only theism provides the rational and purposive intelligence that most naturally accounts for the presence of apparent purpose and design in nature. Thus, theism suggests itself as the best explanation of the teleological appearance of the world.

THE NEW PHYSICO–THEOLOGY II: THE "FINE TUNING" ARGUMENT

In the 1970s, a new version of the Teleological Argument offered further support for Tennant's anthropic universe hypothesis. This argument, known as the "fine-tuning" argument, is based on current physical theory and our understanding of the role that the fundamental constants in our most basic physical laws in determining the character and potentiality contained in our universe. Observation informs us that we live in a universe containing self-conscious rational beings such as ourselves, and thus that the universe in which we live is capable of producing and supporting such beings. All of this seems highly unlikely on the face of it, as exponents of the teleological argument have always asserted. How improbable it is, however, was not calculable until quite recently and the results are really quite astounding.[1]

The fundamental constants are the most basic properties of the fundamental particles that function in our current best explanations for the nature of things. They are called constants because they are the same throughout the universe. These constants are, as Tennant would say "alogical" from the rational point of view; they are neither logically necessary nor knowable *a priori* and, when empirically discovered, remain contingent and logically arbitrary. Each of these constants is also causally independent from the others, so that any or all of them might have varied without affecting

---

[1] See the essays by Robin Collins in Copan and Moser (2003) pages 132–45 and in Manson (2003), especially pages 180–190.

or being affected by the others. Further, although each of these constants for all we know could have had an infinite number of different values, they have quite precise values despite being apparently arbitrary. From the purely natural point of view, there is no reason why these constants ought to have the values they do.

What makes these values interesting and suggestive, say exponents of the "Fine-tuning" argument, is that *if even one of these constants had been even slightly different from what it is the universe as we know it, and ourselves, would have failed to exist*. If we set a computer to work creating simulations of the universe on randomly generated values for these constants, the results would be uniformly uninteresting; nothing like the complex, beautiful and life-friendly universe in which we live would be produced because one or more of the necessary conditions for such a universe would have failed to exist. Indeed, according to some cosmologists, the chances that a universe like this one would be produced by such a random process are extremely long – something on the order of 1 in 10 to the 40th power! At the same time, however, these universal constants only represent the physically necessary conditions for the *bare possibility* of intelligent life in the universe. In order for such to beings to *actually* exist in a universe such as ours, the other necessary and sufficient conditions for intelligent life have to obtain. In turn, we find that the likelihood of those additional conditions being met, even in a huge universe like ours, is also very unlikely. Yet, despite all the odds, intelligent life does exist.

On Tennant's anthropic hypothesis, what seemed arbitrary and contingent now becomes clear: these oddly assorted values, being precisely the ones that are required in order for us to exist, are precisely the values that would have been chosen by an intelligent designer of the universe. On the hypothesis that such a designer exists what appeared surprising, arbitrary and fortuitous becomes intelligible and even to be expected; this, according to Peirce, is the primary sign of a likely hypothesis. Further, in order that the bare possibility of intelligent life might be actualized, a huge universe capable of producing the complex and antecedently improbable environment in which life could develop was also necessary and an intelligent designer intent on producing a universe containing such life would therefore be motivated to produce it. Again, the claim here is not that the universe exists solely to produce beings such as ourselves, only that this is reasonably thought to be one end for which the universe created by an intelligent designer might have created it.

Responses to the Fine-Tuning Argument

Most of evidence upon which the "Fine-Tuning" argument is based was discovered and presented by atheistic scientists who stoutly resisted the apparent theistic implications of that data. Oddly enough, however, the idea that the universe might be an anthropic system did find favour with some of them. The most common response to the data for "fine tuning" was to suggest that the existence of the universe could be explained by something called the *Anthropic Principle*.[1] In fact, several different principles, representing different strategies for "handling" the data for "fine-tuning", have gone by this name. For example, some have suggested that the fact that human beings exist explains the existence of the universe on the grounds that the fact that human beings exist *entails* that all of the necessary and sufficient conditions for the existence of such beings have been met; this is sometimes called the Weak Anthropic Principle. Therefore, we are told, we ought not to be surprised that the conditions for the existence of beings such as ourselves have been met, since if they had not, we would not be here to marvel at that fact! The usual response by advocates of the argument to such claims is that the sort of explanation offered by the Weak Anthropic Principle is unsatisfactory because it fails to provide a properly causal explanation for the fact that the universe is an anthropic system. That the stars twinkle entails that the stars are far away but does not cause their being far away; rather, it is being far away that causes them to twinkle for an Earth-bound observer. Further, the sheer improbability that the universe is an anthropic system on purely naturalistic assumptions ought to be sufficient to make our marvelling at that fact eminently reasonable.

A more extreme Strong Anthropic Principle boldly proclaims that the universe is a teleological system governed by the Anthropic Principle conceived of as something like a universal law. For example, even before the "Fine Tuning" data was published, Canadian metaphysician John Leslie[2] proposed that the existence of the universe could be explained axiologically, i.e. on the ground that it is better than not that the universe should exist, and to postulate that this quasi-moral imperative was built into the very structure of reality, so that a universe like this one must inevitably exist. Cosmologists such as Barrow and Tipler in the 1970's suggested that there was a kind of imperative built into the universe that inevitably requires that human beings be produced, perfected and made (in a sense) immortal. However, very few philosophers or scientists have found this an attractive alternative, given the speculative nature of the SAP.

Other critics have attempted to adapt the Darwinian "chance and necessity" model

---

1 See Barrow and Tipler (1974); for my account here I am largely following Herrick (1999), pages 102–130.
2 See Leslie (1979).

to explain the appearance of design without recourse to a designer. In the 1960's, the Many Worlds Hypothesis and the Oscillating Universe Hypothesis were proposed to explain the existence of a complex world; on these views, there are either an infinite number of simultaneously existing but causally isolated worlds or there has been an infinite series of "bangs" and "crunches." As such, given any probability greater than zero, no matter how small, it is mathematically inevitable that in an infinite amount of time a universe like this one would come to exist. Once again, the existence of such a universe, though initially surprising, proves on analysis to be fully expected. Both of these alternatives remain epistemically possible; however, there is little motivation to embrace either of these conceptions other than to evade the clutches of theism. Further, both are more metaphysically more complex than theism and so less likely to be true on that ground alone.

The Future of the Teleological Argument

In the Hammer *Dracula* movies of the 1950's and 60's, the vampire would always be staked and presumably destroyed at the end of each film. However, at the beginning of the next film in the series, some casual passer-by or thrill-seeking Victorian would come along and remove the stake, causing Dracula to regenerate and launch a new reign of terror. This metaphor reveals both the strength and the weakness of the teleological argument. On the one hand, each version of the teleological argument, whether Thomas's fifth way, Butler's "Clockwork" universe, Paley's argument from adaptation or the modern "Fine Tuning" argument, is derived from and cannot be separated from the reigning scientific paradigm of its time. Because of this, it remains vulnerable to advances in scientific knowledge; thus, as paradigm succeeds paradigm, each particular version of the teleological argument becomes *passé*, the expression of an outdated physical worldview. Yet history teaches us that each succeeding paradigm gives rise to a new version of the argument, one adapted to the exigencies of that paradigm's model of the universe. Due to this fact, claims to the effect that the teleological argument has been refuted are always as premature as claims to the effect that, at long last, we have discovered the final truth about the nature of the physical world. Unless and until we arrive at a scientific conception of things that demonstrates the absolute necessity and inevitability of this universe in such a way as to make all further questions about its origin and structure otiose, we can anticipate that there will be a version of the teleological argument suggested by whatever dominant paradigm happens to reign at any particular time.

Theists, then, can never rest their case for God's existence on any particular version of the teleological argument, since the great likelihood is that the argument in question will go stale after a while along with the theories that motivate it. At the same time, however, this does not mean that their faith in what we might call the *metateleological argument* – i.e. the argument that there will always be some aspects of the world-order that are central and pervasive to it that nevertheless are not explicable in terms of anything either *a priori* or intrinsic to the world-order itself – is necessarily misplaced. This is precisely what we have witnessed in the past and so what it is reasonable for us to anticipate will continue to occur in the future. Stake him as we will, it seems likely that there will come a day when Dracula has risen from the grave.

Chapter Nine

Post-Deductivism and the Rise of Christian Philosophy

Although Swinburne's Inductivism represents a natural response to the "paradigm-shift" away from the Deductivism of the 1950's, it has not proven to be the mainstream of the theistic revival that occurred in the last three decades of the twentieth century. Instead, a much more radical response to the atheistic critique of religious belief, one that eschews the defence of theism *per se* in favour of a distinctive sort of Christian apologetics, has become the dominant position among theistic philosophers of religion. Alvin Plantinga, its major exponent, calls it "Christian Philosophy"; the centrepiece of this philosophy is something he calls "Reformed Epistemology." I prefer to call the Plantingan perspective – propagated across the U.S. by his legion of followers – the Post-Deductive Paradigm or *Post-Deductivism*. As I see it, both the distinctive character and intrinsic radicalism of this perspective consists in its attempts to subvert the presuppositions of the deductivist approach, many of which are shared by inductivists as well.

It has generally been supposed, for example, that philosophy is the search for truth and that, for the philosopher, truth is highest goal of intellectual inquiry, trumping any substantive beliefs that we might have prior to beginning that inquiry. The philosopher was supposed to antecedently possess a love for truth and to cultivate certain virtues, such as objectivity and a willingness to follow the argument wherever it might lead, entailing a certain diffidence with regard to any substantive beliefs one might have. A consequence of this is that a philosopher ought to be willing to adjust or revise his or her beliefs in the face of new evidence. More important than this, however, a philosopher was expected to adopt those beliefs that, on the whole, seem to him or her to be most likely to be true given as complete and thorough a review of the relevant arguments and evidence as is possible or appropriate to the case. While not all philosophers are going to agree, of course, it is at least a requirement that a philosopher believe that he or she has good reasons for what he or she believes and be prepared to make a case for those views. What does seem to be ruled out is that it is permissible for a philosopher – or anyone else for that matter – to hold substantive views about any matter without adequate justification or grounds.

We have already seen how both the neo-Thomists and the analytic atheists of the 1950's applied these ideas to theism and especially to the question of God's existence. Flew's Stratonician principle, for example – the foundation for his presumption of atheism – made it incumbent on theists to either prove God's existence or abandon belief in God on pain of irrationality. While inductivists eschew the rigorous standards demanded by deductivists like Flew, they also tie the rationality of belief in God to considered judgment on the overall evidence. The Post-Deductivist position, however, maintains that belief in God is both permissible and can even be rational *without being based on argument or evidence at all*. A view like this, of course, seems completely counterintuitive and will be a non-starter for most philosophers. Let me attempt to make it more intelligible by laying out some of the historical background of the view.

PROTESTANT PHILOSOPHY BEFORE ANALYSIS

In the last chapter, I briefly described how the happy marriage between science and Christianity ended with Darwin. After an initial spasm of resistance, however, most "mainstream" Protestants and Catholics were able to reconcile themselves to the new evolutionary paradigm. However, for traditional Reformational Protestants – especially those in the Calvinist tradition – Darwinism created a major crisis of faith. For Princeton Theological Seminary's Charles Hodge, the answer to the question asked by his 1874 book "What is Darwinism?" is plain and clear: it is atheism.[1] According to Hodge, Darwinian evolution cannot be reconciled with the literal witness of the Scriptures and for the Christian this is all one needs to know in order to affirm the falsity of Darwin's theory. For a Christian, the Bible is the highest source of truth and, if natural science contradicts that truth, the Christian has no choice but to reject it. The position taken by Hodge was far from universal, even among "evangelical" Protestants. However, many sincere Protestants came to the same conclusion, precipitating the "fundamentalist" movement of the Twentieth Century.

Reformational Protestants could do no better than to look back to the founders of the Reformation, Luther and Calvin themselves, to find the "fundamentalist" view

---

1 Hodge (1994); this book has been continuously in print since its first appearance over 125 years ago and is currently available in facsimile from Michigan Historical Reprints (2006).

articulated in opposition to mediaeval Scholasticism. Luther and Calvin rejected natural theology as part of their critique of Catholic theology, maintaining that the rule of faith is to be found only in Scripture, embraced by faith through the influence of the Holy Spirit. We have already seen, for example, how Barth both rejected natural theology and embraced the notion that the Christian literally lives in a different world, cognitively speaking, from that of the unregenerate non-Christian, such that there is no common ground from which the question of God's existence can be discussed, let alone resolved. For Barth, apologetics of the classic sort is useless: believers do not need it, unbelievers will not be convinced by it. Theology must begin and end with Dogmatics. This does not mean that Barth does not find occasion to discuss most of the traditional issues discussed by philosophers of religion; however, it is always revelation, as understood through Luther's eyes, that has the last word, not neutral reason.

The Dutch Calvinist tradition is at one with Barth in rejecting natural theology and embracing both the fideism and the sufficiency of Scripture as the fount of all truth. Dutch Reformed theologians such as Abraham Kuyper and Herman Bavinck reject all the proofs for God's existence, often using Humean criticisms to refute the traditional arguments for the truth of theism.[1] According to Kuyper and Bavinck, we are justified by faith, and faith is incompatible with proof; so if God's existence could be proved, faith would be unnecessary and with it the possibility of salvation excluded. The failure of all such proofs, then, is a kind of confirmation of Protestant fideism, since it is exactly what we would expect to be the case if the *sola fide* doctrine were true. At the same time, *sola fide* grounds *sola scriptura*; there is no way to God except through faith in Christ, and no way to Christ except through a Spirit–inspired reading of the Scriptures. Since the modern world has neither faith nor a willingness to read the Scriptures through Christian eyes, there is no way of "proving" the claims of Christianity to that world; what the Christian knows through the witness of the Holy Spirit is known in the only way that God has made it possible for us to know that truth. A seemingly unbridgeable gulf separates the regenerate and the unregenerate mind.

Still, there is a modern world to evangelize; the Christian cannot cut him- or herself off in splendid isolation and thereby absolve him- or herself from the task of witnessing Christ to the world. In order to articulate a stance toward the world consistent with their doctrine of incommensurability, Bavinck and Kuyper adopt and

---

1 See Plantinga in Plantinga and Wolterstorff (1978) pages 64–5, 72–3, 87–93 and references.

modify the German philosophical concept of a *worldview*.[1] In their apologetic works, Kuyper and Bavinck emphasize the notion that Christianity is not merely a religion or a set of Scriptural dogmas and doctrines that tell us how to get to Heaven. Instead, Christianity is a comprehensive world-picture, a "world-hypothesis" with its own, Biblically-inspired metaphysics, epistemology, natural history of the world and narrative history of salvation. This Christian worldview is all-embracing and admits nothing beyond its grasp or reach; not even natural science ought to be regarded as autonomous, as independent of the Biblical perspective. For the Christian, all knowledge must be made captive to Christ and the Christian perspective imported into every arena of thought and practice. Implicit in this conception is the notion that there is a distinctly Christian, Bible-based philosophical perspective as well.

The rise of the modern research university at the end of the nineteenth century saw the end of Christian domination in education generally and an increasingly secular cast to higher education both in the United States and in Britain. Indeed, this process was accelerated in the U.S. by the doctrine of separation of Church and State. However, just as there are many Catholic colleges and universities in the U.S., so too are there many small sectarian colleges, seminaries and bible schools, many dating from the nineteenth century, scattered across the U.S., the major concentration of which are in the American Midwest. Most of these schools offer courses in philosophy but demand that these courses be taught from a sectarian Christian perspective. Those engaged in teaching such courses, then, have an incentive to articulate a "Christian" philosophy of some sort. For many of these philosophers, one takes whatever philosophy happens to be at hand and adapts it to Christian purposes. So, to take a typical example, D. Elton Trueblood, a Quaker who taught philosophy for many years at tiny Earlham College, became a widely-read evangelical Christian writer in the 1940's and '50's, producing generic philosophical defences of theism and Christianity.[2] Norman Geisler, another prolific Protestant writer and Baptist seminary president, earned his Ph.D. in Philosophy from Loyola and has articulated his philosophical defence of theism from a largely neo-Thomist perspective.[3] Stuart Hackett, who taught for many years at Wheaton College in Indiana, developed his own philosophical perspective, which he calls "Rational Empiricism" and puts to work in the defence of theism.[4] For all of these thinkers, philosophy retains at least some autonomy and makes some

---

1 On the development of this concept and its application to Christian apologetics, see Naugle (2002), especially chapters 1, 3 and 4.
2 See Trueblood (1960)
3 See Geisler (1979)
4 See Hackett (1957, second edition 1974), especially pages 37–113

appeal to neutral reason as an appropriate arbiter of philosophical views. There are many others as well.

For a distinctively Protestant philosophical system, however, we have to turn to *Presuppositionalism*, articulated primarily by those in the Dutch Reformed tradition strongly influenced by Kuyper and Bavinck. The Presuppositionalists, who take the Bible as the appropriate source of Christian philosophy, base their philosophical perspective and teachings directly on the Bible. A typical, and quite accessible, presentation of this philosophy can be found in the works of the American philosopher G. H. Clark,[1] who taught philosophy at Butler University in Indiana. His metaphilosophy can be looked at as a further articulation of the "Christianity-as-worldview" conception.

For Clark, worldviews are the fundamental unit of philosophical investigation. Each person has a worldview that unifies his or her experience of the world, orders his or her beliefs and animates his or her life as a valuing moral agent. Different worldviews dictate different ways of interpreting experience, different systems of belief and different orientations toward life as expressed in overt behaviour. Since a person's worldview is fundamental to him or to her, it is not itself capable of being evaluated or judged from some neutral perspective outside of itself. Every worldview, then, is self-contained and incommensurable with every other worldview. Further, each worldview will contain some set of beliefs that are central for and foundational to it; these will be the *absolute presuppositions* of that worldview. Since a person's worldview dictates his or her beliefs and a person's worldview is dictated in turn by its presuppositions, it follows that there can be no ground or justification for those presuppositions. Given that they are basic, any attempt to prove them will either be circular or generate an infinite, vicious regress. Presuppositions, then, can only be *chosen*, not proven or justified. To ask for such proof or justification, then, is to commit a category mistake. By the same token, there is no *a priori* constraint on which presuppositions we may choose; the Christian system is as available as any other.

According to Clark, the presupposition of the Christian worldview is "God as revealed in Scripture." Actually, things are more complicated than this. Scripture is what we might call the *epistemic* presupposition for the Christian worldview, whereas God is its *metaphysical* presupposition, i.e. the ultimate principle of reality. Clark, in fact, *embraces* the apparent absurdity of urging that we ought to believe that God

---

1 See Hackett (1957, second edition 1974) pages 154–66.

exists on the basis of the testimony of Scripture.[1] To the charge that this procedure is circular, since we can only have reason for believing that the Scriptures reveal God if we already have independent reason for believing that God exists, Clark responds that all presuppositions are groundless in exactly the same way; we routinely accept the existence of the external world on the basis of the senses despite the fact that the veridicality of the senses presupposes the existence of the external world. For an empiricist of the realist sort, the senses are epistemically basic while the external world is metaphysically so. Either this sort of circularity is unavoidable, or it is acceptable in the former case if acceptable in the latter. Since the demand for a presuppositionless worldview is an empty one, we can do no better in any case.

Nevertheless, this view does not entail relativism or irrationalism. There is only one correct set of presuppositions, those revealed in Scripture. All other worldviews are based on false presuppositions and, insofar as they reach conclusions contrary to Biblical teaching, erroneous in their results. Thus, despite their commitment to incommensurability, Presuppositionalists do not teach that every worldview is as good as every other. Quite the contrary, the Christian worldview is capable of explaining why other worldviews exist despite being false in terms of the *noetic effects of original sin*. In accordance with the Calvinist teaching of total depravity, Clark and the other figures in this tradition maintain that the effects of original sin extend even to our cognitive faculties. As such, our cognitive faculties are *not* reliable and, just as we inevitably fall into sin if we follow our natural bent as fallen human beings, so too will we inevitably fall into error concerning the nature of things and theoretical truth. The unbeliever, dependent for his beliefs on his damaged reason, possesses a blinkered, jaundiced perspective on reality that distorts his intellectual vision. As such, despite the existence of sufficient evidence even in nature to justify belief in God, the unregenerate sinner is unable to apprehend and appreciate that evidence. Again, the believer is thus in a superior position due to the fact that God's Holy Spirit has regenerated his or her cognitive faculties; the believer *knows* what he or she cannot *show* to the unbeliever, any more than a sighted person can explain to a blind person what is it like to experience colour–vision.

Nor does it follow that there is no mode of philosophical witness to non-believers. While it is useless to argue *for* Christianity beyond simply removing palpable errors about what Scripture teaches, it is possible to critique other worldviews *from inside* by the use of *reductio ad absurdum* to expose the contradictions, incoherencies and palpable absurdities entailed by their presuppositions. This Clark does in his volu-

---

1 See Clark's essay in Vos (1971), pages 9–32.

minous writings, culminating in the lectures he gave at Wheaton College in 1967.[1] This procedure constitutes a two-pronged *negative* apologetic intended to show the baselessness of secular critiques of the Gospel by either demonstrating that they flow from presuppositions that are themselves illogical or rest on a mistaken understanding of Biblical teaching. The critic of Christianity can be defeated and silenced, if not converted, by this procedure.

Presuppositionalism is a controversial and much-controverted view, especially in evangelical Christian circles; it is hardly the "mainstream" of conservative Protestant thought.[2] However, I have sketched it as background for the views of Plantinga and Wolterstorff, both of whom came out of the Dutch Reformed tradition and both of whom were products of Calvin College. In fact, despite significant differences, Plantinga's "Christian Philosophy" is strongly similar in spirit to the views of the Presuppositionalists, thus providing a historical context in which find one significant root of his view.

PLANTINGA'S "CHRISTIAN PHILOSOPHY"

Clark expressed a hearty disdain for analytic philosophy; Van Til and the other Presuppositionalists came out of the Continental tradition. By contrast, Alvin Plantinga, Nicholas Wolterstorff and George Mavrodes were all trained as analytic philosophers in secular graduate schools. The influence of analytic philosophy helped make their defence of Christianity much more subtle and sophisticated than that of their Protestant forbearers. Nevertheless, the influence of Bavinck, Kuyper and Van Til can be seen in the writings of all three men. This is most clearly to be seen in the work of Alvin Plantinga in the years after he published *The Nature of Necessity*.[3] Just as Plantinga's commitment to a metaphysical interpretation and application of modal logic in the early seventies represented an advance over his earlier views, so too did his interest in epistemology, which came to the fore in the 1980's and '90's, represent another right turn in the development of his thought consistent with but not altogether to be anticipated on the basis of his earlier work. Let me now attempt to lay out the stages of this development.

---

1 Reprinted in Nash (1968)
2 For further discussion and critique of Presuppositionalism, see Hackett (1957, second edition 1974) pages 250–60, Cowan (2000), especially pages 207–63 and Sproul, Gerstner and Lindlay (1984) pages 183–338.
3 See Plantinga and Wolterstorff (1979) pages 16–93.

Foundationalism and the Ethics of Belief

As I noted earlier, the primary response to Pike's refutation of the deductive argument from evil was to argue that, even if Theism was barely logically coherent, it was still quite improbable given the variety and amount of evil as well as the existence of apparently gratuitous evils. This shift in emphasis created the logical room for the development of Inductivism, as we have seen. However, the response of American protestant philosophers was not, by and large to embrace Inductivism, but instead to attack the presuppositions of the probabilistic argument from evil. The probabilistic argument from evil, it was claimed, rested on a particular account of the ethics of belief, one in which the notions of evidence and rational justification play a key role. According to Plantinga and Wolterstorff, however, this ethics of belief, though shop-worn through familiarity, is vulnerable to philosophical critique and with it, the demands for an explanation for evil in general or in even particular cases. The critic's case, then, turns out to rest on a disputable ethics of belief whose demands are not, in the end, obligatory on the theist. As such, the theist cannot and ought not be faulted for failing to meet them, nor accused of irrationality for refusing to try. This will become clearer as we actually consider the position within the context of the ethics of belief.

In Chapter One we noted W. K. Clifford's principle that it is wrong, always and everywhere, to believe any proposition without adequate evidence. This, when combined with Flew's Stratonician Presumption, i.e. the claim that the burden of proof lies on the person making the positive claim, gives rise to the presumption of (negative) atheism. On this view, it is a violation of one's doxastic obligations to persist in religious belief in the face of the failure of philosophical defenders of theism to carry the burden of proof; as such, to knowingly and willingly do so is to be *positively irrational*. An inductivist like Swinburne can agree with this, but claim that the burden of proof can be carried without providing what Flew demanded, a sound deductive proof of God's existence from self-evident first principles. But the Post-Deductivist like Plantinga attacks this view at much more fundamental level, claiming that the Cliffordian ethics of belief cannot be sustained. In particular, Plantinga claims that it might be rational to believe in God without any proof or evidence whatsoever.[1]

---

[1] See Plantinga in Delaney (1979), Plantinga and Wolterstorff (1983) and Plantinga (2004) pages 16–93.

EVIDENTIALISM AND FOUNDATIONALISM

Evidentialism, according to Plantinga, is the view that a belief is rational only to the extent that it is justified by evidence. According to one classical articulation of the Evidentialist thesis, there are only two possible sources of cognitive evidence, i.e. direct presentations of sense and self-evident truths of reason. The Evidentialist thesis then asserts that one is rationally justified in accepting only those beliefs that can be justified by evidence derived from one of these two sources; beliefs of any other sort, based on whatever grounds, are not rationally justified and thus not worthy of rational credence. Evidentialism thus depends on a traditional but now thought to be highly problematic view known as *Foundationalism*. Foundationalism in epistemology is the position that the possibility of human knowledge depends on our being able to identify some set of propositions in our set of beliefs that are capable of conferring justification on other beliefs without in turn requiring to be justified by any other, more fundamental beliefs. This set of beliefs will serve as the foundation for the other beliefs that can be justified by reference to them and those beliefs will be justified to the extent that they are supported by that foundation.

Plantinga, however, maintains that Evidentialism, thus stated, is self-refuting because it is neither self-evidently true, nor evident to the senses, nor deducible from evidence of either of these sorts. As such, if we apply Evidentialism to itself, the Evidentialist thesis turns out not to be worthy of rational credence. Evidentialism, then, fails as a foundation for Cliffordian ethics of belief and this in turn undermines its claims concerning our doxastic obligations. Thus, the religious believer cannot be convicted on those grounds of any epistemic impropriety, even if he or she accepts those religious beliefs on the basis of no reasons or evidence whatsoever.

Indeed, for most Christians, religious belief is a matter of faith and one's faith-commitment is unconditional and, ideally at least, unrevisable. Plantinga endorses the "reformed objection to natural theology" to be found in Calvin, Bavinck and Barth, that to adopt the Thomist (or, for that matter, Swinburnean) position in the philosophy of religion is to treat belief in God as though it were a conditional, provisional or derivative belief that is beholden to proof or evidence of some kind and that this is inconsistent with any sort of genuine Christian faith. Someone who believed in God only because he or she thought that it was justified by neutral evidence and who was prepared to abandon that belief if he or she could be convinced that what he or she took to be evidence was no good after all, according to these Reformed thinkers, would not possess genuine faith at all. They would evince only a tepid, "diffident" belief that even a Hume could approve of. Natural theology, then, rests on a mistake;

to the extent that a philosophical defence of religious belief is even possible, let alone desirable, it must restrict itself to a largely negative apologetic that defends only the thesis that there is no reason not to suppose that belief in God is *properly basic* for the believer, i.e. rationally permissible for him or her to hold without the need for any evidence or proof whatsoever.

NEGATIVE APOLOGETICS AND THE PROBLEM OF EVIL

At least initially, Plantinga saw his apologetic project in a manner very similar to that adopt by analytic atheists like Flew within the old Deductivist paradigm in the philosophy of religion. Since the believer lives by faith and not by sight, he or she makes no claim to effect that those beliefs are justified by neutral evidence and thus makes no claims that require to be justified in that way. As such, the religious believer need not defend any positive claims whatsoever; instead, at most what is needed is a defence against the claims of the critic and it is sufficient to turn these objections aside to simply show that they will not work as deductive disproofs of God's existence or for the other characteristic beliefs of Christianity. Even the claim that belief in God is properly basic was initially regarded by Plantinga in this way, i.e. as one that could be maintained philosophically solely on the negative ground that it could not be shown that it was *not* properly basic.

One context in which this strategy was applied (with some semblance of success to judge from its widespread popularity) was with regard to the probabilistic argument from evil that supplanted the older, deductive argument from evil. In 1979, William L. Rowe refocused the on-going debate over the reasonableness of belief in God in the face of evil with his landmark paper "The Problem of Evil and Some Varieties of Atheism."[1] Rowe varies from the earlier presentations of the probabilistic argument from evil by basing his argument of the existence of apparently gratuitous evils, as follows:

1. An omnipotent, omniscient and omnibenevolent God would prevent every gratuitous evil, permitting only those evils that are necessary for the existence of some greater good.
2. There are *apparently* gratuitous evils.
3. Therefore, there is no God.

To illustrate premise 2, Rowe envisages a hypothetical scenario (sometimes called

---

1 Reprinted in Howard–Snyder (1996), pages 1–11.

the "Bambi" case) in which a fawn is caught in a forest fire, badly burned and then lingers in agony for a few days before dying of dehydration. Although this is a hypothetical case, Rowe supposes that cases like this occur in the real world. If so, it would appear in such cases that there is no higher good, or indeed, any good at all that such an occurrence would subserve; given this, then in accordance with Swinburne's principle of credulity, the *prima facie* best explanation for the existence of apparently gratuitous evils is that such evils do in fact exist. However, since God, as described, would not permit such evils, if they exist God does not. Rowe emphasizes that this is an inductive rather than a deductive argument. There is no way to prove that there are any actually gratuitous evils; the logical possibility always remains that there is *some* explanation for every evil that we observe. However, it is not *reasonable* to believe this in the face of apparently gratuitous evils, examples of which may be multiplied indefinitely.

In 1996, Rowe's paper served as the focus for a collection entitled *The Evidential Problem of Evil*, edited by Daniel Howard-Snyder.[1] Although numerous other philosophers contributed to the collection, including Swinburne, Paul Draper and Richard Gale, the lion's share of the discussion concerned Rowe's paper and the primary response to it reflected the Post-Deductivist commitment to negative apologetics. Instead of arguing that God might be morally justified in permitting some gratuitous evils or to denying that such evils occur, the majority of the papers on the theistic side evinced the "hard-nosed" approach reminiscent of Pike's stance in "Hume on Evil", i.e. that the theist is in no way obliged to provide any theodical explanation of any of the evils in the world and need not have any idea of what the reasons might be that justify God in permitting the evils we observe around us in the world. In other words, the Post-Deductivist Christian philosophers disputed the claim that apparently gratuitous evils are in any evidence for the existence of actually gratuitous ones.

The major exponent of this position in this collection was Stephen Wykstra, who in his paper "Rowe's Noseeum Arguments from Evil"[2] tries to undercut the force of Rowe's argument from apparently gratuitous evils. Essentially, Wykstra argues that appearances only provide presumptive evidence for a substantive claim in those cases in which we would reasonably expect to see something different from what we in fact observe if the claim in question was false, something that obviously applies in the case of positive experiences but is a trickier matter where evidence of absence is

---

[1] See Howard–Snyder (1996) where this approach predominates among those defending theism against Rowe s version of the argument from evil.
[2] In Howard–Snyder (1996), pages 126–150.

concerned. For example, suppose I wonder if there are aphids on my rose-bushes. I go to my kitchen window and, looking out, observe my rose-bushes through the glass at a distance of about fifty feet. I don't see any aphids when I do this, but of course it would be silly for me to conclude in those circumstances that there are no aphids on my rose-bushes. In this case, given the size of aphids and taking into account both the medium and my distance from the rose-bushes, the fact that I fail to see any aphids provides no evidence whatsoever, presumptive or otherwise, with regard to the question of whether or not they have aphids or not. This is because, even if the aphids were there, I would not reasonably expect to be able to see them under those conditions. Thus, in this case, the fact that I don't see any aphids (i.e. there appear to be no aphids) is no proof whatsoever that there aren't aphids on the rose–bush.

Wykstra claims that one can argue in a similar fashion that apparently gratuitous evils are evidence for the existence of actually gratuitous ones only if it is reasonable for me to believe that if there were reasons for God to permit those apparently gratuitous evils that we would be privy to them. Wykstra maintains that Rowe cannot prove that this is so, and that therefore his version of the problem of evil fails. Thus, Wykstra's contention is that apparently gratuitous evils constitute no evidence *at all* for the non-existence of the theistic God. Of course, the believer trusts in divine providence and accepts the notion that God's understanding exceeds our own and that all things that happen ultimately serve His good ends, often in ways that are inscrutable to us. Thus, while there is a problem of evil, that problem is essentially a *pastoral* one that arises in the care of souls whose faith has been tested or challenged by the evils they have experienced or heard about; strictly speaking, however, there is no *theological* problem of evil nor does anything much hang on our speculations about the reasons that God might have for permitting evils to occur. On this view, theodicy is neither a theoretical nor a practical necessity for the Christian.

The foregoing, of course, does not summarize the entire debate about Rowe's argument, which is ongoing and much more sophisticated than I can usefully present here. The reader is advised to consult the relevant literature him- or herself.[1] Here I am only concerned to illustrate how the Post-Deductivist apologetic operates in contrast to, e.g. traditional natural theology or Swinburne's Inductivist system. Essentially, Post-Deductivists attempt to undermine the analytic atheist's arguments by challenging the (often apparently plausible) presuppositions of those arguments in order to undercut the atheist's challenge rather than to answer it. In so doing, they are attempt-

---

1 For example, an important recent contribution that came into my hands too late for discussion here is Van Inwagen (2006).

ing to do what Kant claimed to be doing in his philosophy, i.e. restricting the claims of reason in order to make room for the claims of faith.

Plantinga's "Reformed Epistemology"

Although a negative apologetic seems to be the most natural expression of the Protestant philosophical orientation, it nevertheless remains that the mandate of "Christian Philosophy" is to engage in philosophical reflection from a Christian point of view, so that it was natural for Plantinga to move forward and to attempt to craft what can only be described as a Christian epistemology. Besides, the central claim of Plantinga's defence of the rationality of religious belief was that belief in God is properly basic for the believer. However, this naturally leads one to ask what makes a belief *properly* as opposed to merely *de facto* basic. Consider, for example, the standard objection to the claim that belief in God is properly basic for a Christian, called the Great Pumpkin objection.[1] Couldn't believers in the Great Pumpkin, or Satanists, or exponents of Nazi racist ideology claim that their beliefs are properly basic for them as well? Are there no standards or limits on what can count as properly basic? If not, isn't Plantinga committed to a kind of relativism and doesn't his position reduce to the Presuppositionalist position that one's fundamental beliefs are ultimately a matter of choice? Plantinga's initial response to the Great Pumpkin objection was to deny that these implications follow and, in the "hard nosed" style of Pike's response to the problem of evil, to deny that there was any need for the Christian to provide any account of proper basicality even while rejecting the claim that Great Pumpkinists, Satanists and Nazi can claim that their beliefs are properly basic. The apparent arbitrariness of this claim, however, makes one uneasy about this; at any rate, Plantinga does go on to attempt to justify the claim that belief in God is properly basic, and not just *de facto* basic, for the Christian in a way that excludes these other possibilities. The story is a long one and not one that can be easily summarized; in what follows I can give only a sketch of Plantinga's view and recommend that one read his own works to get the full picture of his account.

Warrant, Externalism and Proper Function

Beginning in the 1990's, Plantinga published a trilogy of books in epistemology, a subject in which he had not previously worked. It began with a book called *Warrant:*

---

1 See Martin (1990) pages 342–5 and Parsons (1990) pages 45–50; the name for this objection is Plantinga's own: see Plantinga 1979.

the Current Debate,[1] was quickly followed by a companion volume *Warrant and Proper Function*[2] and, after an interval of several years, completed with *Warranted Christian Belief* in 2004.[3] The first book and nearly all of the second are purely "secular" productions in which Plantinga's evangelical Christianity plays no overt part. However, he slowly transitions from the secular to the Christian context, tying the secular and Christian perspectives together in the final volume.

Warrant: the Current Debate is essentially a survey of contemporary epistemology and an exercise in ground-clearing. By *warrant* Plantinga intends to designate whatever it is that converts true belief into knowledge. Plantinga begins by continuing his attack on Foundationalism, taking as his stalking horse Roderick Chisholm's sophisticated defence of classical internalist epistemology according to which a belief's being warranted requires that the truth-conditions for one's beliefs be accessible to and appropriated by the believer as a condition for his knowing them. He concludes, unsurprisingly, that Foundationalism is hopeless. From this, and the famous Gettier problem, he appears to draw three conclusions. First of all, whatever warrant is, it is not *rational justification in terms of evidence or argument*. This conception of warrant, tied as it is to Foundationalist internalism, cannot survive the critique of that conception. Secondly, the way forward in epistemology is to adopt the externalist perspective, according to which one's being warranted in believing anything is largely a matter of how that belief was produced. The major externalist epistemology, called *Reliabilism*, maintains that one's beliefs are warranted if they are *caused* in the right way, i.e. by the operation of some process that (generally) produces true beliefs. It does not follow, nor is it necessary according to externalists, that the believer have access to or even have any reason to believe that his or her beliefs are warranted. Thirdly, following the lead of the Scottish Realist philosopher Thomas Reid, Plantinga de-centres discursive reason as the predominant cognitive faculty in favour of a view that treats the deliverances of all of our cognitive faculties (e.g. sense-perception, memory, Hume's "inductive habit", etc.) as equally basic and autonomous. The claims of sense-perception, memory and so on are thus neither subject to nor in need of epistemic support from our faculty of discursive reason; each makes its own legitimate claim on us and has its own internal standards and procedures for evaluating the relevant form of immediate data upon which it works.

Though these conclusions put Plantinga in the mainstream of contemporary epis-

---

1 Plantinga (1993a)
2 Plantinga (1993b)
3 Plantinga (2004)

temology, it does not follow that he is satisfied with any of the extant epistemological theories, whether externalist, coherentist or probabilist. Plantinga reviews a dozen different major contemporary epistemological theories of all these types and rejects them all. Despite the great variety of the theories he considers, however, his criticism of all of these theories is remarkably similar, amounting merely to variations on a theme. In each case, Plantinga simply argues that, whatever the standards for warrant the theory in question promotes, it is possible for all of those conditions to be met by a belief or set of beliefs and yet for that belief or beliefs to be grossly false. From this, Plantinga concludes more than simply that all of these theories are false; instead, he seems to conclude that all attempts to specify what warrant consists in are wrong-headed.

In *Warrant and Proper Function*, Plantinga reduces the externalist position to the bare–bones view that a belief is warranted just in case it was produced by a cognitive faculty that was a) designed to yield (generally) true beliefs and which b) functions properly, i.e. as it was intended to in accordance with its "design-plan", in the production of specific beliefs. Plantinga eschews any attempt to provide any substantive account of warrant or what "proper functioning" amounts to in the case of any specific cognitive faculty and, given his commitment to the externalist point of view in epistemology, this is a both a consistent and probably sensible line to take. In the end, the conviction that our cognitive faculties are in fact sources of true belief is largely a matter of epistemic faith. However, in the final chapter of *Warrant and Proper Function*, and almost as an aside, Plantinga makes the controversial claim that we have no reason whatsoever for supposing that Darwinian evolution operating by itself would endow us with cognitive faculties capable of arriving at any substantive, true theoretical beliefs about the world – including evolution itself.[1] Plantinga thus suggests that if our faith in our cognitive faculties is to be credible, we ought to suppose that evolution by itself is not the sole designer of our cognitive faculties. Instead, says Plantinga, if you want to be a naturalist, you ought to be a theist! This claim, the germ of Plantinga's critique of naturalism, has become the focus of an extensive literature[2] but as it is ancillary to Plantinga's primary project, we will have to bypass this development here.

Proper Basicality and Warranted Christian Belief

The foregoing gives us the rudiments for a general account, in Plantingan terms, of

---
1 See Plantinga (1993b) pages 216–37.
2 See Beilby (2002).

proper basicality. A belief is properly basic if it is the spontaneous production of any one of our autonomous cognitive faculties and passes muster according to the internal standards of evaluation appropriate to that context. Each of our cognitive faculties produces such beliefs: sense-perception produces beliefs about the external world, memory about the lived past, the "inductive habit" beliefs about the likely course of the future, and so on. Each of these faculties, however, is notoriously fallible despite being reliable in the main and there are well known "defeaters" for claims of each distinct type that are capable of overturning beliefs from whatever faculty these are derived. The standard examples of such defeaters are internal to each of our autonomous cognitive faculties, such as when I think I see a ghost but subsequently discover that it was only a sheet flapping in the breeze on a stormy night; however, sometimes the deliverances of one faculty can be used to trump another, as when my current sense-experience of an old home movie trumps one of my putative childhood memories. For the most part, however, our spontaneous beliefs pass muster, being neither defeated nor even requiring revision in the light of subsequent deliveries of our cognitive faculties and this gives us some reason to think that our faith in these faculties is not entirely misplaced. Nor is it always the case that one of my basic beliefs is "defeated" by neutral evidence sufficient to convince a disinterested third person that this is the case. Despite the fallibility of memory, if I clearly remember that I was hiking by myself near Mt. Rainier yesterday, I can certainly claim to know that I did not rob a bank in Seattle at that same time, despite sincere eyewitness testimony to the effect that I was doing so sufficient to convince a neutral observer.

On this general account, the Christian's belief that God exists, the core belief of theism, will be properly basic for him or her just in case that belief is the spontaneous product of a reliable and properly functioning cognitive faculty. Since this belief is not the product of any of our other, largely uncontroversial cognitive faculties such as sense-perception, such a belief does not appear to be a likely candidate for a properly basic belief. However, here is where the "Reformed" element in Reformed Epistemology obtrudes. Inspired by a suggestion of Calvin's, taken in the context of Reid's Scottish Philosophy, Plantinga proposes that there is a special cognitive faculty (the *Sensus Divinitatis*)[1] that produces the conviction that there is a God in all rational beings. Despite the cognitive effects of original sin, that blind the unregenerate sinner to the presence of God in the world, Calvinists have generally wanted to claim that God's existence is somehow clearly evident to every human being, so that sinners cannot plead ignorance of God's existence as an excuse for their failure to

---

1 Plantinga (2004) pages 167–86.

live lives of faith. Calvin thus postulated a vague, direct awareness of God, somehow sufficient to convict us of wilful rebellion against God but insufficient to provide traditional epistemic justification for that belief. While this appears to be entirely *ad hoc* in Calvin's case, Plantinga nevertheless adopts it as an additional cognitive faculty that operates to produce spontaneous beliefs about God, including the belief that God exists. This *sensus divinitatis* provides the *grounds* for beliefs about God in the form of inner conviction about the "God-relatedness" of ourselves and the world in general to God. Most of the "data" providing the grounds for traditional arguments for God's existence, such as the contingency of the world, the order and apparent design of the world, the sense of moral obligation, the innate desire for meaning and purpose in life, etc. as well as events occurring in our individual lives that strike us as providential or in some way a response on the part of God to our situation are the result of the operation of this faculty. For the Christian, the conviction that there is a God resulting from the testimony of the Scriptures would be an additional example of its operation.

Plantinga concludes that, if there is such a faculty and if it operates reliably, then belief in God is a both basic and a warranted belief as well, thus a properly basic belief for the Christian theist. Of course, that belief must pass muster by resisting any proposed defeaters brought against it by atheistic critics of Christianity. However, for this purpose it will be sufficient to employ the devices of negative apologetics. This Plantinga (and his legions of followers) claim to be able to do and, indeed, to have done. In that case, belief in God will not only be both basic and warranted, but fully rational as well. In this way, theism is thus vindicated in a way that meets the model for belief in God demanded by evangelical Protestantism, thus finding a middle way between rationalism and fideism.

The Future of "Christian Philosophy"

The "Christian Philosophy" of Plantinga and Wolterstorff is a philosophical research program that portends the transformation of all of philosophy from a Christian, Post-Deductivist point of view, not just the philosophy of religion. Plantinga, for one, has strongly encouraged younger Christian philosophers to develop theories in other areas of philosophy drawn from and reflecting Christian principles and perspectives.[1] Wolterstorff has made similar pleas with regard to social philosophy, political theory and the philosophy of economics.[2] More than this both have also suggested that

---

1 See Plantinga (1984), (1994) and (1995)
2 Wolterstorff (1976, second edition) Part II, pages 111–46.

Christian scholars of every sort eschew neutrality and conduct their researches from a distinctively Christian point of view, though one finds it hard to imagine the shape a distinctively Christian mycology or herpetology, for example, would take. Whether these challenges will be taken up and what results, if any, they may produce remains to be seen. Thus far, there are few indications that this is happening.

In a more recent development, as Plantinga has grown older, his allegiance to the once-rigid Protestant opposition to natural theology appears to have weakened. Although Plantinga continues to maintain that arguments for God's existence are not necessary for belief in God either to be true, warranted or rational, this does not mean, he says, that no such arguments exist. Plantinga, in fact, thinks that there may be such arguments and, in an unpublished lecture, sketches out two dozen arguments, with variants, drawn from a variety of thinkers and branches of philosophy.[1] Further, he claims now to see some limited value in natural theology, on the grounds that such arguments, while not universally compelling, may be compelling to some people, with the likely result that different arguments will carry weight with different people. Times have changed, he notes; to believe in God is no longer regarded, even by all college professors, as an infallible sign of hypocrisy, stupidity or irrationality. Some may even be open to persuasion and one or another of these arguments may play a part in an effecting conversion in such people. In this way, natural theology may have a role to play in evangelization and thus is not wholly to be despised, however superfluous it may be for those who already believe.

---

1 See his lecture notes for a presentation at Wheaton College entitled 'Two Dozen (or so) Theistic Arguments' on–line at www.homestead.com/philofreligion/files/Theisticarguments.html – to date apparently unpublished.

Chapter Ten

Philosophy of Religion Today

Our survey of contemporary philosophy of religion is complete and seems to come in a timely fashion, given that most of the figures that I have been discussing are either recently deceased or, even if still hard at work, either retired or close to retirement age. One anticipates that a new chapter in the history of the philosophy of religion is about to be written, as views once fresh and novel a few decades ago begin to take on the appearance of calcified "systems" ready for neat summary and shelving in order that they may become objects of study for philosophers of the future. Even so, we are not yet at the point where we can see the likely shape of the future of the discipline and I for one am not inclined to speculate about what will happen next in its development. Given the time left to me, I will watch with interest how the future goes. In anticipation of that future, however, let me set out the lay of the land as I see it in the first decade of the new millennium. I shall begin by noting the state of theistic philosophy today, then of contemporary atheism. I shall conclude with my general assessment of the state of the discipline at the present time – and there I will cease.

CONTEMPORARY THEISTIC PHILOSOPHY

Although contemporary philosophy of religion began in Britain at a time when British philosophers dominated Anglophone thought, the leading edge of contemporary philosophy of religion in the new millennium is decidedly American; even Swinburne's successor as Nolloth Professor, Brian Leftow, is an American. In what follows, then, I will be largely discussing the state of theism as we find it in the U.S. At the present time, we are approaching the end of a period of steady growth in prominence, of both theistic philosophy of religion and of the number of theists in American philosophy. Whereas theism was considered very much a dead letter in the 1960's and militant atheism almost *de rigueur* among American philosophers, a kind of party line to which all philosophers were expected to adhere, things are very much different today.

Theism has been espoused by a number of prominent philosophers at major universities and the philosophical defence of theism, as the body of this book has documented, is much more solid now than at any time in the recent past. Theists are also much more strongly organized in the academic world than at any time in the past.

The oldest philosophical organization composed primarily of theists is the American Catholic Philosophical Association, founded in 1926, with a current membership of over one thousand. The ACPA sponsors annual meeting, awards the Aquinas Medal annually (recent recipients have included Peter Geach and Michael Dummett) and publishes the *American Catholic Philosophical Quarterly,* formerly the *New Scholasticism.* Although neo-Thomists and Aquinas scholars still play a prominent role in the life and governance of the ACPA, the new, Post-Vatican II pluralism of the Catholic Church is well represented, with philosophers of all stripes, including the Continental and Post-Modernist traditions, in attendance. In addition, a number of prominent analytic philosophers are members of the ACPA, as well as a number of non-Catholics.

The growth of theism within the philosophical community is well-evidenced by the founding of the Society for Christian Philosophy in 1978. Philosophers with any sort of Christian religious commitment were few and isolated in the 1960's and '70's, so the founding of the SCP was a major event for Christian philosophers. Originally, the SCP met as part of the regional meetings of the American Philosophical Association, where satellite sessions of many small special–interest study groups (such as the North American Jaspers Society and the American Society for Value Inquiry) are held. In time, however, the SCP has become large enough to sponsor three annual meetings in its own right (on the model of the APA), usually at small sectarian colleges. It has published its own peer–reviewed journal, *Faith and Philosophy*, which accepts submissions both by theists and atheists, since 1983. Most of the major figures of contemporary Christian philosophy – Plantinga, Wolterstorff, Mavrodes, Peter Van Inwagen, William Alston and Robert Adams, just to name a few – have published in its pages. It currently boasts about 1,400 members; there is also a Canadian SCP as well. Although it is an ecumenical Christian organization, it is largely Protestant and exponents of analytic theism, especially Plantinga's "Christian Philosophy" constitute its core membership. In an effort to widen its membership, Linda Zagzebski, a prominent Catholic analytic philosopher, was elected president in 2005 and immediately began an effort to recruit Catholics into the SCP. In addition to their scholarly work, members of the SCP have made missions to Russia and China in an effort to aid awareness of the rational grounds for theism and Christianity. They have even established a library in Wuhan, China named for Norman Kretzmann, the prominent Aquinas scholar who died in 1998.

We may also mention the Evangelical Philosophical Society, founded in 1974 and claiming a membership of around eight hundred. It also publishes a peer-reviewed journal, *Philosophia Christi*, the current incarnation of which was founded in 1998. The EPS meets annually in conjunction with the much larger Evangelical Theological Society. The EPS is a sectarian philosophical society; admittance to its ranks in contingent on signing a statement accepting the inerrancy of Scripture "in its original autographs." It receives the lion's share of its support from BIOLA University (formerly the Bible Institute of Los Angeles) and Liberty University in Virginia. Both its governance and the editorial board of *Philosophia Christi* are exclusively Protestant. The EPS has recently attracted some adverse publicity for the prominence it has afforded in its journal and meetings to Intelligent Design theory (sometimes in conjunction with the Seattle-based Discovery Institute, the major exponent of this view, which is dismissed by its opponents – and the federal courts – as "the New Creationism.")

CONTEMPORARY ATHEISTIC PHILOSOPHY

In December of 2004, the philosophical community (and even world beyond) was surprised by the announcement by Antony Flew he had changed his mind and was now persuaded that God, at any rate the God of the philosophers, exists.[1] His position most closely resembles deism and does not carry with it any religious commitment; nevertheless, his reasons for changing his views on this topic were primarily philosophical: he cites in particular the work of Swinburne and the "Fine Tuning" version of the teleological argument. It is certainly a tribute to the work done by theistic philosophers that they have contributed to this change of view in someone so strongly associated with the atheist cause.[2]

Of course, atheistic philosophy has hardly disappeared since the revival of theism. The APA, for example, has a membership of about 10,400, the great majority of whom do not belong to any of the aforementioned organizations and the majority of whom would cheerfully describe themselves as atheists. However, the relationship

---

[1] Flew s interview with Gary Habermas was slated for publication in the Winter, 2005 issue of *Philosophia Christi*; the text is available on line at http://www.illustramedia.com./IDArticles/flew–interview.

[2] In 2006, Flew was awarded – and accepted – the Philip E. Johnson award from BIOLA University. The award, named for the prominent creationist who was its first recipient, was given to Flew for his contributions to the cause of rationality and freedom of thought in academia.

between atheism and theism has become somewhat more complex since the advent of the theistic revival. For the most part, philosophers who have been exposed to the writings of Plantinga, Swinburne and other prominent theistic philosophers, though in many cases unconvinced, have become less confident in the transparent falsity of theism and less dismissive of religion in general. As such, many philosophers today would be better described as religiously indifferent rather than militantly atheistic as was the norm forty years ago. By the same token, religious commitment is no longer the "career-breaker" that it once was and something wisely kept hidden until one had attained tenure. Although atheism is still by far the majority view among philosophers, most philosophers are more tolerant of religious belief than they once were and the influence of old-time militant atheists appears to be on the wane. As such, it seems to me that in contemporary philosophy of religion we can identify two distinct groups of atheists, the heirs of the postivistically-tinged militant atheism of the 1950's and what are sometimes called "Friendly Atheists." Both groups continue to be prominent in the philosophy of religion, though neither is a large or dominant as it once was; within present–day philosophy of religion, theism is currently the dominant view.

Anti-Theism

One wing of contemporary atheistic philosophy of religion might be called the anti-theistic wing. This consists of philosophers whose roots are in the logical positivist tradition and the early analytic atheist critique of theism. These figures continue to espouse the basic lines of argument introduced by those movements and maintains that the efforts of theistic philosophers to rehabilitate theism are all for naught and indeed merely retreads of older views known to be false since the time of Hume. These "hard-liners" are unwilling to make any concessions to analytic theism and attack every attempt to defend theism as worthy only of swift and dismissive refutation.

The most prominent philosopher in this camp is Michael Martin, *emeritus* professor of philosophy at Boston University. A life-long atheist, Martin worked primarily as an analytic philosopher of science until he was jolted from his "dogmatic slumber" by contemporary analytic theism. Since that time, he has devoted the bulk of his scholarly efforts to the philosophical critique of theism and Christianity. His magisterial *Atheism: A Philosophical Defense*[1] is an encyclopaedic compendium of philosophical arguments against theism. To this, Martin has added books refuting Christianity and Christian apologetics and arguing that both objective ethics and the meaning of

---

1 Martin (1990)

life can be secured even in a physicalistic universe.[1] A tireless polemicist, Martin has carried on a large number of internet debates with theists and sectarian Christians of all stripes, including the Presuppositionalists. Although his works are marked by an intransigence that borders in many cases on question-begging and a fondness for the superficial "quick kill", Martin's writings definitely ought to be studied by theistic philosophers both as something to stimulate thought and against which to test their mettle. Another, younger philosopher who appears to be the heir apparent to Martin, repeating his general line and arguments, is Keith Parsons.[2]

In this connection, we might also mention the work of Paul Kurtz, who was for many years Professor of Philosophy at SUNY Buffalo. Kurtz is not an analytic philosopher, but comes out of the American naturalist tradition that once dominated Columbia and NYU, where Kurtz studied under Sidney Hook. Although he has written extensively, Kurtz is more prominent as an activist than as a scholar and has worked tirelessly to promote "rationalism" and free thought. He popularized the term "secular humanism" as the name for a positive philosophical position, helped write the humanist manifestoes, founded and edits the magazine *Free Inquiry* and, in 1969, founded Prometheus Press, devoted to reprinting philosophical classics in inexpensive paperback editions as well as anti-religious writings by famous authors and thinkers, many of which have been out of print for many years. He has had a hand in founding a number of humanist organizations and societies and lectures extensively on humanism, free thought and against both belief in the paranormal and religion. Another of Kurtz's projects is the peer-reviewed academic journal *Philo*, also published since 1998. Although the editorial board reads like a *Who's Who* of atheistic philosophy, prominent theists such as Plantinga and Peter Van Inwagen are also members. Like *Faith and Philosophy*, *Philo* publishes submissions by both theists and atheists, although there is a decided preponderance in favour of atheism.

In the internet world, the Secular Web, headlining Internet Infidels, is probably the most philosophically sophisticated of the many websites and blogs devoted to secularism, humanism and metaphysical naturalism. It is peer-reviewed and prints on-line essays by both theists and atheists. On the other side, there are innumerable websites for Christian apologetics and Christian philosophy of every possible stripe; however, as with the anti-religious websites, good examples are hard to find. Nevertheless, the philosophy page at Christian Cadre.com lists a number of good ones, as well as the apologetics and philosophy pages at the Leadership University web site.

---

1 Martin (1991), (2002) and (2006)
2 See Parsons (1990)

FRIENDLY ATHEISM

Not all atheistic philosophers necessarily regard theism as more than merely false, but somehow wilfully irrational and perhaps even wicked. In his 1979 article on the problem of evil, William L. Rowe coined the phrase "Friendly Atheism" to name the view according to which, although theism is false that at least some theists may be rationally justified in believing that God exists. This, according to Rowe, is not a paradoxical position to take, for *being rationally justified* in believing that P not equivalent to *knowing* that P: I can be rationally justified in believing that no one has survived a plane crash at sea if no survivors have been found within twenty–four hours; even so, that belief may be false as you, floating in the sea in your life-vest, may be all too well aware. Something similar could hold in the case of the theist as well; the theist believes that he or she has grounds sufficient to justify belief in God and thus reasonably believes, on the basis of the evidence, that theism is true. The atheist disagrees about that, maintaining that those grounds are not sufficient to justify belief in God, but is able to see how, from the theist's point of view, this might seem to be the case and that the theist's avowal is therefore sincere. In other words, the theist is wrong but not guilty of any epistemic impropriety or wilful irrationality. Of course, it remains for the theist to view the atheist in the same way, i.e. as wrong but not wilfully irrational – or, at any rate, some atheists, which would probably include Rowe himself.

Although there is no group of philosophers who are self-proclaimed "friendly atheists", it seems as though Rowe, Richard Gale and a number of younger philosophers of religion, such as Paul Draper of Florida International University and the Australian philosopher Graham Oppy (who describes himself as an agnostic) roughly fit this description and reflect this "friendlier" attitude in their writings. They are generally more respectful of theists than their predecessors and more circumscribed in their claims, often presenting their arguments (as does Rowe) as problems or questions for theists rather than as refutations of theism, and reserving final judgment on the issues raised. These generally moderate and thoughtful critiques of theism are no less challenging than those of earlier times and contemporary theistic philosophers would do well to respond to them in kind. One might even look forward to the day when both atheistic and theistic philosophers can meet on a plane of mutual respect and discuss the major questions of the philosophy of religion without heat, rancour or mutual contempt. But that, I suppose, is utopian.

TOWARD A FRIENDLIER ATHEISM

How friendly can friendly atheism be? Rowe's version is fairly circumscribed and is extended only to those philosophers, like Swinburne, perhaps, who are fully cognizant of and apparently sensitive to the force of the atheist's critique and yet still willing and able to make out a case for theism plausible enough to pass muster with the unprejudiced as constituting enough proof to make it reasonable to believe while falling short of conclusive proof and so compatible with unbelief. On these terms, the ordinary religious believer could never count as rationally justified in believing in God, not being a trained and sophisticated philosopher of religion. By contrast, a Plantingan maintains that being rationally justified in believing in God is not a matter of belief or evidence at all, since belief in God is properly basic, like the belief that I had breakfast this morning. Between these two points of view there still seems to be a considerable distance.

However we may mediate this dispute, it does seem to me that, after a review of the course of the dialectic within the philosophy of religion in the last fifty years, theistic philosophers have done more than enough to re-establish the viability of theism, even in our modern scientific world. The objections to theism that seemed so crushing in the 1950's have subsequently proven to be less serious than was previously thought. The arguments for God's existence have been rehabilitated and the argument from evil, though still formidable, has not proven be to the last word on whether God exists. For my own part, I think that a disinterested, impartial observer would have to conclude that theistic philosophers have achieved rough dialectic parity with atheistic ones, at least within the analytic tradition. As such, theism has to be seen as a viable option for philosophers. Further, the religious believer, though not a trained philosopher, can draw comfort from this fact. Even if lack of time, training and talent or interest prevent the believer from confirming this for himself, he may take it on authority that a rational case for theism can be made or acquaint him- or herself with a popularized account of what philosophers are prepared to articulate and defend at a more sophisticated level. Thus, the religious believer's *blik* can thereby borrow on account the capital gained the believing philosopher's investment in the philosophical defence of theism.

Nor is this a unique situation or a case of special pleading. There are a large number of philosophical issues concerning which it is quite reasonable to take different and incompatible positions without losing one's status as a member of the philosophical community. Consider the following:

> Do numbers exist?
> Is there free will?
> Is utilitarianism the correct moral theory?
> Is retribution or deterrence the proper foundation for punishment?
> Ought distribution to be made on the basis of merit or equality?
> Is beauty subjective or an objective feature of the aesthetic object?

One will find equally well-respected philosophers on either side of these questions, debating and refining arguments that have been around since the early centuries of Western philosophical speculation. Why ought we not to include "Does God exist?" among questions of this sort, for which it is possible to hold either the positive or the negative position without being suspected of irrationality? The only reason for doing so would be if there was no plausible case whatever for one of the positions on the question and, if what I have depicted as the historical facts is anywhere near to being accurate this is simply not the case.

The friendlier atheism I envisage is one in which there is a presumption in favour of the rationality of individual religious belief that can be defeated or overridden by evidence to the contrary. Corresponding to this there is would also be a friendly theism that makes the same concession to the atheist on the same condition; just as not every theist is qualified to be a party to the debate over God's existence, the same holds for some atheists as well. We are a long way from achieving anything like this, but perhaps this is what would most accurately reflect the actual state of the evidence in our time. Radicals on both sides will undoubtedly disagree, but that it to be expected. In the end what matters is the judgment of those who are capable of objectively viewing that evidence sympathetically from both sides of the issue and it is to that judgment that I will most willingly submit.

Bibliography

Adams, Robert Merrihew (1994), *Leibniz: Determinist, Theist, Idealist*, New York, Oxford University Press

Adler, Mortimer J., (1980) *How to Think about God*, New York, Macmillan

Alston, William P. (1989a) *Divine Nature and Human Language*, Ithaca, NY, Cornell University Press

—— (1989b) *Epistemic Justification*, Ithaca, NY, Cornell University Press

—— (1991) *Perceiving God*, Ithaca, NY, Cornell University Press

—— (1993) *The Reliability of Sense-perception*, Ithaca, NY, Cornell University Press

Anderson, Douglas R. (1995) *Strands of System*, West Lafayette, IN, Purdue University Press

Anderson, James F. (1965) *St. Augustine on Being*, the Hague, Martinus Nijhoff Anselm of Canterbury, St. (1962) *Basic Writing* (edited by S. N. Deane), Chicago, IL, Open Court

Audi, Robert and Richard Wainwright (1986), *Rationality, Religious Belief and Moral Commitment*, Ithaca, NY, Cornell University Press

Augustine, St. (1997) *On Christian Doctrine*, Upper Saddle River, NJ, Prentice–Hall

Austin, J. L. (1955) *Sense and Sensibilia*, Oxford, Clarendon Press

Ayer, A. J. (1946) *Language, Truth and Logic*, London, V. Gollancz

—— (1940) *Foundations of Empirical Knowledge*, London, Macmillan

—— (1959) *Logical Positivism*, Glencoe, IL, Free Press

Barbour, Ian (1974) *Myths, Models and Paradigms*, New York, Harper and Row

Barrow, John and Frank Tipler (1986) *The Anthropic Cosmological Principle*, New York, Oxford

Barth, Karl (1961) *Anselm: Fides Quarens Intellectum*, New York, Meridian

—— (1962) *Church Dogmatics: A Selection*, New York, Harper Torchbooks

Basinger, David and Randall Basinger, *Predestination and Free Will*, Grand Rapids, MI, IVP

Beilby, James (2002) *Naturalism Defeated?* Ithaca, New York, Cornell University Press

Benz, Ernst (1966) *Evolution and Christian Hope*, New York, Doubleday

Berlin, Isaiah (1934), "Verifiability in Principle" *PAS* 39, pages 225–48

Bertocci, Peter (1970) *The Person God Is*, London, Allen and Unwin

Blanshard, Brand (1968) *Reason and Analysis*, Chicago, IL, Open Court

—— (1974) *Reason and Belief*, London, Allen and Unwin

Braithwaite, Richard (1955) *An Empiricist's view of the Nature of Religious Belief*, Cambridge, England, Cambridge University Press

Brams, Stephen (1983) *Superior Beings*, New York, Springer–Verlag

Buijs, Joseph A. (1988) *Maimonides: A Collection of Critical Essays*, Notre Dame, IN, Notre Dame University Press

Burrill, Donald (1967) *The Cosmological Argument*, Garden City, NY, Anchor Books

Butler, Joseph (1736) *The Analogy of Religion*, Kessinger Publishing (no date)

—— (1992) *Catechism of the Catholic Church*, New York, Libreria Editrice Vaticana

Clarke, Samuel (1998) *A Demonstration of the Being and Attributes of God*, New York, Cambridge University Press

Clarke, W. Norris (2001) *The One and the Many*, Notre Dame, IN, Notre Dame University Press

Clifford, W. K. (1999) *The Ethics of Belief and Other Essays*, Amherst, NY, Prometheus Books

Copan, Paul and William Lane Craig (2004) *Creation Out of Nothing*, Grand Rapids, MI Baker Academic

Copan, Paul and Paul K. Moser (2003) *The Rationality of Theism*, London, Routlege

Cottingham, John, Robert Stoothoff and Dugald Murdoch (1985) *The Philosophical Writings of Descartes*, Three Volumes, New York, Cambridge University Press

Cowan, Stephen B., ed., *Five Views on Apologetics*, Grand Rapids, MI, Zondervan, 2000

Craig, William Lane (1979) *The Kalam Cosmological Argument*, Eugene, OR, Wipf and Stock

—— (2000a), *The Tenseless Theory of Time*, New York, Springer Verlag

—— (2000b) *The Tensed Theory of Time*, New York, Springer Verlag

—— (2001), *Time and Eternity*, New York, Crossways Books

Craig, William Lane and J. P. Moreland (2003), *Philosophical Foundations for a Christian Worldview*, Downer's Grove, IL, InterVarsity Press

Craig, William Lane and Quentin Smith (1993), *Theism, Atheism and Big Bang Cosmology*, Oxford, Clarendon Press

Cupitt, Don (2001) *Taking Leave of God*, London, SCM Press

Darwin, Charles (1995) *The Origin of Species*, London, Gramercy

Davis, Stephen T. (1983) *Logic and the Nature of God*, London, Palgrave Macmillan

—— (1997) *God, Reason and Theistic Proofs*, Grand Rapids, MI, Wm. B. Eerdmans

Delaney, Cornelius (1979) *Rationality and Religious Belief*, Notre Dame, IN, Notre Dame University Press

Denzinger, Henry (1954) *Sources of Catholic Dogma*, (31st Edition, ed. Karl Rahner) Fitzwilliam, NH, Loreto Publications

Drange, Theodore (1998) *Nonbelief and Evil* Amherst, NY, Prometheus Books

Dupuis, Jacques and J. Neuner, S. J. (2001) *The Christian Faith*, New York, Alba House

Emmet, Dorothy (1946) *The Nature of Metaphysical Thinking*, London, Macmillan

Farmer, H. H. (1943) *Towards Belief in God*, London, Macmillan

Farrer, Austin (1943) *Finite and Infinite*, London, Dacre Press

—— (1948) *The Glass of Vision*, London, Dacre Press

Ferre, Frederick (1961), *Language, Logic and God*, New York, Harper and Brothers

Flew, Antony and Alasdair Macintyre (1955) *New Essays in Philosophical Theology*, London, SCM Publishing

Flew, Antony (1966) *God and Philosophy*, London, Hutchinson

—— (1976) *The Presumption of Atheism and Other Essays*, New York, Barnes and Noble

Findlay, J. N. (1963) *Language, Mind and Values*, London, George Allen and Unwin

—— (1970) *Ascent to the Absolute*, London, Allen and Unwin

Franks Davis, Caroline (1989) *The Evidential Force of Religious Experience*, Oxford, Clarendon Press

Gale, Richard (1991) *On the Existence and Nature of God*, New York, Cambridge University Press

Garrigou–Lagrange, Reginald (1934) *God: His Existence and His Nature* (Two Volumes), St. Louis, MO, B. Herder Book Co.

Geach, Peter and Elizabeth Anscombe (1961) *Three Philosophers*, London, Blackwell

Geach, Peter (1977) *Providence and Evil*, New York, Cambridge University Press

Geisler, Norman (1979) *Philosophy of Religion*, Grand Rapids, MI, Zondervan

Gellman, Jerome (1998) *Experience of God and the Rationality of Religious Belief*, Ithaca, NY, Cornell University Press

Gerson, Lloyd P. (1994) *God and Greek Philosophy*, London, Routledge

Gill, Jerry H. (1968) *Philosophy Today: No. 2*, New York, Macmillan

Guthrie, Kenneth Sylvan (1987) *The Pythagorean Source Book*, Grand Rapids, MI, Phanes Press

Gutting, Gary (1982) *Religious Belief and Religious Skepticism*, Notre Dame, IN, Notre Dame University Press

Hackett, Stuart (1957) *The Resurrection of Theism*, Grand Rapids, MI, Baker Book House

Hare, Peter H. and E. H. Madden (1968) *Evil and the Concept of God*, Springfield, IL, C. C. Thomas

Hartshorne, Charles (1941) *Man's Vision of God*, Chicago, Willett, Clark and Company

—— (1962) *The Logic of Perfection*, LaSalle, IL, Open Court Publishing Company

—— (1965) *Anselm's Discovery*, LaSalle, IL, Open Court Publishing Company

—— (1967) *A Natural Theology for Our Time*, LaSalle, IL, Open Court Publishing Company

Hasker, William (1989) *God, Time and Knowledge*, Ithaca, NY, Cornell University Press

Hebblethwaite, Peter (2005) *Philosophical Theology and Christian Doctrine*, London, Blackwell

Helm, Paul (1997) *Faith and Understanding*, Grand Rapids, MI, Eerdmans

Hepburn, Ronald (1958) *Christianity and Paradox*, London, Watts

Herrick, Paul (1999) *Reason and Worldview*, New York, Harcourt

Hick, John and Everett McGill (1967) *The Many–Faced Argument*, New York, Macmillan

Hick, John (1957) *Faith and Knowledge*, Ithaca, NY, Cornell University Press

—— (1970) *Evil and the God of Love*, London, Collins

—— (1977) *The Myth of God Incarnate*, Westminster, John Knox Press

—— (1993) *The Metaphor of God Incarnate*, Westminster, John Knox Press

Hodge, Charles (1994) *What is Darwinism?* Grand Rapids, MI, Baker Book House

Hoffmann, Joshua and Gary Rosenkrantz (2002) *The Divine Attributes*, London, Blackwell

Hook, Sidney (1961a) *The Quest for Being*, New York, St. Martin's Press

—— (1961b) *Religious Experience and Truth*, New York, NYU Press

Howard-Snyder, Daniel (1996) *The Evidential Argument from Evil*, Bloomington, IN, University of Indiana Press

Hudson, Deal and Dennis Moran (1992), *The Future of Thomism*, Notre Dame, IN, Notre Dame University Press

Hume, David (1980) *A Treatise of Human Nature*, Oxford, Clarendon Press

—— (1984) *Dialogues Concerning Natural Religion*, Indianapolis, IN, Hackett

James, William (1979) *The Will to Believe and Other Essays*, Cambridge, MA, Harvard University Press

Joyce, G. H. (1922) *Principles of Natural Theology*, London, Longmans, Green and Company

John, Helen James, SND (1966) *The Thomist Spectrum*, New York, Fordham University Press

Katz, Steven T. (1979) *Mysticism and Philosophical Analysis*, New York, Oxford University Press

Kant, Immanuel (1934), *Critique of Pure Reason*, London, J. M. Dent and Sons

Klemke, E. D. (2000) *A Defense of Realism*, New York, Humanity Books

Kenny, Anthony (1969) *The Five Ways*, New York, Shocken Books

Kennedy, Leonard (1988) *Thomistic Papers, Vol. 4*, Houston, TX, Center for Thomistic Studies

Kuklick, Bruce (1985) *Churchmen and Philosophers*, New Haven, CN, Yale University Press

Leslie, John (1979) *Value and Existence*, Oxford, Blackwell

Lewis, C. I. and C. H. Langford (1932) *Symbolic Logic*, New York, The Century Company

Lewis, H. D. (1962) *Our Experience of God*, London, Macmillan

Long, Eugene T. (2000) *Twentieth Century Western Philosophy of Religion*, Boston, MA, Kluwer Academic Publishers

Mackie, J. L. (1982) *The Miracle of Theism*, Oxford, Clarendon Press

Marcus, Ruth Barcan (1993) *Modalities: Philosophical Essays*, New York, Oxford

Martin, C. B. (1959) *Religious Belief*, Ithaca, NY, Cornell University Press

Martin, Michael (1990) *Atheism: A Philosophical Defense*, Philadelphia, PA,

—— Temple University Press

—— (1993) *The Case against Christianity*, Philadelphia, PA, Temple University Press

—— (2002) *Atheism, Morality and Meaning*, Amherst, New York, Prometheus Press

—— (2006) *The Cambridge Companion to Atheism*, New York, Cambridge University Press

Martin, Michael and Ricki Monnier (2003) *The Impossibility of God*, Amherst, NY, Prometheus Books

Martin, Raymond and Christopher Bernard (2003) *God Matters*, New York, Pearson Longmans

Mather, Cotton (1994) *The Christian Philosopher*, Urbana, IL, University of Illinois Press

Mavrodes, George (1970) *Belief in God*, New York, Random House

McInerny, Ralph (1961) *The Logic of Analogy*, The Hague, Martinus Nijhoff

—— (1968) *Studies in Analogy*, The Hague, Martinus Nijhoff

—— (1999) *Aquinas and Analogy*, Washington, D.C., Catholic University of America Press

—— (2006) *Praeambula Fidei*, Washington, D.C., Catholic University of America Press

McLeod, Mark (1984), *Rationality and Theistic Belief*, Ithaca, NY, Cornell University Press

Melchart, Norman (2007) *The Great Conversation*, Fifth Edition, New York, Oxford University Press

Mitchell, Basil (1957) *Faith and Logic*, London, Allen and Unwin

—— (1973) *The Justification of Religious Belief*, London, Macmillan

Mondin, Battista (1963) *The Principle of Analogy in Protestant and Catholic Theology*, The Hague, Martinus Nijhoff

Montagnes, Bernard (2004) *The Doctrine of the Analogy of Being according to St. Thomas*

Aquinas, Milwaukee, WI, Marquette University Press

Morris, Thomas V. (1986) *The Logic of God Incarnate*, Ithaca, NY, Cornell University Press

—— (1988) *Divine and Human Action*, Ithaca, NY, Cornell University Press

—— (1989) *Anselmian Explanations*, Notre Dame, IN, Notre Dame University Press

—— (1991) *Our Idea of God*, Notre Dame, IN, Notre Dame University Press

Nielsen, Kai (1971) *Contemporary Critiques of Religion*, New York, Herder and Herder

—— (1983) *An Introduction to the Philosophy of Religion*, London, Macmillan

Naugle, David K. (2002) *Worldview: History of a Concept*, Grand Rapids, MI, Wm. B. Eerdmans

Nash, Ronald H. (1968) *The Philosophy of G. H. Clark*, Philadelphia, PA, Presbyterian and Reformed

Owen, H. P. (1971) *Concepts of Deity*, London, Macmillan

Owens, Joseph (1980) *St. Thomas Aquinas on the Existence of God*, Albany, NY,
—— SUNY Press

—— (1993) *Cognition*, Houston, TX, Center for Thomistic Studies

Pap, Arthur and Paul Edwards (1973) *A Modern Introduction to Philosophy*, NY, The Free Press

Parsons, Keith (1990) *God and the Burden of Proof*, Amherst, NY, Prometheus Books

Peterson, Michael and Raymond Van Arragon (2003), *Contemporary Debates in the Philosophy of Religion*, Oxford, Blackwell

Phillips, D. Z. (1967) *Religion and Understanding*, Oxford, Blackwell

—— (1976) *Religion without Explanation*, Oxford, Blackwell

Phillips, R. P. (1941) *Modern Thomistic Philosophy*, London, Washbourne and Oates

Pike, Nelson (1965) *God and Evil*, Englewood Cliffs, NJ, Prentice–Hall

Pinnock, Clark (1989) *The Grace of God and the Will of Man*, Grand Rapids, MI, IVP

Plantinga, Alvin (1965) *The Ontological Argument*, Garden City, NY, Anchor Books

—— (1967) *God and Other Minds*, Ithaca, NY, Cornell University Press

—— (1974) *The Nature of Necessity*, Oxford, Clarendon Press

—— (1975) *God, Freedom and Evil*, London, Allen and Unwin

—— (1993a) *Warrant: The Current Debate*, New York, Oxford University Press

—— (1993b) *Warrant and Proper Function*, New York, Oxford University Press

—— (2004) *Warranted Christian Belief*, New York, Oxford University Press

Plantinga, Alvin and Nicholas Wolterstorff (1979), *Faith and Rationality*, Notre Dame, IN, Notre Dame University Press

Prevost, Robert (1990) *Probability and Theistic Explanation*, New York, Oxford University Press

Prior, A. N. (1957) *Time and Modality*, Oxford, Clarendon Press

Pseudo–Dionysius (1987) *The Complete Works*, New York, Paulist Press

Ramsey, Ian T. (1957) *Religious Language*, London, SCM Press

—— (1961) *Prospect for Metaphysics*, New York, Philosophical Library

—— (1964) *Models and Mystery*, London, Oxford University Press

—— (1965) *Christian Discourse*, London, Oxford University Press

—— (1973) *Models for Divine Activity*, London, SCM Press

—— (1974) *Christian Empiricism*, London, Sheldon Press

Ratzinger, Josef (1985) *'In the Beginning...'* Grand Rapids, MI, Wm. B. Eerdmans

Reale, Giovanni (1987) *From the Beginnings to Socrates*, Albany, SUNY Press

Robinson, John A. T. (1963) *Honest to God*, London, SCM Press

Ross, James F. (1969) *Philosophical Theology*, Indianapolis, IN, Bobbs–Merrill

—— (1981) *Portraying Analogy*, New York, Cambridge University Press

Rowe, William (1975) *The Cosmological Argument*, Princeton, NJ, Princeton University Press

Russell, Bertrand (1956) *Logic and Knowledge*, London, Allen and Unwin

—— (1957) *Why I am not a Christian*, New York, Simon and Schuster

Ryder, John (1994) *American Philosophical Naturalism in the Twentieth Century*, Amherst, NY, Prometheus Press

Sahakian, William (1968) *Outline–History of Philosophy*, New York, Barnes and Noble

Schellenberg, J. N. (2006) *Divine Hiddenness and Human Reason*, Ithaca, NY, Cornell University press

Schilpp, P. A. (1942) *The Philosophy of G. E. Moore*, Evanston, IL, Northwestern University Press

Scriven, Michael (1966) *Primary Philosophy*, New York, McGraw–Hill

Searle, John (1992) *The Rediscovery of the Mind*, Cambridge, MA, MIT Press

Sell, Alan P. F. (1988) *Philosophy of Religion 1875–1980*, London, Croom Helm

Sennett, James F. (1998) *The Analytic Theist*, Grand Rapids, MI, Wm. B. Eerdmans

Sleigh, R. C., Jr. (1972) *Necessary Truth*, Englewood Cliffs, NJ, Prentice–Hall

Sluga, Hans and David Stern (1996) *The Cambridge Companion to Wittgenstein*, New York, Cambridge University Press

Smart, Ninian (1969) *Philosophers and Religious Truth*, London, SCM Press

Soames, Scott (2003) *Philosophical Analysis in the Twentieth Century*, Princeton, NJ, Princeton University Press

Sobel, Jordan Howard (2004) *Logic and Theism*, New York, Cambridge University Press

Sproul, R. C., John Gerstner and Arthur Lindsley (1984), *Classical Apologetics*, Grand Rapids, MI, Zondervan

Steinkraus, Warren (1966) *New Studies in Berkeley's Philosophy*, New York, Holt, Rinehart and Winston

Swinburne, Richard (1970) *The Concept of Miracle*, New York, St. Martin's Press

—— (1973) *Introduction to Confirmation Theory*, London, Methuen

—— (1977) *The Coherence of Theism*, Oxford, Clarendon Press

—— (1979) *The Existence of God*, Oxford, Clarendon Press

—— (1981) *Faith and Reason*, Oxford, Clarendon Press

—— (1986) *The Evolution of the Soul*, Oxford, Clarendon Press

—— (1989) *Responsibility and Atonement*, Oxford, Clarendon Press

—— (1991) *The Existence of God* (revised edition), Oxford, Clarendon Press

—— (1992) *Revelation*, Oxford, Clarendon Press

—— (1994) *The Christian God*, Oxford, Clarendon Press

—— (1996) *Does God Exist?* Oxford, Clarendon Press

—— (1997) *Simplicity as Evidence of Truth*, Milwaukee, WI, Marquette University Press

—— (1998) *Providence and the Problem of Evil*, Oxford, Clarendon Press

—— (2001) *Epistemic Justification*, Oxford, Clarendon Press

—— (2002) *The Resurrection of God Incarnate*, Oxford, Clarendon Press

—— (2004) *The Existence of God* (second edition), Oxford, Clarendon Press

Swinburne, Richard and Sidney Shoemaker (1984) *Personal Identity*, Oxford, Basil Blackwell

Tennant, F. R. (1930) *Philosophical Theology*, Cambridge, Cambridge University Press

Thomas Aquinas, St. (1964), *Summa Theologiae*, Cambridge, Blackfriars

—— (1965) *On Being and Essence*, Notre Dame, IN, Notre Dame University Press

—— (1968) *On the Unicity of the Intellect*, Milwaukee, WI, Marquette University Press

Thomson, Judith Jarvis (1987) *On Being and Saying*, Cambridge, MA, MIT Press

Tracy, Thomas F. (1994) *The God Who Acts*, College Station, PA, Penn State University Press

Trueblood, D. Elton (1957) *Philosophy of Religion*, New York, Harper

Urban, Linwood and Douglas Walton (1978) *The Power of God*, New York, Oxford University Press

Urmson, J. O. (1956) *Philosophical Analysis*, Oxford, Clarendon Press

Van Buren, Paul (1963) *The Secular Meaning of the Gospel*, New York, Macmillan

Van Inwagen, Peter (1995) *God, Freedom and Mystery*, Ithaca, NY, Cornell University Press

—— (2006) *The Problem of Evil*, Oxford, Clarendon Press

Vesey, G. N. A. (1972) *Talk of God*, London, Macmillan

Vos, Howard (1968) *Can I Trust the Bible?* Chicago, Moody Publishing

Whitehead, Alfred North (1929) *Process and Reality*, Cambridge, Cambridge University Press

Wild, John (1948) *Introduction to Realistic Philosophy*, New York, Harpers

Wisdom, John (1963) *Philosophy and Psychoanalysis*, Oxford, Basil Blackwell

Wolterstorff, Nicholas (1984) *Reason within the Limits of Religion*, Grand Rapids, MI, Wm. B. Eerdmans

—— (1996) *John Locke and the Ethics of Belief*, Cambridge, Cambridge University Press

—— (2001) *Thomas Reid and the Story of Epistemology*, Cambridge, Cambridge University Press

Yandell, Keith (1984) *Christianity and Philosophy*, Grand Rapids, MI, W. B. Eerdmans

Zagzebski, Linda (1993) *Reflective Faith*, Notre Dame, IN, Notre Dame University Press

—— (1996) *The Dilemma of Foreknowledge and Freedom*, New York, Oxford University Press

Also available from www.humanities-ebooks.co.uk

Philosophy Insights

An Introduction to Critical Theory
An Introduction to Rhetorical Terms
American Pragmatism
Barthes
Critical Thinking
Metaethics Examined *
Thinking Ethically in Business
Existentialism
Modern Feminist Theory
Formal Logic
Heidegger
Contemporary Philosophy of Religion *
Philosophy of Sport
Plato
Wittgenstein

Full Length Ebooks

Sibylle Baumbach, *Shakespeare and the Art of Physiognomy* *
John Beer, *The Achievement of E M Forster*
John Beer, *Coleridge the Visionary*
Jared Curtis, ed., *The Fenwick Notes of William Wordsworth* *
Richard Gravil, *Master Narratives: Tellers and Telling in the English Novel*
Richard Gravil and Molly Lefebure, *The Coleridge Connection: Essays for Thomas McFarland*
John K. Hale, *Milton as Multilingual: Selected Essays 1982–2004*
John Lennard, *Of Modern Dragons and other essays on Genre Fiction* *
Colin Nicholson, *Fivefathers: Interviews with late Twentieth-Century Scottish Poets*
W J B Owen, *Understanding 'The Prelude'*
Keith Sagar, *D. H. Lawrence: Poet* *
William Wordsworth, *The Prose Works of William Wordsworth*, Volume 1 *
William Wordsworth, *The Convention of Cintra*
The Poems of William Wordsworth: Collected Reading Texts from the Cornell Wordsworth *
The Cornell Wordsworth: A Supplement *

* printed version available

www.ingramcontent.com/pod-product-compliance
Lightning Source LLC
Chambersburg PA
CBHW080920180426
43192CB00040B/2559